CW01455536

Volume 5

Inspiring Next
H2H Innovation

Ripi Singh

THIS BOOK SERIES BRINGS
A FEW THINGS FOR EVERYONE,
AND EVERYTHING FOR THE FEW

Research 2015-2021.
Created Aug 2021.
Expiry June 2026.

Author Royalties go to
Ocean Cleanup.

www.InspiringNext.com/Books

Inspiring Next H2H Innovation

Volume 5 – Human Ideas to Serve Human Needs

The term H2H inspired by https://bryankramer.com/

ISBN: 979-8-4712-8883-6

Dedicated

to

My father, Chief Engineer Manmohan Singh,

for

Taking me with him to his workplace every month for
early development of two things he believed to be the most important –
MENTAL MUSCLE and ETHICS.

I was just 10 at that time.

Acknowledgments

In 2019, a good friend, Vaibhav Garg, inspired me to write my innovation methodology in form of a book series. First four volumes were brought to market in 2020 during the pandemic. Another good friend, Bill McClain always challenged me to look at human side of innovation. This year I looked back into the original series and picked on various human aspects. A light bulb went on *"Innovation is a Human-to-Human Activity."* Rick Fernandez and Frank Voehl encouraged me to write a chapter on this topic for *"Global Innovation Science Handbook II"* to be published in 2022. Some of the content matured while writing papers with Marybeth Miceli on gender, with Traci Clifford on ethics, and with Vaibhav Garg on decision making. The seed can be traced back to a question from Brent Robertson in 2018 on human value from innovation. *I owe gratitude to these individuals for nudging me in the direction that is often ignored – HUMANS.*

Association with other ISO team of innovation experts has been a wonderful learning experience. I am so glad to know Prof. Pierre Deplanche (France), Federico Meneghello (Italy), Prof. Jin Chen (China), James Bromely (U.K.), Magnus Hakvåg (Norway), Irene Makar and Sorin Cohn (Canada), Harlan Bannett and Robin Rowe, (USA).

The content of the Inspiring Next series comes from the years of research on innovation and experience working with clients around the world. Some wonderful individuals who put their faith in early versions of the innovation Framework and applied it to their businesses include Dr. Pavan Suri (Singapore & USA), Dr.-Ing Carsten Könke (Germany), Dr. Johannes Vrana (Germany), Prof. Ali Bazzi (Lebanon & USA), Serge Dos Santos (France), Ranvir Singh Rathore, Dr. Anukram Mishra (India), and Lax Srinivasan (India), Prof. Krishna Pattipati, Dr. Khaled Hassouna, Michael Hoagland, Robert Renz, Bryan Mattimore, Chirag Thaker, Joe Pesticci, Paul Sessions, Brian Kench, Don Locke, Kate Jopling, Tim Maurer, Rich Dorans, Michael Rocheleau, Don Judson, and Mark O'Brien (all from the USA). I am grateful for learnings from all.

Going back to the early years of my coaching practice, few individuals gave me the confidence to keep moving whenever I was experiencing my lows. Kevin Bouley has always been there to show me hope, connecting me with the right set of individuals, engaging me in intellectually stimulating activities, and showcasing my work to his network. Dr. Pawan Suri and Dr. Rick Pettit never hesitated to help me recalibrate. Rob Berman has been a strong emotional supporter and branding coach.

I attribute the foundations in research and technology management to a decade of learning through United Technologies Leadership Trainings encouraged by Paul Adams, John Zimmerman, and Dan Eigenbrode. Ann Gowdey has been a mentor and coach for almost 15 years, encouraging me to think bigger, helping me transition from an engineer to a manager, to an executive, and then an entrepreneur. Dr. Gopi Katragadda and Dr. G.P. Singh were my former leadership mentors. Late Prof. A.K. Rao, Prof. T.S. Ramamurthy, Prof. B. Dattaguru, Prof. A.R. Ingraffea, Prof. V.S. Malhotra, Prof. S.C. Sharma, and Prof. S.N. Atluri, were my engineering teachers through the graduate program and early career. Their leadership style still inspires me to do the right thing in the right way, for the organization and the people, no matter what. Often, I just get to an answer by asking *"What would Dattaguru or G.P. do in this situation?"* Just after Coronavirus, I quickly adapted the process G.P. followed soon after 9/11 for his business.

I would like to acknowledge the good that came out of a few naysayers, who pushed me to both improve the models and how I express them.

My lovely wife Anu Kaur and my son AJ Singh, who have both been by my side, encouraging me to excel for almost three decades now. Let's not forget all those who are helping us deal with the Coronavirus through innovations in medicine and service.

– *Ripi Singh*, Sept 03, 2021.

Foreword

Innovation is broken, or at least struggling. It needs to find ways to crack through corporate politics or bureaucratic silos, to move from defense to offense, to nurture real breakthrough, and to drive new ways to add value.

In *Ripi Singh's H2H Innovation Manual*, one of America's leading strategic innovation consultants and teachers offers coaching and guidance with many concrete and pragmatic steps – steps that can unlock and drive day-to-day innovation in your business, which can help you gain and maintain a competitive advantage.

H2H Innovation combines what is best in classic innovation theories with a uniquely new human-centered strategic model. It shows leaders how to focus innovation that creates the products of visionary genius without the necessity for actual genius. It provides practical tools and guidance on building and leading the teams, working conditions, organizational structures, and cultures. The author illustrates a roadmap to the periphery and organizational margins at which real innovation takes place.

H2H Innovation is a framework to counter failure. It directs you, the reader, to the consumer, who will tell you how to innovate the benefits to create a future you can own. This book invites you to 'think different' to become a change leader, to go the 'other way' to get to the 'right place.'

In today's innovation infrastructure, the role that the human plays is being downplayed by other authors, and this book explains why the human factor in innovation processes is more important now than ever before. We have entered an era in which talent-driven innovation is the only sustainable source of competitive advantage for many companies and countries. Today, knowledge, information, and technology are widely distributed, increasingly commodities, and globally accessible. Those who know best what to do with these building blocks gain a competitive edge.

As innovation takes center stage in the world's economies, it has never been more important to explore the innovator's craft—the innovative thinking and know-how applied by insightful and determined business leaders, brilliant scientists and engineers, master entrepreneurs, creative organizations, and champions of change.

The opportunity that many executives are missing is the need to identify those in the organization that have the needed competencies to be innovative, and to develop those important skills they are weak in; and to arrange them into innovation teams where together they can fill any voids that the team members have using the strengths of the others.

As Ripi Singh explains in this book, it is the human needs that should first be determined, and then use them to drive the innovation efforts. It is the human decisions and their exercise of controls that will guide the technological or process innovations. Technology is only a tool that needs to be harnessed by the human in command. It is the inclusion of the human being in the process that leads to better strategic innovation.

During this whole process the humans will face an ethical dilemma, when they will need to choose between artificial intelligence and people intelligence and knowledge management. Ripi does a great job of explaining this conundrum and help our leaders, regulators, and government decide.

In summary, we need new rules and tools of innovation for faster and better solutions and higher returns on investment. The growing number of opportunities for innovation means that we need to engage intellectually with a much wider and diverse population. It has never been more important to teach people and organizations how to out-imagine, out-create, and out-innovate in a human-to-human mindset.

We must innovate or evaporate – and learn how best to manage the innovation process to achieve the speed, efficiency, cost-effectiveness, and outcomes that will deliver competitive advantage, economic prosperity, higher standards of living, and a better quality of life.

Frank Voehl (Chair) and *Rick Fernandez* (Vice Chair)
USA, TAG/TC 279; ISO 56000 (Innovation Management) Sept 04, 2021

Table of Contents

1. Introduction

After a keynote lecture on *Fourth Industrial Revolution* focusing heavily on automation to a large group of high school students in 2020, an adolescent mind asked a simple question, "*What will be my role in the workplace in 10 years from now. Will I still be valuable?*" So, I retraced some of my presentation to show her places where she is still crucial. Later, back in the office, going through the pitch deck again, I discovered human is in almost every aspect of innovation. From ideation to fulfilling the purpose. I scanned through my research content from the last 7 years and started writing this book. The term H2H[1] resonated with me.

> Innovation is an H2H Activity.

Digital Revolution

The Fourth Industrial Revolution has put innovation at the center stage of discussion across the world since 2015. The technology-driven change has already been fast and furious, coming from all directions. This pace of change is creating an impression that humans are becoming redundant. Although we need a suite of processes to develop, adopt, and apply digital technologies that are fusing with the physical reality; we also need empathy, creativity, and a purpose that serves humans.

---

[1] Human to Human: #H2H; Bryan Kramer; E-Book; 2014.

Do We Need Innovation?

Humans strive for assistance, prosperity, comfort, and security at various levels. This seems to be a primal need, as defined by Abraham Maslow in 1943, published as a social psychological model on human motivation. This provides us with an insight into the 'why' of all innovations.

The global pandemic, Covid-19, pushed everyone out of their comfort zone. Every country scrambled to manage the health of the population while trying to juggle the economic realities from widespread lockdowns. Creativity at home and innovations in the workplace witnessed enormous opportunities coming out of human survival instincts. It is as if the world has gotten a crash course on crisis innovation.

The next few years will be an era for the innovator to bring a new normal to the world, fueled by novel business models, industry 4.0 technologies, and a social purpose.

Is Innovation Hard?

We perceive it to be hard because of the uncertainty and risk of novel ideas and experimentation. Thinking and attempting something different, with potentially little or no short-term reward, can be emotionally draining. Our natural tendency is to fall back on known methods to arrive at solutions. In most of the work environments, we tag not making mistakes or avoiding an embarrassing failure as outstanding performance. However, this is an unavoidable part of experimentation. In my experience, the biggest barrier to innovation is leadership lacking the courage to go with the minority opinion or weak market signals. The moment we fall into driving the consensus amongst a group of responsible managers, we end up with an average acceptable next step, that everyone can see; at the cost of disengaging the visionaries and their opinions.

> We the humans make innovation harder on ourselves.

Can Innovation be Made Easy?

Yes, when we agree on a process where the risk of exploration is managed and build a mindset where diverse ideas and lessons (failures) are welcome, we can bring innovation into our culture. We can take a portfolio approach where the total output is way more when accounting for some failures (lessons), as compared to limited attempts with guaranteed success. Ethical considerations, however, will continue to be the tough part, hard to address.

The approach to innovation presented in the first four volumes of Inspiring Next Innovation series integrates strategic innovation and tactical execution within a common framework. It is based on a core process, from purpose-driven ideation to monetization, which is enhanced by a suite of enabling tools and tips that bring discipline to various aspects of innovation management. This Framework asserts that innovation can be much more affordable and accelerated through a disciplined approach, now fully supported by the International Organization of Standards (ISO).

A Snapshot of H2H Innovation

The intent of the first 4 volumes of Inspiring Next Innovation Series is captured on the cover of Volume-3, as shown below. It reflects a structured approach to innovation with purpose at the center; neatly surrounded by project, profiles, people, and inspiring set of questions.

Observing carefully, these are all human aspects to creativity for a human need, with all those volumes handling the human piece either implicitly or subtly. This volume amplifies the heart and soul of innovation, along with a recap of basic innovation processes.

Inspiring Next Innovation Framework

Volume 3

What if … innovation is structured ?

Why not ?
How about ?
What if ?

Robust
Trendsetter
Forecaster
Follower
Aware

Ripi Singh

Innovation management is generally discussed as a process. Until 2020, I have been talking about innovation as a combination of purpose, process, and mindset; and even suggesting process for arriving at purpose and building the mindset. When the young mind from Goa opened my eyes to the possibility of human being at the center of innovation, it became quite clear that:

(a) **Purpose** ought to serve some human value, need, or desire.

(b) **Process** begins with identification of a match making between a consumer need and creativity, and the steps are full of choices and decisions we make under uncertainty. The entire process is full of interactions between humans and machines, requiring a certain form of leadership and diversity to be competitive.

(c) **Mindset**, of course, is a human trait.

This human-to-human engagement is summarized here with discussions throughout the rest of the book. Happy reading.

Let's Take a Selfie

You can also do this online for tracking and analysis as well as updated content. https://.InspiringNext.com/Books/Selfie.

I can see the role of humans in

- ☐ Defining the purpose.
- ☐ Creating strategy.
- ☐ Generating ideas.
- ☐ Understanding market needs and consumer empathy.
- ☐ Making hard choices.
- ☐ Product design and development.
- ☐ Choosing the right over wrong.
- ☐ Helping social cause.
- ☐ Leading teams through uncertainty.
- ☐ Manufacturing and supply chain management.
- ☐ Custom manufacturing.
- ☐ Quality Assurance.
- ☐ Co-working with production machines and learning machines.
- ☐ Sales and Marketing.
- ☐ Handling accounts.
- ☐ Training employees.
- ☐ Assuring regulatory compliance.
- ☐ Circular economy.
- ☐ Bringing useful content such as this book to readers.
- ☐ Keeping a check on artificial intelligence.
- ☐ Childcare development.
- ☐ Healthcare systems development.
- ☐
- ☐
- ☐
- ☐

2.   History of Revolutions

REVOLUTIONS ARE THE LOCOMOTIVES OF HISTORY
— KARL MARX

While growing up in a small town in the Himalayas, the most advanced piece of technology in our house was a radio of the size of a microwave. It used to take 5 minutes to warm up and had just 4 different bands – one AM and 3 SW (Short Wave). We had not heard of FM radio. Then slowly it got smaller as transistors replaced vacuum tubes. Then we got an audio cassette player with a magnetic tape. The Vinyl disc and cassette players got replaced by CDs and now we have digital files (.mp3). That is a revolution. Simultaneously, we can have so many channels from around the world through services like Pandora. On video side, I recall movies on long photo spools, which had to be changed every 30 minutes. And now we are on to digital streaming. This is a revolution.

The first phone instrument to come to our house had no way to dial. As you pick up, it calls a manual operator who would connect you to the desired party. Operator knew every phone owner by name, but supported only 5 calls at a time, because she had only 5 cables. So, we were asked to hang up after a few minutes because someone else was waiting for the connector cable to get free. When new phone came with a rotary dial, we got a 2-digit phone number '34.' As the network grew, it became '234.' Moving to a city, we had a four-digit number. Long-distance calls would typically take hours to days to connect through an operator. Now we have cell phones with free international video calling facility, and we don't even need to remember the phone numbers. This is revolution.

I started my engineering education in India with log tables in 1982, graduated on main a frame computer Dec-Alpha10, moving on to HP workstation for post-doc research at Georgia tech with a ftp connection with NASA by 1992. This is revolution.

We used to visit friends by walking up to their house and knocking on the door. With phones came the culture of calling ahead. Now we send a text to find out if it is a good time to call. This is also revolution, or the flip side of revolution, if you like an active social lifestyle.

Our knowledge of the human body and health was limited. Everything fell between flu, infection, fracture, cancer, and heart attack. Visiting a doctor in India was like a party room with all other patients in the same room, and no privacy at all. Sometimes the doctor would attend to 3 patients simultaneously, like a bartender in a pub. X-ray machine was high technology. This sector has significantly changed how we care for health.

A lot has changed since World War II and has changed rapidly with digitization. Different thought leaders are defining major shifts differently. Let us look at four different perspectives:

(1) Innovation Waves,
(2) Industrial Revolutions,
(3) Social Revolutions, and
(4) Wealth-based Eras.

Six Long Waves of Innovation

Coined by economist Joseph Schumpeter in 1942, the theory of "creative destruction" suggests that business cycles operate under long waves of innovation[2]. Specifically, as markets are disrupted, key clusters of industries have outsized effects on the economy.

---

[2] Long Waves: The History of Innovation Cycles; Dorothy Neufeld; https://www.visualcapitalist.com/the-history-of-innovation-cycles/; June 30, 2021.

First wave (1785-1845) emerged when waterpower became instrumental in manufacturing paper, textiles, and iron goods. Unlike the mills of the past, full-sized dams fed turbines through complex belt systems. Advances in textiles brought the first factory, and cities expanded.

Second wave (1845-1900) came from significant advancements in rail, steam, and steel. The rail industry alone affected countless industries, from iron and oil to steel and copper. Great railway monopolies were formed.

Third wave (1900-1950) emerged from electricity powering light and telephone communication and dominated the first half of the 1900s. Henry Ford introduced the Model T, and the assembly line transformed the auto industry. Automobiles became closely linked to the expansion of the American metropolis.

Fourth wave (1950-1990) was when aviation revolutionized travel.

Fifth wave (1990-2020) came from the internet boom upending barriers to information. New media changed political discourse, news cycles, and communications. The internet ushered in a new frontier of globalization, a borderless landscape of digital information flows.

Sixth wave (Since 2020) is marked by digital transformation, including Artificial Intelligence, Internet of Things, Robotics, and Drones, which will likely paint an entirely new picture. Physical goods and services will likely be digitized. The time to complete tasks could shift from hours to even seconds. Clean tech could come to the forefront. At the heart of each technological innovation is solving complex problems, and climate concerns are becoming increasingly pressing. Lower costs in solar PV and wind are also predicating efficiency advantages.

To the economist Schumpeter, technological innovations boosted economic growth and improved living standards. Like the Big Tech behemoths of today, the rail industry had the power to control prices and push out competitors during the 19th century. At the peak, listed shares of rail companies on the New York Stock Exchange made up 60% of total stock market capitalization.

Four Industrial Revolutions

Over the last three centuries, humanity has seen significant changes in lifestyle, driven by three industrial revolutions; a lot more than previous three millennia. At this time in our history, we are going through the fourth revolution, in which the physical assets are getting connected with their digital twin through IIoT, creating smart products, processes, and even factories. Machines are beginning to learn and assist in our cognitive function. Small handheld devices are gaining the perception of a life support system. Change is happening faster than our ability to adopt.

The term 'Industrie 4.0' originally came from a team of scientists developing a high-tech strategy for the German Government[3] in 2011. It became popular when Klaus Schwab, executive chairperson of the World Economic Forum, introduced the phrase to a wider audience in 2015 and published an article in Foreign Affairs[4].

First industrial revolution brought a change from handcrafted forms of production to the mechanization of production with steam engines or regenerative energy sources such as water. Many other steam-powered machines transformed the society with trains, mechanization of manufacturing and loads of unwanted smog.

Second industrial revolution triggered by electric power, enabled new industries and mechanical production engineering. We mastered the control of physical materials and products, through use of conveyers and mass production lines, over a few decades. New manufacturing systems and electrical/chemical inventions enabled the assembly line, led to the era of mass production, including the negative externalities like asbestos and carbon-dioxide.

---

[3] Industrie 4.0: Mit dem Internet der Dinge auf dem Weg zur 4. industriellen Revolution; H. Kagermann, W.-D Lukas, W. Wahlster; VDI-Nachrichten 13, (2) 2011.

[4] The Fourth Industrial Revolution, What It Means and How to Respond; Klaus Schwab; https://www.foreignaffairs.com/articles/2015-12-12/fourth-industrial-revolution; December 12, 2015.

Third industrial revolution came from development of computers, which allowed automated control of industrial production and revolutionized data processing. Machine connectivity and the birth of the Internet; the big game-changer in the ways information is handled and shared, and the evolutions to e-anything versions of previously brick and mortar environments only, resulting in far more automation and the undesirable social divides. We mastered data creation and management with the digital space.

Fourth industrial revolution is harnessing the potential of digital-physical integration. A good example of the digital-physical integration is a self-driving car. The car gathers the data from multiple cameras and sensors to determine its position, velocity, and separation to other cars. It uses the data in real-time to take physical actions with an intent to reach the destination without collision or passenger discomfort.

A similar change is happening in industrial manufacturing and maintenance. Manufacturing shops are installing sensors to monitor production, collecting the data from all kinds of manufacturing, and handling machines. They are connecting Enterprise Resource Planning (ERP) and Manufacturing Execution Systems (MES) to simplify, enhance, and secure industrial production. This streamlines supply chains, and allows new, cheaper, and safer products. In addition, there is a growing desire to make these cyber-physical systems learn from experience, adopt to variation in inputs, make select decisions, and act autonomously to accomplish an objective. A lot is discussed and kept current under Plattform Industrie 4.0 initiative[5].

In fact, every sector is witnessing digital transformation – health care, education, transportation, logistics, home, office, shopping, you name it.

---

[5] Plattform Industrie 4.0, https://www.plattform-i40.de/PI40/Navigation/DE/Home/home.html

What differentiates Industry 4.0 from Digital Revolution

The 3rd revolution was digitization. The 4th is digital transformation. The transition state in between is called digitalization. They are defined as:

Digitization encompasses various methods to convert analog information into binary numbers. Example – Moving from a typewriter to digital form of text.

Digitalization is using digitized form to simplify specific operations. With digital text, the word processing simplifies operations like search and replace, spell check, cross references, track changes and compare documents. Currently, AI based tools being integrated, like translation tools, or grammar checking tools, are still digitalization – even that they are way advanced – but they are still implemented to simplify specific operations.

Digital Transformation takes the idea of digitalization to a completely new level, making collaboration and connectivity agnostic, opening new business models, and enabling eco-system growth. The digital transformation of word processing begins with collaborative content development systems possible from different developers, and with intelligent augmentation.

The fourth revolution is more about meaningful integration of digitalized systems. The portfolio of over a dozen technologies includes meaningful data collection using digital twin, digital thread, digital weave, Industrial Internet of Things (IIoT), and semantic interoperability. Technologies such as 5G, revision safe storage using blockchain, enable new ways of data transfer. Cloud computing, AI, Big Data, mobile devices, and Quantum Computers make interpretation meaningful and efficient. All this can be easily visualized using extended reality and dashboards. Finally, multiple technologies like Additive manufacturing, Simulation, Reconstruction, and Digitization enable automation, data processing and purposeful application. These are all viewed and deployed in a new light within the fourth revolution.

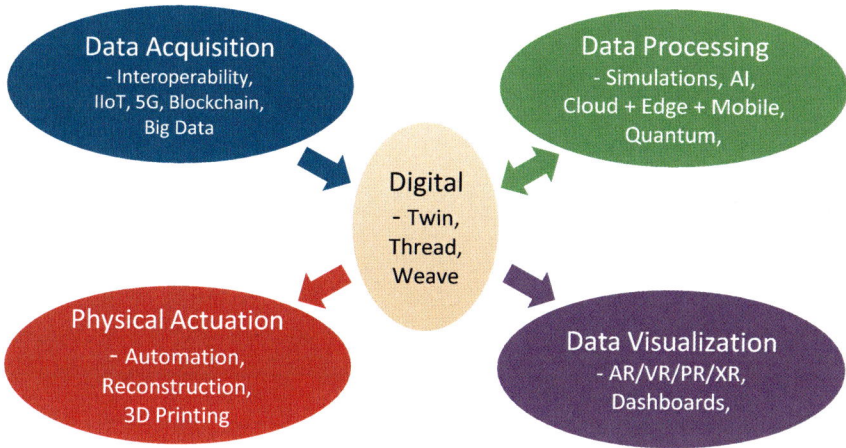

For all the technologies listed above, somebody might argue that none of those are new; and there is an element of truth to that. Industry 4.0 is not a single technology; it is a suite of cyber-physical technologies deployed for a purpose. The fourth revolution is not a discrete event; it is a phase over which the portfolio of value-add digital technologies is coming together to change the way humans work and live, produce and consume, learn, and stay healthy. In some spheres of industrial domains and geographical regions, even the third revolution is still under way.

The emerging reality is that the closed-loop networking between machines, computers, and materials enables production of individual components tailored to the needs of the customer, commonly referred as mass customization. So now you can have the economies of scale benefit without compromising the personalization typical of pre-industrial age, where every product was unique. This fourth revolution takes us from conformity to individualism.

Automation and artificial intelligence have created a general misconception that Industry 4.0 will make humans redundant. I think it moves humanity to engage in more fulfilling and meaningful activities and take much of the repetitive hard work to machines.

Industrial revolutions push humans up the Maslow pyramid.

With global disparities in the economic health, the widespread adoption of industry 4.0 has a long way to go. Over the last few decades, concerns around excessive focus on machines taking over industrial processes for economic value creation have raised the eyebrows of forward-thinking leaders and those concerned about social conditions.

A possible next disruption in digital-physical world could be when manufacturing robots, AI, and autonomous vehicles collude to understand human needs. Then autonomously create factories that design and manufacture innovative products and deliver to humans, create energy plants and hospitals to serve communities. They even maintain law and order because the idle mind might become the devil's workshop. Will that be the fifth revolution? We discuss that in Chapter-11.

The Flip Side of Industrial Revolutions

We have all realized that the innovations and industrial revolutions driven by commercial interests have come with a mixed bag. Commerce has not been particularly good at addressing diverse social outcomes of such revolutions. The first industrial revolution ravaged the countryside, contributed to colonization and slavery. The second and third revolutions created wealth disparity, wars, and robbed the planet of many of its natural resources. It created an era of misinformation, a crippling education system, a digital divide across generation, and lots of environmental effects so hard to reverse. The fourth revolution, if not handled properly, can completely take away privacy and security, make us slave to an emotion-free machine. It has a risk of forcing a human to compromise on ethical and moral values, and some other things we may not have perceived today. We can already see the early signs of such trends, which must be regulated now, before it is too late. In brief, while the revolutions helped build a better economy and lifestyle on an average, humanity paid a heavy price to create new social issues.

The United Nations (UN) Sustainable Development Goals (SDG) cannot get enough traction with politically focused governments, getting just lip service from large corporations, failing to resonate with small business; all leading to plan revisions such as **Decade of Action**[6].

Over the past century, some of the scientific/technical inventions have created non-scientific concerns in the society. Such issues also cause acceptance delays and denials by a significant percentage of our society. We see that every day now, around biotechnology innovations. However, as responsible scientists and engineers, we should tackle such concerns head on through education and community engagement, looking for responsible new ways to solve problems. Scientific collaboration should be done with an open mind engaging diverse perspectives – all perspectives that impact human well-being, human experience, and human interactions, including psychology, sociology, necessary social reforms.

There is certainly a need for purpose-driven business and technology innovation. The 'Conscious Capitalism' is all about addressing that aspect[7]. The next generation, now growing up under an economy of abundance, smart phones, and a lot more aware of sustainability issues, gives me hope that this revolution (social and industrial) will address humanity with a heightened sense of purpose and responsibility.

Five Social Revolutions

After the declaration of Industry 4.0 by Europe, the Japanese Science and Technology Basic Plan[8] proposed the term Society 5.0 in 2016. It calls for the application of technology in a manner that concurrently brings both economic development and solutions to social problems. It ensues

---

[6] https://www.un.org/sustainabledevelopment/decade-of-action/

[7] https://www.consciouscapitalism.org/

[8] The 5th Science and Technology Basic Plan; Government of Japan; http://www8.cao.go.jp/cstp/english/basic/5thbasicplan.pdf; 2016.

technology for the sake of society and not just for business reasons. In some sense, addressing humanitarian needs in driving technology.

Taking a long view of history, Japan has defined:

Society 1.0 as groups of people hunting and gathering in harmonious coexistence with nature.

Society 2.0 as forming groups based on agricultural cultivation, increasing organization and nation-building.

Society 3.0 promotes industrialization through the Industrial Revolution, making mass production possible. This (Society 3.0) was driven by 1st industrial revolution and stayed through the 2nd industrial revolution with invention of electricity and mass production.

Society 4.0 as an information society that realizes increasing added value by connecting intangible assets as information networks. This was driven by 3rd industrial revolution.

Society 5.0 is an information society built upon Society 4.0, aiming for a prosperous human-centered society. This ought to be the purpose of the 4th industrial revolution as discussed in my previous book[9].

In some sense, innovations and industrial revolutions have fueled societal transformations until now. In Society 5.0, we may see a reversal of this philosophy. We should define the lifestyle we want to live and drive the industrial revolution from such a need. Focus on purpose at society level rather than technology or industry level or business considerations.

Interestingly, Japan used a different numbering scheme for the revolutions in society. For the industrial revolutions, handcraft is the basis and is therefore not given a number. The basis of society, hunting and coexistence with nature, is given the number "1.0" by Japan.

---

[9] Inspiring Next Innovation Purpose; Ripi Singh; Book, OutSkirts Press; Sept 2020.

Society 5.0 – A Human-centered Society

In Society 5.0, all people receive high-quality services and lead a comfortable, lively life that considers their diversity, such as age, gender, region, or language. It is called Society 5.0 to identify a new society created by transformations led by scientific and technological innovations (Industry 4.0) and the sharing economy.

So far, our priorities in social, economic, and organizational systems have resulted in gaps in products and services that individuals receive because of individual skills and other reasons. In contrast, Society 5.0 achieves an advanced convergence between cyberspace and physical space, which enables robots and big data-based Artificial Intelligence (AI) to act or support the work and adjustments that people have done so far acting as an agent. By creating this new value, only the products/services that are needed for the people who need them at the right time can be provided, optimizing the entire social and organizational system.

This is a society that focuses on everyone and not a future that is controlled and monitored by AI and robots. Japan is leading the world.

In the information society (Society 4.0), the exchange of knowledge and information flow across the board was not sufficient, and cooperation was difficult. Social reforms (innovations) in Society 5.0 create a future-oriented society that eliminates the existing feeling of stagnation, a society whose members respect each other and across generations. Big data collected by the IoT is transformed by AI into a new form of intelligence that reaches every corner of society. Based on health and medical data from a universal health system and a wealth of operational data from many production facilities, Japan has an environment that is rich in real and usable raw data for the current market economy and industry. It remains to be seen if other countries will follow a similar philosophy.

What Differentiates Society 5.0 from the Information Society?

Society 5.0 achieves its purpose through the convergence of cyberspace and physical space. In the Information Society 4.0, people collect, search, retrieve, and analyze the data using cloud services. In Society 5.0, people, things, and systems in cyberspace are interconnected. A sizeable amount of information is collected by sensors in physical space to be stored and managed in cyberspace. This big data is analyzed by AI that surpasses human analytical capabilities in cyberspace. It allows optimal results to be returned to the physical space for human consumption. In this way, a new value for industry and society is created that was previously not possible. Smart living, mobility, and healthcare are all manifestations of this.

> Society 5.0 provides a purpose to Industry 4.0.

Five Eras

Merle and Davis[10] have a slightly different take on major shifts in the history of humanity and have indicated the next likely revolution as well. They defined the four eras of human activity in terms of wealth creation and accumulation, along with the disruptive innovations that changed the very essence of human activity around the world. Although each of the four eras were quite different, there are some common themes that help foresee the Fifth Era. Disruptions can fundamentally change how people spend their time. New and quite different wealth creation opportunities emerge. The wealth does not automatically accrue to the best-positioned and most successful players of the prior era. It is possible to see a new era coming and position yourself for the next phase of wealth creation. The challenge is that this needs to be a conscious choice, as prior wealth creation strategies may

---

[10] Corporate Innovation in the Fifth Era; M C Le Merle and A Davis; Book, Cartwright, 2017.

not be relevant in the subsequent era. Each of the Era had its own series of breakthroughs (or revolution). Their definition is:

Hunter-Gatherer Era (Prior to 11,000 BC) The dominant societal mode was a tribal group (family groups), helping each other within the tribe, but fighting with other groups, gathering, and collecting the abundance of nature (fish and plant foods). This meant no accumulation of materialistic wealth in the hands of the few rich.

Agrarian Era (About 11,000 BC to ~1400AD) was characterized by high productivity crops (of that time), local animal husbandry, domestication, irrigation, farming tools (muscle operated), and storage. The second agrarian phase saw well-organized empires (Persian Achaemenid Empire, Han Empire in China, and the Roman Empire) becoming the hub of wealth accumulation, with ruling few who rose to dominate. Wealth was primarily in form of precious metals (Gold) and real estate, whose accumulation was a driver of many battles around the world.

Mercantile Era (~1400 AD to ~1800 AD) was characterized by novel forms of transportation, and global convergence, exchange of plants and animals, and then common forms of currency and methods of exchange in the global economic scale. The increased emphasis on trade led to wealth in form of material goods around the world. This era also brought about large military power to secure trading routes and real estate and control the trading networks.

Industrial Era (~1800 AD to ~2000 AD) is the series of first three industrial revolutions already discussed, starting with steam, electricity, steel, machines, and finally computers. This led to better living situation, workplace, healthcare, education, transportation, and life expectancy. The wealth creation has been with corporate leaders and their financiers, including the public as corporate share-holdings.

Fifth Era (Since ~2000 AD) is what we see now as digital revolutions, biotechnology, and others. The key characteristics here are data connectivity, intelligent machines, the quantum world, and all the scientific advances down to nano-materials and genetic engineering. The dominant players today seem to accumulate wealth in form of data that can be monetized. Data also allows confluence of multiple seemingly diverse items, creating compounding of innovations at unprecedented rates. We are at the intersection of digital revolution and biotechnology revolution and future is rapidly unfolding.

You can see some overlap between these eras, and with each subsequent era some groups continued to live in prior era(s), but most of the human society changed radically with a new mode of wealth accumulation. We may still see foragers in the rainforest, agrarians on some continents, and mercantile traders everywhere. However, the world today is dominated by industrialization and now digitalization.

The other aspect is that the eras change over generations and is always messy. In this transition between the Industrial and Fifth Era today, no one can predict the future exactly, but we can be sure that it will create exciting alternative forms of wealth and wealth creation opportunities.

> We do not seem to know enough to even give it a name!

The Alignment

The graphic below aligns the waves of innovation, industrial revolutions, social revolutions, and the eras. There is a bit of misalignment of the numbering schema because of the basis of revolutions. However, you would see the 'fifth' is almost getting aligned. If we ignore how we defined the historical changes, we can look ahead and prepare for what's coming...

What causes the misalignment is the way revolutions are defined. We can choose other criterion, food, education, healthcare, and these would be different. For the rest of the book, we will only use Industry 4.0 or Society 5.0 model for conversation.

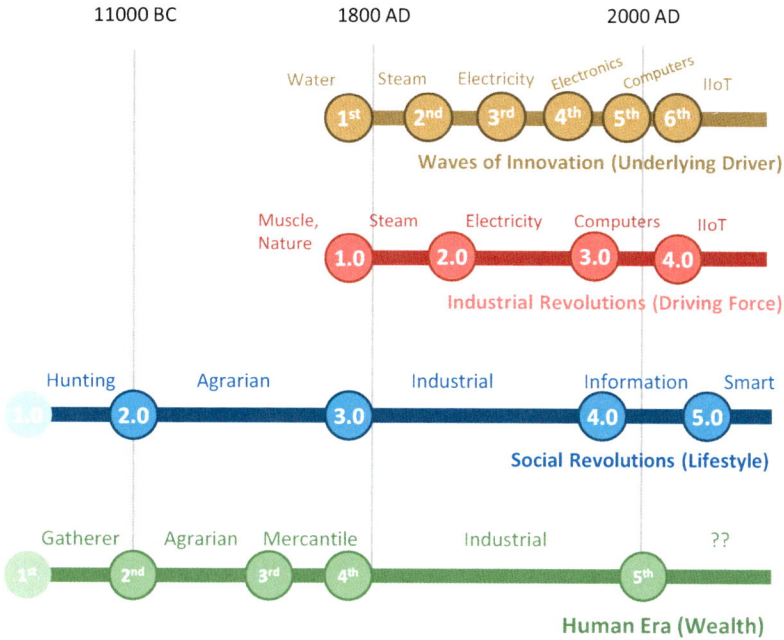

| | 11000 BC | | 1800 AD | | 2000 AD | |

Waves of Innovation (Underlying Driver)
Water — Steam — Electricity — Electronics — Computers — IIoT
1st 2nd 3rd 4th 5th 6th

Industrial Revolutions (Driving Force)
Muscle, Nature — Steam — Electricity — Computers — IIoT
1.0 2.0 3.0 4.0

Social Revolutions (Lifestyle)
Hunting — Agrarian — Industrial — Information — Smart
1.0 2.0 3.0 4.0 5.0

Human Era (Wealth)
Gatherer — Agrarian — Mercantile — Industrial — ??
1st 2nd 3rd 4th 5th

The shift is happening in favor of humans. As my colleague from ISO 56000 James Bromely (Scotland) says Global mindset is becoming GLocal (Adapting global approaches to local regions). Decision-making baby boomers are yielding to millennials with new set of values. Positive-results only exclusive-Leadership is yielding to 'all-results for all' consensus. Financial profit is being edged by societal value. Belen Suarez (Spain) calls it moving from ego-systems to eco-systems.

Let's Summarize

Innovations change our life every day, slightly. We call it evolution. The rate of change depends on how different evolutions build on each other. When fundamentals are altered, we call it a revolution or an era. Until now, these have been defined by historians. Current changes are being defined in real time to actively control what happens to us, in the future; and that makes current times an exciting period to live in.

Let's Take a Selfie

My favorite model for change is

- ☐ The 6 waves of innovation.
- ☐ The 4 industrial revolutions.
- ☐ The 5 social revolutions.
- ☐ The 5 eras.
- ☐ It does not matter, since the promise of a better living is the same in all.

Waves of Innovations – Our state is

- ☐ We are still in the 5th wave, I just heard about these.
- ☐ We have started our journey into the 6th wave.
- ☐ We understand the importance of the 6th wave in helping humans.

Industrial Revolutions – Our state is

- ☐ We are still in the 3rd revolution, I just heard about the 4th.
- ☐ We have started our journey into the 4th revolution.
- ☐ We understand the importance of the 4th revolution in helping humans.
- ☐ We are in a wait and watch mode to adopt digital transformation.

Social Revolutions – Our state is

- ☐ We are still in the Society 4.0 mindset and would like to learn more.
- ☐ We have started our journey into the Society 5.0.
- ☐ We understand and dislike the philosophical model of Society 5.0.
- ☐ Digital Transformation is the only way to meet the intent of Society 5.0.

Fifth Era – Our state is

- ☐ It is just a name given by a thought leader to encompass all the changes.
- ☐ There is something serious happening, so fast, and it is a different era.
- ☐ The 5th era is exciting and thrilling.
- ☐ The 5th era is scary and stressful.
- ☐ I still do not understand what the fuss is about.

3.   Forms of Innovation

One day in 1978, growing up in a village in India, I learned that someone in the neighborhood had purchased a radio that also showed a movie picture. My curiosity pushed me to learn more, and I had my first look at this big box, which we later learned was called a television. My father explained the terms invention, scientist, and inventor; and I realized that is what I wanted to be. He got me 'Meccano'–a model construction system to build creative toys by putting pieces together. For many years, I was a living room (re)inventor assembling working models of earthmoving machinery. Today, we use the term *innovation,* with so many definitions floating around.

Definition of Innovation

Crossan and Apaydin[11] defined innovation as:

> *Production or adoption, assimilation, and exploitation of*
> *a value-added novelty in economic and social spheres;*
> *renewal and enlargement of products, services, and markets;*
> *development of new methods of production; and*
> *establishment of new management systems.*
> *It is both a process and an outcome.*

---

[11] A Multidimensional Framework of Organizational Innovation: A Systematic Review of The Literature; M M Crossan and M Apaydin; J of Mgmt Stu, Vol 47, pp 1154; 2010.

This definition is the most comprehensive, as it captures several important aspects of innovation: it includes both internally conceived and externally adopted innovation (production or adoption). It highlights innovation as more than a creative process, by including application (exploitation). It emphasizes intended benefits (value-added) at one or more levels of analysis. It leaves open the possibility that innovation may refer to a relative novelty of an innovation as opposed to the absolute. An innovation may be common practice in other organizations, but it would still be considered as such if it is new to the unit under research. It draws attention to the two roles of innovation (a process and an outcome), the keyword being *'outcome.'* The definition is quite open and implicitly shows that innovation engages humans and machines in creating an outcome.

International Organization for Standardization (ISO) has recently converged on a simple set of terms and descriptors[12] for innovation management.

> Innovation is "New or changed entity, realizing or redistributing value."
>
> Novelty and value are relative to, and determined by, the perception of the organization and relevant interested parties. An innovation can be a product, service, process, model, method, etc. Innovation is an outcome. The word 'innovation' sometimes refers to activities or processes resulting in, or aiming for, innovation. When 'innovation' is used in this sense, it should always be used with some form of qualifier, e.g., innovation activities. (ISO 56000:2020 Clause 3.1.1)

New or changed entity corresponds to a new or an improved product or process, or a combination thereof, that differs significantly from previous products or processes. Realizing or redistributing value indicates that it has been made available to potential users or brought into use.

---

[12] ISO 56000:2020 – Innovation Management – Fundamentals and Vocabulary; www.iso.org; 2020.

In this context, the concept of innovation is characterized by novelty and value, and both are necessary and sufficient. To realize value, the entity must be introduced, deployed, adopted, or used to a certain extent.

> Invention without the manifestation of value is not innovation.

The value of an innovation may be perceived differently, at different times, by different categories of users and consumers throughout a particular value stream or a specific network. Value can be either or both financial and non-financial, such as revenues, savings, productivity, sustainability, satisfaction, empowerment, engagement, trust, or experience. Individual value perception highly depends on the individual purpose.

My involvement in ISO process development has convinced me that humans are an intrinsic part of the process, identifying context, providing leadership, managing operations, and improving continuously, to realize or redistribute value.

Additional definitions, to help you grasp the breadth of the term, are in Appendix. Having researched so many of these definitions, I am one of those who believe that it has become a bit of a buzzword and perhaps we should not be looking for a precise definition. Subsequent subsections will show that the meaning will vary based on circumstance, application, domain, purpose, and a few other factors.

In the meantime, if we accept that there are multiple correct definitions of innovation, then we can view it from various angles and viewpoints. An innovation can have one or more attributes describing what, how, and why it is innovated. These attributes could provide a broader context or specific purpose. Let us define a few types of innovation with certain distinguishing attributes. These are not unique; in fact, some innovations can be a combination of multiple other innovations and we can classify some under multiple categories. You are welcome to add your preferred category, after reviewing these.

Innovations Classified on Scope

From a high-level, I view the realization of value at different levels: individual, organizational, and markets or consumers.

Workbench Innovation for Personal Efficiency and Effectiveness

Most individuals are continuously improving their work (and even life). I will call it *Workbench Innovation or Point of Action Innovation*. For example, when you create an Excel Macro to speed up repeated calculations, create a widget to hold your workpiece in place reducing variation, or devise a new recipe for a dessert. This benefits an individual or an employee and the organization may never realize its impact. It is happening in every organization all the time, and most of it goes unnoticed or unappreciated. However, building this is foundational to a mindset of innovation, which involves a conscious effort towards developing Innovative Processes, Products, Services, and Business Models.

Process Innovation for Bottom line

Most companies are continuously improving the tools, methods, models, and processes used to design, develop, and produce a product or deliver a service to a customer. This is generally focused on reducing risk, cost, and improving quality and turn time; improving the company's profit margins. For example, automation in material handling to create a 24/7 operation, or re-arranging a manufacturing cell for production and delivery activity. Typically, this helps improve the organization's productivity, net profits, and employee engagement. Market or customer may not see much benefit, other than a potential price drop.

Process innovation typically requires low investment and has low returns. It can be easily seen, justified, and usually forms the bulk of the innovation portfolio with many companies.

Product or Service Innovation for Top Line

This constitutes innovation in technology and product performance or a novel service, which creates a market differentiator and affects net sales. For example, a new microwave, or an automobile, or laundry service that combines cleaning and minor repairs. Typically, this helps improve revenues through better customer experience. Depending upon the application, this can have a much broader impact. Some innovations can change our lifestyle, such as a smartphone or a Global Positioning System (GPS). Product innovation requires higher investment with possibly much higher returns, at higher risk levels, over an extended period. All of us need to be conscious of the impact of our products on society and the environment, while innovating. This will be discussed at length later in the purpose of innovation.

Broadly, the term product in this book includes service as well. A simple differentiator – a service cannot be created without engaging a customer or a consumer.

Business Model Innovation for Market Recapture

Business model innovation is an art of creating value out of the same product or service by engaging with the customer differently. For example, power by the hour from Rolls Royce, where instead of selling the jet-engine to the airline, you maintain the engine and sell the power; or Uber – a novel way of connecting excess supply with demand through existing technology. Typically, business model innovation provides higher returns for very low investment. Unfortunately, they are short-lived, unless supported by product innovation. A brief life span emanates from its inability to intellectually protect itself from being copied.

Innovations Classified on Attributes

Once again, the innovation may create different levels of value, at a different pace, under varied scenarios of collaborative and budgetary constraints. Let us recap a few that were discussed in detail in Volume-2[13].

Evolutionary Innovation (Small Improvement)

Evolutionary Innovation is when you make an incremental change to an existing product, service, or a process to stay competitive. It typically draws upon user feedback, lessons learned, or quick improvements just to go one-up in the marketplace. Examples: a new smartphone with twice the memory, higher screen resolution, a refrigerator with better internal lights, or a smoother automatically closing door. It is a 'must-do' in today's business environment. All those who stopped doing this are already out of business.

Eco-adaptive Innovation (Translation)

Eco-adaptive Innovation (Translation) is when you take a successful product from one eco-system and adapt it to work in another. Examples: adapting a German Porsche car for USA roads, a USA refrigerator modified for Indian households, or a menu of a well-established fast-food chain in the USA altered to suit the local taste buds in African countries. This is typically driven by a desire to enter new markets.

Peripheral Innovation (Adjacent)

Peripheral Innovation (Adjacent) is when you create new products as peripheral devices, accessories, and adjacent services. This is done to enhance the value of the core product through compatibility and convenience, with options to purchase, upgrade, discard, and even use with a competitor's or white labeled products. e.g., a carry case for the camera.

---

[13] Inspiring next Innovation Value Chain; Ripi Singh; Book, Outskirts Press; 2020.

Crisis Innovation (Emergency)

Crisis Innovation (Emergency) is when you have extremely limited time to solve a problem, possibly to save a few human lives at stake. Examples: Return of Apollo 13 in 1970, Rescue of chili miners in 2010, and innovations around handling the Coronavirus outbreak in 2020. Competency, emotional control, and some levels of readiness are required.

Burst Innovation (Rapid Fire)

Burst Innovation (Rapid Fire) is when you have a business crisis on hand, with some direct impact on employment, service deliveries, or the environment. Examples: a bailout of a reputed airline heading into bankruptcy, Containment of British Petroleum Oil Spill. These are driven by a desire to control financial losses, or turnaround a business.

Bold Innovation (Multi-Faceted and Integrated)

Bold Innovation (Multi-Faceted and Integrated) is when the effort is enormous in magnitude, requiring serious integration of multiple innovations to come together. Examples: Human mission to Mars, or a floating city. These are driven by a few bold visionaries, willing to take the risk and drive investments that most would think insane.

Frugal Innovation (Resource Starved)

Frugal Innovation (Resource Starved) is when the budget is low, and quality is of little consequence. Examples: you create a makeshift rooftop rack for your car to carry stuff for vacation, and now it lasts forever. We can also call this a 'Hack Job.' Affordable prototyping to prove a concept is not to be confused with frugal innovation brought into practice.

Open Innovation (External Participation)

Open Innovation (External Participation) is when you engage external entities or individuals outside the boundaries of an organization without serious constraints on knowledge-sharing to accelerate the creation of new products. Examples: P&G program called Connect and Develop, where together with OraLabs produced a new lip balm called CoverGirl.

At times, multiple parties come together to share solution development. An example is the Global Human Body Modeling Consortium, where seven auto companies created digital human models to replace costly test dummies and better understand human body injuries in auto accidents.

Classified Innovation (Secrecy)

Classified Innovation (Secrecy) is when you work on something highly confidential, and you must not disclose it even to the closest of your relations. Examples: Strategic Defense Initiative or Skunkworks of Lockheed Martin. Typically, these are in national defense projects, to gain military superiority. Within the business world, most of Merger and Acquisition activities are kept close to the chest by a few people. This is the exact opposite of open innovation.

Breakthrough Innovation (Significantly New)

Breakthrough Innovation (Significantly New) is when there is a high degree of change or impact, related to an organization, process, technology, product, or service. Examples: Paying for insurance by the mile based on a plug-in telematics device. Breakthrough innovation is at the other end of the continuum to evolutionary or incremental innovation.

Disruptive Innovation (Turning Point)

Disruption is defined when a significant fraction of potential customers adopts something new or when a fundamental breakthrough or value proposition leads to a change in lifestyle. It usually involves a new business model, though not always. Typically, this type of innovation initially addresses a less demanding need with lower performance, but eventually displaces established offerings. These are generally more cost-effective, needing lot fewer resources, and are offered at a lower cost. Disruptive innovation will often hurt some other businesses. Netflix killed Blockbuster.

There is another term called Radical innovation. Different people use it interchangeably with Breakthrough or Disruptive innovations. Is it somewhere in between?

Responsible Innovation (Socially Conscious)

Responsible Innovation (Socially Conscious) is when an approach to innovation anticipates and assesses potential implications and societal expectations; intending to foster the design of inclusive and sustainable research. In some sense, this distinguishes Good from Bad innovation; akin to saying, 'do the right thing.'

I believe, most of the innovation types discussed above should also attempt to be *a Responsible type* except Crisis Innovation, when human lives are at risk. The social responsibility should be a piece of the purposeful innovation.

Open-source Innovation (Social & Free)

Open-source Innovation (Social & Free) is about creating a new product design for social good, using openly available resources, and freely giving away the design so anyone can produce for use where they need and when. Multiple contributors and beneficiaries get connected using geographical or virtual platforms. In some sense, it is a combination of Crisis, Frugal, and Responsible innovations with no business model associated with it. The Covid-19 pandemic brought out a lot of open-source innovation to address a shortage of hand sanitizers, ventilators, and hospital beds, in 2020.

Dark Innovation (Unwanted)

Dark Innovation (Unwanted) is exactly the opposite of responsible innovation. This is about new products or new use of an existing product with a purpose to hurt people, their property, their reputation; or to hurt a community, faith, country, or even deliberately impact the environment or planet sustainability. The intent is important here. Many innovations provide an opportunity for dark applications that are illegal or unethical. That does not make the innovations 'dark innovation.'

The unintentional side effect due to lack of awareness of a well-intentioned innovation is not to be confused with dark innovation either. However, once you become aware, you need to activate your moral compass.

Distinct Innovation

We can put any adjective ahead of the term 'innovation' to describe the innovative activity or context or outcome, with the sole purpose of being specific. You can think of and define 'Free Innovation', 'Fast Innovation', 'Academic Innovation', 'Sharp Innovation', 'Bull**** Innovation', or maybe not.

Various forms of innovation discussed in this section are compared on a few parameters at some relative contextual levels below.

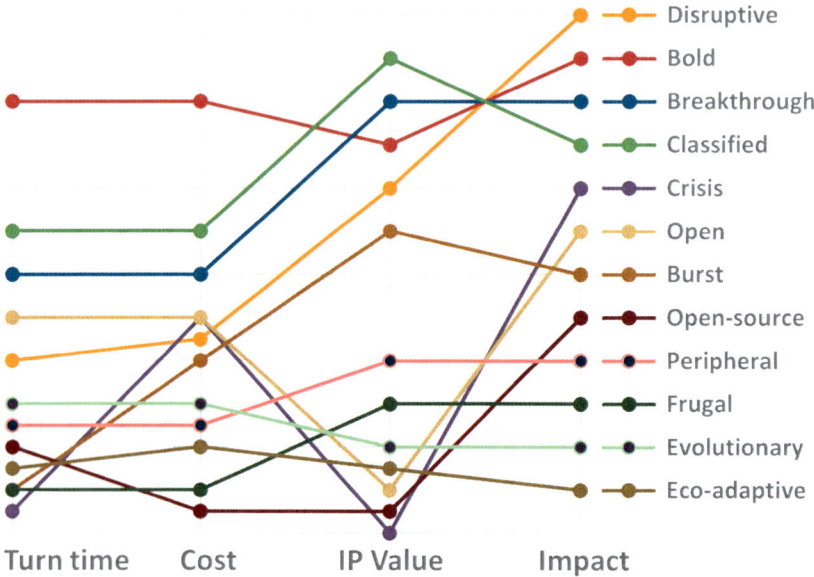

The identification of these parameters that could provide a meaningful comparison across classifications may not be an exact science. After discussions with a few expert peers, we narrowed it to Turn time, Cost, Intellectual Value, and Impact. The visual here shows these in relative terms just to provide a perspective, which is not based on data.

In the Context of the Automobile Industry

Let us just look at the most familiar industry – automobile and connect a few of the classifications above. We could think of mobility, if we wish to go back in time, and project into the future. Over 5000 years ago, man learned how to ride a horse for mobility (disruptive). The uses spread to the agriculture and battlefield (eco-adaptive). Then came the chariot (radical) around 2000 B.C., which allowed multiple warfighters to move swiftly with the power of multiple horses. Four-wheeled wagons were used in bronze age with Europe providing a comfortable seating(evolutionary) as there is historical evidence that the platforms were suspended elastically. Carriage, coaches, and wagons went through evolutionary innovations for comfort, steering, and stability for many centuries. These basic forms also went through a series of eco-adaptive and peripheral innovations for various uses and terrains.

A breakthrough or a disruption happened when the horse was replaced by a steam engine, sitting underneath the carriage, in early machines. Series of evolutions started moving the entire thing towards automobiles of today. Comfort, safety, stability, control, and cost have been the key drivers. Every year, every new model has a few additional features (evolutionary). Introducing an Airbag could be considered a breakthrough for safety. Going from 4 to 6 airbags is evolutionary. An active braking system is a breakthrough technology today. When you take a car designed for the USA market to India, you must re-do the suspension for Indian roads and change to right-hand drive (eco-adaptive). Design of rooftop rack for sports package, or a tow dolly, are peripheral innovations.

There were a lot of Burst Innovations in the industry, when President Obama offered bailout packages to the big auto manufacturers in 2009. Yes, they were evolutionary at the technology level, but the speed and scope were to help recover from a business crisis. Innovations in design methods and assembly lines can be categorized as process innovations. A brand new powerful automated manufacturing machine could be a breakthrough innovation for the machine manufacturer, and process innovation for the automobile manufacturer. When there is a machine tool breakdown causing a delivery pressure, a machinist quickly hacks a new tool to get going. This will be a frugal innovation, or workbench innovation, Car lease, rental car, and ride-sharing, belong to the business model innovation. Creative arrangements with suppliers can be process or business model innovations.

When the manufacturer is called in to secretly modify an existing car model for military applications with certain capabilities for the battlefield, it would be a classified innovation. On the other spectrum, if a car company openly solicits ideas for their next model, this would be an open innovation.

When material scientists came up with fiber-reinforced plastics, it was a breakthrough for them. However, the application in automobile bumper is evolutionary for the car. The revisions to design, manufacturing, and quality checks in the factory for such a bumper are process innovations. Most car users will not even notice the new material in the bumper until they have to take the car to the body shop, who might create an innovative business model to repair it.

When a bad guy uses the car as a car bomb or to ram through a crowd, it is an example of a dark innovation. When Toyota had an issue with sticky pedals and lives were being lost, the solution required a crisis innovation. The Eisenhower Interstate Highway System authorized in 1956 is an example of a bold innovation. Tesla is more of a breakthrough innovation. Throughout the evolution of the automobile industry, manufacturers have been doing responsible innovations – reducing emissions and improving passenger safety.

There have been a series of breakthroughs in other sectors such as visual recognition, cloud computing, networking, GPS, that are finding their way into automobile safety and control, bringing us to a driverless car. We can call it a disruptive innovation because it is going to change our lifestyle altogether. The ripples may adversely affect many sectors such as parking lots, highways, Dept of Motor Vehicles, insurance, highway patrol, emergency rooms, injury lawyers, and others.

Thus, we could say that the mobility can be characterized by a few desirable aspects such as speed, safety, stability, cost, and comfort. These are continuously pushing changes in design, manufacturing, and business models. The changes can be small, large, or lateral. I would say, driverless cars are short-lived. Once mobility gets automated, there is no reason to stick to the ground. We will go for personal drones. The technology is there. We just need a bold vision, safety regulations, and an ethical pursuit.

In the Context of the Covid-19

The world has seen a significant amount of innovation over the last 18 months in trying to survive the Coronavirus pandemic. This has mostly been in the broad category of Crisis Innovation to save lives such as the rapid design of ventilators from locally available stock and 3D printed face shields. A low-cost ventilator (~$4) in India is an example of a frugal innovation. Adapter that enables one ventilator to work on 2 patients is an eco-adaptive innovation. Making that ventilator design or digital files for 3D printable parts available to the public is soliciting open-source innovations. Soliciting ideas through web-portals for solutions for devices and vaccines is another example of an open innovation. Deployment of Naval assets Mercy and Comfort (large medical carrier class ships) to Los Angeles and New York is eco-adaptive. Adapting hydroxychloroquine for Coronavirus might be another eco-adaptive. Rapid development and acceptance of mRNA vaccines is an example of burst innovation. Making of face masks from fabric at home, is an example of workbench innovation.

Innovations to fight Covid-19 have clearly been an H2H endeavor.

Creativity, Invention, R&D, Innovation, and Revolution

Creativity is the ability to conceive an original idea, a concept, or a solution to a problem. When supplemented with processes to deliver value, it becomes innovation. Art and music are creative activities. A new musical number is generally not referred to as innovation.

The invention is primarily characterized by novelty. However, an innovation must realize and deliver value. An invention can lead to innovation, but innovation does not have to start with an invention.

Research is exploratory or investigative activity to create new knowledge. Development is a systematic set of planned activities to transform requirements into products through existing knowledge and new research. R&D should pave a way to innovation, when combined with a business model to deliver value.

Innovations are transformative by nature, for both the organization and their value chain from suppliers to the consumers. Over the life span, an organization will see multiple forms of innovations described in the sections above. Evolutionary innovations ought to be there with periods of breakthroughs and bursts depending upon how business understands and predicts the market.

Revolution results from a significant shift in fundamentals. Industrial revolutions were fueled by steam, electricity, computers, and digitalization. A very simple comparison of evolution and revolution is tabulated below.

Evolution (Same fundamental)	Revolution (New fundamentals)
Improved product design	Breakthrough products
Deals with aging problem	Deals with obsolescence
Need to sharpen your skills	Need to develop new skill set
Creates new jobs	Creates new industries
Improves cost structures	Creates new business models

Various classifications of innovations are not the only way to distinguish them. You are welcome to create ones that work best for your organization. One thing to remember is that each of these types requires a unique approach, and some of them are even diametrically opposite in constraints and expected outcomes.

Innovator Profiles

All the above classifications are based on attributes of actions or outcomes. They have not yet addressed the two frequently asked questions:

1. Is there a yardstick to assess how innovative is your company?
2. Is there a systematic way of becoming more innovative?

Here is my proposal for the classification of an organization using a profile from a market perspective.

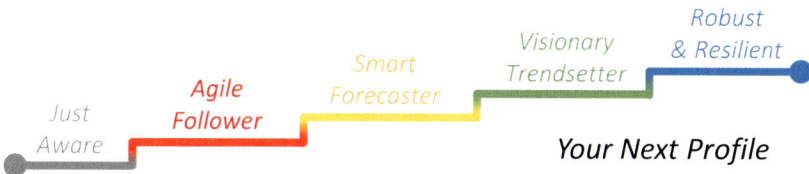

Just Aware

These are the companies that have successfully innovated and **know how** to. They continuously struggle to sustain it and keep losing to the competition. Often, the primary reason for being so is overly inflated self-worth from being innovative 'once upon a time' and not being able to develop enough of an outward perspective. Kodak, Blackberry, and Blockbuster are well-known examples. During one of my keynote talks, the audience loved the closing remark, *"Netflix'it or get Blockbusted!"*

Agile Follower

These companies innovate profitably in **response to market demand** and successfully compete on cost and time to market. They are listening to the customers, benchmarking themselves against the competition, and continue working hard to compete directly. Typically, they are good at '*How*' and are actively listening to the customer for '*What*.' Most companies fall into this category.

Smart Forecaster

These companies consistently innovate in **anticipation of market demand** and try to be amongst the first few in the marketplace to easily recover their investment. They empathize with the customer to understand the unarticulated needs, invest in competitive intelligence to predict their moves, and compete on offering continuously increasing value ahead of the competition. They typically understand the '*What*' and the '*How*' and are seeking '*Why*.' Examples include Airbus, Ford, Sony, and other such companies.

Visionary Trendsetter

These companies are natural at innovation and **create a demand** with new products and services. They educate the customers on '*Why and How*' of their offerings, while making the competition irrelevant. They start with '*A Why Not.*' For example, SpaceX, Lockheed Martin, Cox, Pepsi, Tesla.

Robust and Resilient

These companies consistently deliver profitable innovation in the face of uncertainty; they are the trendsetters, who have also built so much branding, talent, and cash reserves they can absorb any emerging disruption, even when sometimes missing a trendsetting scenario. They have developed **some immunity** to market forces. These are Google, Apple, Amazon, … class.

I urge you to self-assess where you are today and where would you like to be, to get full value. This is a good starting point for any innovation journey.

Just a note of caution, not everyone needs to be a *Visionary Trendsetter.* There is nothing wrong in being a *Smart Forecaster,* which offers stability and growth at an affordable risk. Being a *Trendsetter* entails a lot of risk, and is not for everyone, or every occasion.

Let's Summarize

Different experts have different perspectives on what innovation is and what it is not. I have shared a few definitions and types to provide a perspective that I believe to be a relatively simple to comprehend and apply. Some of my fellow experts say innovation is a process, others call it a skill or a competency. I think it is … **a human mindset** … that inspires to challenge assumptions, break away from generally accepted norms, explore new options, experiment, and learn from failures, and eventually create a new value for someone; be it a single user or the entire humanity. The realization of value is the ultimate objective; desired impact, and the rationale for organizations to engage in innovative activities.

During my early days of innovation, I used to say, *"Learning to innovate is like learning to paint or play a piano. There are both logic and art to it. You can pick up the logic in a day, but the mind-memory-muscle coordination takes months of practice. You can learn it. It is not the privilege of just the gifted few."*

Over the past few years, I come to realize that another metaphor fits even better. *"Innovation is like a sport – a team sport, a contact sport, played in the market arena. You don't win every game, but if you practice regularly with a coach, your success rate keeps getting better."*

> *Just like a sport, music, or art, innovation is a human activity.*

39

Let's Take a Selfie

My level of engagement in new initiatives is generally (Mark with x)

☐ *Tolerance* – I will take the pain of change, so I survive another day.

☐ *Acceptance* – I understand what is happening and accept it, reluctantly.

☐ *Compliance* – I will do the minimum required to avoid penalty.

☐ *Commitment* – I will do whatever it takes to deliver, ethically.

☐ *Obsession* – I am willing to lose everything to succeed (sacrificial).

I think we are …

☐ *Onetime Innovators* – Successful start-up, scale-up, and stagnated.

☐ *Returning Innovators* – Innovated, stagnated, and now turning around.

☐ *Serendipitous Innovators* – It is all hit and trial, and survival.

☐ *Consistent Innovators* – Profitably innovating in sync with the market.

☐ *Occasional Innovators* – Whenever competency and opportunity meet.

☐ *Crisis Innovators* – Innovative whenever desperate to survive.

☐ *None of the above* – A new kind called …

Generally, I work with …

☐ *Data* – Numbers arranged in some readable form, so it makes sense.

☐ *Information* – Understanding derived from data (trends, cause-effect).

☐ *Knowledge* – Understanding of facts (information + observer).

☐ *Wisdom* – Optimum actionable judgment (based on knowledge+action).

☐ *Intelligence* – Interpreting the known (use of knowledge+anticipation).

☐ *Vision* – Envisage the future, based on wisdom/experience/knowledge.

☐ *People* only.

☐ *Alone.*

I think we have a bias towards (mark with an x) …

Near-term	O O O O O	Far-term
Tangible	O O O O O	Intangible
Reactive	O O O O O	Pro-active
Productivity	O O O O O	Innovation
Incremental	O O O O O	Step change
Machines	O O O O O	Humans

I am reading this book to help me develop …

☐ *Myself* – Develop new appreciation of role of humans in innovation.
☐ *Process* – Optimize role of human in our innovation process.
☐ *Enterprise* – Take the company to a new level of human performance.
☐ … add your own

I recollect having innovated the following at work/home.

Processes

Products

Business models

I think, our organization's innovation profile is …

☐ *Aware* – Know how to innovate.

☐   In between.

☐ *Agile Follower* – Innovating in response to market demand.

☐   In between.

☐ *Smart Forecaster* – Innovating in anticipation of market demand.

☐   In between.

☐ *Visionary Trendsetter* – Innovating and creating market demand.

☐   In between.

☐ *Robust & Resilient* – We got the world under control.

☐ I still cannot tell.

From the following list, my choice of top 5 innovations is …

☐ Printing Press
☐ Light Bulb
☐ Airplane
☐ PC / Internet
☐ Vaccines
☐ Automobile
☐ Clock
☐ Telephone
☐ Refrigeration
☐ Camera

☐ Wheel
☐ Compass
☐ Automobile
☐ Steam Engine
☐ Concrete
☐ Petrol
☐ Railways
☐ Airplane
☐ Fire
☐ Nail / Tools
☐ Light bulb

☐ Battery
☐ Telegraph
☐ Steel
☐ Transistor
☐ Antibiotic
☐ X-Ray
☐ TV
☐ Credit Card
☐ ATM
☐ Guns
☐ Films

I see innovation as a …

☐ Business function – B2B activity.

☐ Business function – B2C or B2H activity.

☐ Business function – H2H activity.

☐ H2H Activity – with business opportunities.

4. Innovation Purpose: Human Needs

A NOBLE PURPOSE INSPIRES SACRIFICE, STIMULATES INNOVATION, AND ENCOURAGES PERSEVERANCE.

— GARY HAMEL

Throughout my school days, all vacations were a 2-week trip to my grandfather's farmhouse in northern India. The farm was about 10 miles from the town and employed over 15 workers, who practically lived on the land. My grandfather took care of the workers' housing, medical needs, and food. He worked very hard for 38 years after a full service with Indian Army to establish the local infrastructure; getting the government to bring roads, electricity, bank, irrigation, school, and public transport in the region. He also worked with a local bank, food market merchants, and a tractor dealer to create a win-win-win model bringing mechanization to the local farming setup. He changed the economic conditions of over 100,000 people across a 50-mile radius, and perhaps a generation after that. Although we do not have a base in that region anymore, they treat us like kings, if we drive through that region. All because my grandfather had a purpose, and he lived for it.

Hierarchical Purpose Model

In the business world, startups are invariably innovative, emerging out of an entrepreneur's purpose or passion. They scale up into a business with a formal structure, which then slides into the abyss of financial objectives. Unfortunately, the purpose now gets buried under some 'mission statement' that very few employees understand. Most of the employees frequently walk past the mission statement on the wall to address their boss or customer's immediate need. Innovation becomes an enabling tool with an emphasis on speed and cost. The larger the organization, the deeper this abyss gets.

Then comes the annual cycle of revising the business strategy; supposed to guide the teams on how to compete successfully in the marketplace. New products, services, or new markets is one of those guidelines. Innovation and strategy are often mistakenly viewed as separate approaches, and I hear CEO's saying, "*let's get our strategy first, and then we will work on innovation.*" That is as good a sign of an aging organization as any.

> *Purposeful innovation* is the best strategy.

Innovation is not just a keyword or an action to support strategy. Purposeful innovation is the way for an organization to be forward looking and deliver true lasting value, besides financial responsibility and sustainability. Ray Stasieczko says, "*Innovative organizations understand the importance of relevant products; while dying organization stay obsessed with selling the relevancy of their soon to be obsolete products.*" Innovation is the most important factor in economic viability, technology adoption, social well-being, and sustainable development.

The purpose comes from the heart of the leadership, and it can be at various levels, broadly classified below:

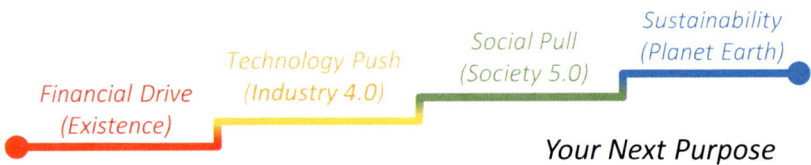

Financial Drive (Existence) — *Technology Push (Industry 4.0)* — *Social Pull (Society 5.0)* — *Sustainability (Planet Earth)*

Your Next Purpose

Financial Drive

Where the purpose is to provide enough sales and profit margins, to stay in business, and perhaps grow. I find this to be the lowest level of purpose, although mostly described, justified, and referred to under the context of

Business decisions. I would prefer to call it merely an objective so you can exist for a larger purpose, … to create value in some form.

Management in the 20th century was, in large part, the art of strategic planning. You gathered information about markets, competitors, and other trends and then planned accordingly. Strategy was like a game of chess. You planned each move in response to a changing board and anticipation of competitors' moves. Primary tools include Voice of the Customer (VOC), Strength, Weakness, Opportunities, and Threats (SWOT), Continuous Product Improvement, and Business Model Innovation.

Today, the technology cycles move faster than planning cycles ever could, so we need to take a more Bayesian approach to strategy. Instead of trying to get every move right — which is impossible in today's environment — we need to become less wrong over time. Essentially, we need to treat strategy like a role-playing game, taking quests that earn us experience and artifacts along the way.

That means, we will need to plan differently. Besides strategic planning, or planning based on things we know, or we think we know; we need to start innovation planning or planning based on things we need to learn to solve new and important problems.

> Today, you may plan the journey as much as you like,
> but you must prepare for unanticipated diversions.

A significant question in this age of rapid innovation is "*What will Make Your Business Irrelevant in 5 Years?*" Hint: market forces, technology, talent, business model, or these big four (Amazon, Google, Apple, Elon Musk) endeavors that have emerged from zero to the top in about 25 years; half a career span for most of us these days.

You do not plan the journey as much as you prepare for it. I would prefer to use the terms *'Strategic Readiness'* over *'Strategic Planning.'*

Technology Push – Industry 4.0 [14]

When the purpose is to successfully develop, leverage, enable, exploit the cyber-physical integration into process, product, service, or business application. It is OK to have a technology development as a defined purpose, but it makes a lot more sense to connect it with an impact on everyday living.

The original portfolio of technologies within Industry 4.0 had Big Data and Analytics, Autonomous Robots, Simulation, Horizontal and Vertical Systems Integration, Industrial Internet of Things, Augmented Reality, Cybersecurity, Cloud, and Additive Manufacturing. Now it should also include Artificial Intelligence (AI), Blockchain, Voice Control and Assistance, Quantum Computers, and 5G. Digital Twin and Digital Thread which connect the cyber and physical spaces are the key to creating value through relevant applications.

Industry 4.0 offers tremendous opportunities at various levels from cleaning the oceans down to desktop effectiveness or point of action. Different profiles look at technology differently.

Agile Followers watch & adopt as and when they see maturity and value.
Smart Forecasters are a little ahead of the game adopting, tweaking, & leveraging these to create new products and services.
Visionary Trendsetters develop these technologies and show the value through application.

Interestingly, the companies with a financial purpose frown upon these technology projects as a cost driver. While those with social or sustainability purposes like to leverage these technologies as tools. Industry 4.0 is scary or cute to those who are still working to discover their purpose.

Technology for the sake of technology could be a purpose for the techies; however, the leaders ought to think of making life a little better for

---

humans, across all domains of everyday living – home, city, work, manufacturing, healthcare, mobility, … towards the next revolution …

Social Pull – Society 5.0 [15]

When the purpose is to create a better life for human beings. This is the Japanese perspective and response to Germany's Industry 4.0; Cyber-Physical-Human confluence to create a smart society. This is the onset of purposeful innovation, and it now makes sense. Technology for the sake of technology or money only brings us halfway. Application for the benefit of humanity is where it ought to lead us.

Portfolio of leading social pulls include smart living (homes and city), smart healthcare (eHealth, mHealth, wearables, ambient assisted living), smart mobility (indoor, outdoor, intra-city, inter-city, cross-continent), smart grid and renewables (substations, mobile, meters, appliance) and smart workplace (factory, office).

Society 5.0 is an attempt to create a human-centered society that balances economic advancement with the resolution of social problems by a system that highly integrates cyberspace and physical space. Social reform (innovation) in Society 5.0 will achieve a forward-looking society that breaks down the existing sense of stagnation, a society whose members have mutual respect, transcending the generations, and a society in which everybody can lead an active and enjoyable life. All the technologies in Industry 4.0 and supporting business models have the potential for social transformation.

> Eventually, if everything around you is *smart*,
> Would you still need another purpose? Of course.

---

[15] https://www8.cao.go.jp/cstp/english/society5_0/index.html

Sustainable Development[16]

This is where your purpose goes beyond humanity and addresses the sustainability of the ecosystem on our planet for a long time to come. True sustainability[17] requires a balance of economic, social, and environmental factors in equal harmony. Sustainable development is defined as *'Development that meets the needs of the present without compromising the ability of future generations to meet their own needs.'*

United Nations (UN) document called Brundtland Report[18] provided early guidance on the subject in 1987. **Humanity can make development sustainable.** The concept of sustainable development implies limits – not absolute limits but limitations imposed by the present state of technology and social organization on environmental resources and by the ability of the biosphere to absorb the effects of human activities. This understanding and evolution continued with eight 'Millennium Development Goals' for the period 2000-2015 and now a set of 17 Sustainable Development Goals for the period 2015-2030. These 17 goals are somewhat hierarchical. The first few are basic and more relevant to the developing countries. The ecological and spiritual goals are more relevant for the developed countries currently.

Progress is being made in many places, but, overall, action to meet the Goals is not yet advancing at the speed or scale required. The 'Decade of Action 2020-2030' calls for accelerating sustainable solutions to all the world's biggest challenges – ranging from poverty and gender to climate change, inequality, and closing the finance gap.

Earth Overshoot Day: Experts at the Global Footprint Network are monitoring the world's ecological footprint each year and pinpointing the

---

[16] https://sustainabledevelopment.un.org
[17] What is Sustainability and What is Sustainable Development?
https://circularecology.com/sustainability-and-sustainable-development.html; May 2020.
[18] Our Common Future; Report of the World Commission on Environment and Development: Brundtland Report; https://sustainabledevelopment.un.org/content/documents/5987our-common-future.pdf; UN 1987.

day that we have officially demanded more from nature than what the Earth can regenerate. This day is referred to as Earth Overshoot Day[19]. It is computed by dividing the planet's bio-capacity (the amount of ecological resources the earth can generate that year), by humanity's ecological footprint (humanity's demand for that year).

The planet's capacity to sustain resource use and waste production was breached in 1970. And it has been sliding in the wrong direction ever since. The only periods of rollback or positive movement have been during the three recessions: 1981-82, 1990-91, and 2007-09; and 2020 because of the Coronavirus pandemic. In 2019, it fell on July 29, which means humanity consumed 1.7 times what Earth gave us. Lockdowns due to Covid-19 pushed it to Aug 24 in 2020, which has now returned to July 29, 2021. Another interesting perspective is that the prosperous countries have much more impact on Earth Overshoot Day. For the USA as a country, it was March 14, 2021. Imagine, if your budget = 4.9 x sales, and you are forced to use your reserves because your annual revenues only lasted for the first 2.5 months!

An easy inference is when the economy is good, we consume the planet more. So, the **industrial revolutions**, which are giving **society** a false sense of happiness, have certainly led to an adverse impact on our **planet's** ecological balance. It is time to balance economic and ecological systems.

The number #1 challenge is that the goals are too big and daunting. Each one of us can easily convince ourselves that we cannot make a difference. It is for government bodies, large corporations, and philanthropists to save the planet. Well, not really, it ought to be everybody's job. Policies help implement actions that are otherwise not easily adopted – but these policies do not come about without collective input. Each of us, individually, through our needs, wishes, and demands convey a message of what is acceptable to consume and produce. Corporate innovators capture the

---

[19] This section from https://www.footprintnetwork.org/ and https://www.overshootday.org/; Aug 2020.

message via surveys, focus groups and demand analysis to decide where to invest and what products to bring to society. Products are a social pull. We should do our share to educate everyone around us with personal messages.

Country Overshoot Days 2021

When would Earth Overshoot Day land if the world's population lived like...

Source: National Footprint and Biocapacity Accounts, 2021 Edition
data.footprintnetwork.org

EARTH OVERSHOOT DAY

Global Footprint Network
Advancing the Science of Sustainability

Even in the corporate sector the sentiment is slowly changing. Major investment firms are integrating sustainability issues into their investing criteria. Business Roundtable released a new statement in 2019 on the purpose of a corporation signed by 181 CEOs who commit to lead their companies for the benefit of all stakeholders: customers, employees, suppliers, communities, and shareholders. One of the five commitments is to protect the environment by embracing **sustainable practices.**

Some Examples

Amazon Mission – To build a place where people can come to find and discover anything, they might want to buy online. Lead with 3 core ideas – lots of choice, fast delivery, and competitive pricing.

Apple Purpose – To empower creative exploration and self-expression.

Apple Mission – To bring the best user experience to its customers through its innovative hardware, software, and services.

David Packard's speech to Hewlett Packard in 1960 – Purpose is like a guiding star on the horizon – forever pursued but never reached. Yet although purpose itself does not change; it does inspire change. The very fact that the purpose cannot be fully realized means that an organization can never stop stimulating change and progress.

Google Mission – Organize the world's information and make it universally accessible & useful.

Tesla Mission – Accelerating the world's transition to sustainable ~~transport~~ energy.

Volvo Purpose – An Automobile is driven by people. Safety is and must be the basic principle in all design work. – Cofounders in 1939.

Purpose and Humanity

A well thought out innovation program should aim for positive contribution on all fronts that matter to individuals, society, or the ecological system, to the extent of human knowledge. As we learn more, we must quickly shift away from stable economic business models to more purposeful execution, even if it has short-term uncertainty and economic implications. For example, moving away from single-use plastic bottles, shifting to electric mobility, renewable energy, etc.

My endeavor with all my clients is to think social and environmental aspects of every business decision, even if it is not their business purpose, it ought to be at least a constraint.

Let's Summarize

In the fast-changing world, the best way to stay relevant is to have a purposeful business, a purpose that helps humans in the short-term and long-terms. It helps continuously re-align value proposition because the focus is not on tasks, projects, initiatives, or fiscal objectives. It is a lot easier and more palatable to digest the failure of an effort when the eye is on a bigger goal.

Human purpose helps redefine the playing field, because it assumes a lot less, has fewer boundaries, and opens the mind. When I was working on simulating structural failures, I had a certain market opportunity in my field of view. The day I redefined my purpose to be *aviation safety* it turned out to be 100 times bigger; and I ventured into risk-based inspection, life cycle management, human factors; all with structural simulation as the centerpiece. That is the power of the purpose.

The traditional view of the mission statement is to align the organization in terms of priorities and focus, creating efficiency and effectiveness, engaging employees, and retaining customers. That is not enough. When you upgrade your thinking from mission to purpose, you also upgrade alignment to trust in relationships with employees and customers.

Leaders and companies that have effectively defined corporate purpose typically have done so with one of two approaches[20] – retrospective or prospective. The retrospective approach builds on a firm's existing reason for being. It requires that you look back, codify organizational and cultural DNA, and make sense of the firm's past. The focus of the discovery process is internal. In the prospective approach, you look ahead and ask what you wish to accomplish and impact in the future. I do not expect you to rewrite your purpose in terms of planet sustainability. But I do sincerely hope that

---

[20] Put Purpose at the Core of Your Strategy; T W Malnight, I Buche, and C Dhanaraj; https://hbr.org/2019/09/put-purpose-at-the-core-of-your-strategy; HBR, Sept-Oct 2019.

whatever innovation purpose you may choose to pursue next, you are at least aware of its impact on humans, society, and sustainability; and you will do the right thing in the right way.

If you had already identified next technology (Industry 4.0) or next smart thing (Society 5.0) as a purpose, you might see those in light of moving the date, so you are working towards a more meaningful purpose.

In other words, you will choose to pursue Responsible Innovation.

If you wish to go deeper into the models discussed here,
Please refer to Volume-1 **Inspiring Next Innovation Purpose.**

Let's Take a Selfie

 # The purpose of my life or our business is at this level

☐ I still cannot wrap my head around this.
☐ Financial growth, one way or the other, Legally and Ethically.
☐ Technology push, whatever can find market acceptance.
☐ Technology push to improve the quality of human life.
☐ Bring people together to make good things happen for society.
☐ Technology push to support UN Sustainable Development Goals.
☐ … Add your own

 # I can see an opportunity and a threat to my business from the following technologies

☐ Internet of Things.
☐ Artificial Intelligence.
☐ Robotics and Automation.
☐ Additive Manufacturing (3D Printing).
☐ Augmented Reality.
☐ Competitors who start using these before I can understand them.
☐ … Add your own
☐

 # I can see a social opportunity in the following industries and applications:

☐ Smart living (Home, City, Mobility, etc.).
☐ Better healthcare and hospitality services.
☐ Advanced learning and education.
☐ Smart manufacturing and exotic materials.
☐ Better environment (Air, Water, etc.).
☐ Better animal life (on land, in water).
☐ … Add your own.

I will bring others along with me, in my pursuit of a purpose

☐ Train, support, and reward my employees to support our purpose.
☐ Products, processes, and business models, to promote our purpose.
☐ Educate & set expectations with suppliers who understand our purpose.
☐ Recognize and extra support to customers who appreciate our purpose.
☐ Educate regulatory bodies that seek our counsel.
☐ Include promotors, influencer, and sponsors.
☐ … Add your own

My Purpose (Statement)

Purpose Validation: Keep iterating the above statement until the answer to all the following questions is Yes.

☐ Is it compelling enough to make me change my vacation plans?
☐ Is there anything similar that I enjoyed during my school and college?
☐ If I do not do this by the age of 60, will I regret it?
☐ Is this the most important thing to me other than my family and health?
☐ Do I have the competency and personality to successfully pursue it?

My Purpose-Profile Journey looks like

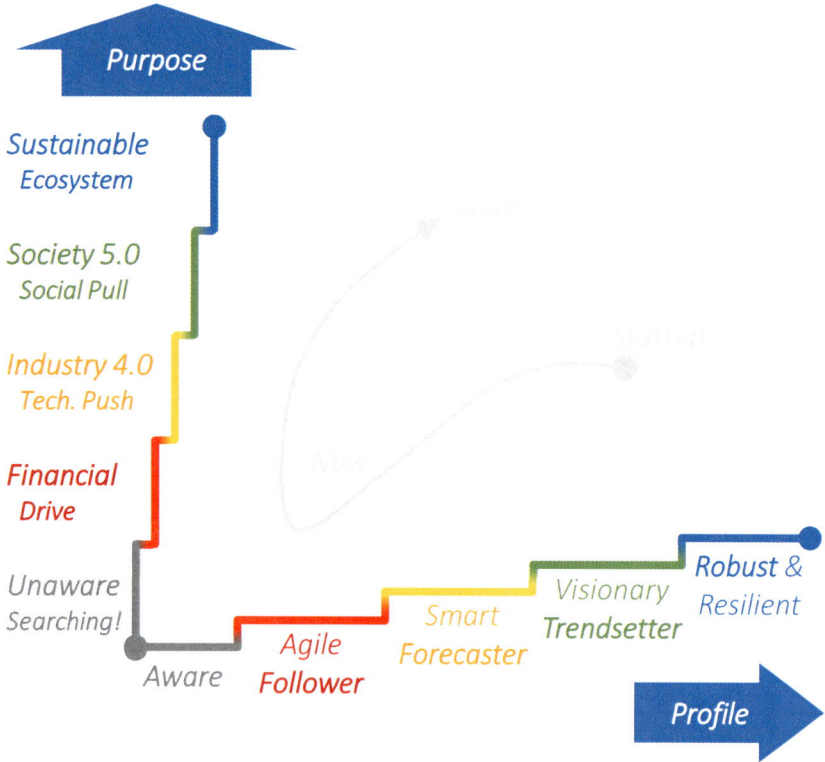

Can you plot your journey on this chart? The light gray is a very typical journey that I come across and is deliberately kept very light to allow you to draw your own line in this chart.

5. *Innovation Value Chain: Human Driven*

*INNOVATION IS THE PROCESS OF TURNING IDEAS INTO
MANUFACTURABLE AND MARKETABLE FORM
— WATTS HUMPREY*

In 1995, with a team of aerospace graduate students, we took on a challenge to build a *Flying Tiffin* – a box to carry food across the university campus. Today, we would call it a pizza-drone, which was not a popular term back then in India. We sketched around a dozen helicopter type configurations, picked an attractive one, did our preliminary design, and started our search for a financial sponsor. Once, we realized we may not get all the funding we need, we started brainstorming on what parts can we afford and how? Luckily, we managed to excite a local two-wheeler manufacturer, TVS Motor Company, to offer us a used 4.5HP engine free of cost; though prohibitively heavy for any flight vehicle. That brought us back to the drawing board for resizing around the only engine we had. The helicopter became heavier, larger, at the cost of food box becoming smaller. Taneja Aerospace, an upcoming manufacturer, offered us a small amount of money to build the airframe in exchange for our service to create and host their website – a big deal at that time and place. We then cannibalized a control system from an old materials test lab equipment sitting unused with

a friend and resolved the last of our financial concerns. The shape and size of the control system took out any remaining room and weight margin for the food box. We could see a flying machine in our future with no payload capacity to carry anything. Another round of iteration and we gave up the look and feel of the

machine to at least have enough room for a sandwich. The team went over a dozen learning iterations, and were still excited to follow through, but they ran out of time. The academic semester was over, and the students graduated. The following year, another batch of students picked up the engine, the controls, redesigned the airframe for a better look and feel, and with larger payload capacity—a result of a fresh set of minds and eyes. Just before they graduated, they rolled out a fine-looking helicopter from the local hangar (workshop) to an exciting celebration, knowing very well that the rotors were not balanced to the level required for a safe flight. That machine never flew, but the project served the purpose – *taught two batches of graduate students as to what innovation entails.*

Simplified Innovation Value Chain

Innovation Value Chain can be described as a series of connected steps, which lead to an innovative product, service, or business model. Successful outcomes typically require an innovator to make assumptions at each step, validate or challenge them at the next step, go back if required, continuously build upon new lessons, and iteratively closeout on the purpose.

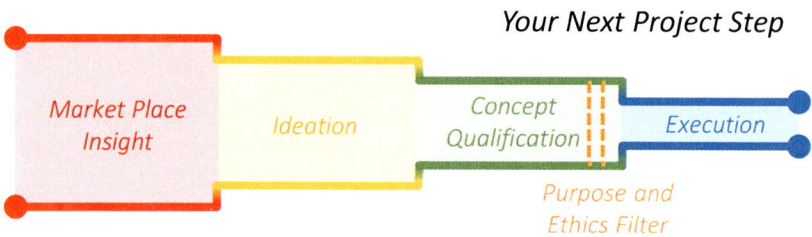

In its simplest form, an innovation is about visualization of the end solution for a customer, starting with a lot of ideas or opportunities; screening them down to a few qualified projects; and then ethically executing them to a successful delivery, or some new learning (Failure).

The beginning of an innovation process is always very hazy. It is an accidental or deliberate matchmaking between an idea and the problem it can solve. It is sometimes difficult to separate, which came first. Generally, the individuals and startups get an idea and start exploring the market opportunity, while the corporate innovations search for ideas to go after a market opportunity. In either case, almost everyone goes through several iterative cycles before converging on any idea-market combination worthy of a pursuit.

Each of these steps requires human creativity and decision making under uncertainty. It requires working with other humans with diverse perspectives. It requires project management to continuously adapt and leadership courage to take risks and accept failures.

Value Chain as a Multilayer Filter

This multistep activity from market insight to market capture is like a multilayer filter. At each step, you remove the options that may not work. From experience, we all know that out of 100s of ideas only a handful will qualify for execution. At this stage, you could either create a portfolio of projects, or use a criterion for prioritization.

Marketing folks might see this as a funnel, which is a poor metaphor because in a funnel everything that gets in from the top gets out at the bottom. In a well-designed filter, only the desired material comes out. In the case of the innovation value chain, the filter design is the innovation management process and the human reviewer, who comes with experience, bias, illusions, and desires.

Inspiring Next Innovation Value Chain (Volume-2) provides details on each of these layers of filters. How do various innovation profiles capture and use marketplace insight? How are different ideation techniques way more effective than traditional brainstorming? How do you create a Value Proposition and Qualify new Concepts? How do you assess and mitigate risk in exploration?

Deep Market Insight

When the objective is to take a new product or a service to the market, then you need a good insight into what opportunities exist out there and what are you competing against. This marketplace insight is an absolute pre-requisite to fulfill any desire or purpose to influence it.

Customer insight: The first major step in a structured innovation is to define a problem worth solving. The opportunities are all around us, in every little action starting with wake up and coffee to flying across the world for business or pleasure. Every day, we see, hear, use, or talk about new products from toothbrushes to Space Station. Most often they appear so obvious and simple in hindsight, and yet we never asked for it or thought about it, staying busy doing the same thing, the same way, in our habitual routine.

Competitor insight: The other step is to see what already exists or is in works to solve the problem you have identified. Once again, there is a competition, or an incumbent solution resisting change to start with; and when you make something new, it invites new competitors to the market.

Agile followers focus on what is currently happening in the marketplace and compete on price, quality, and experience.

Smart Forecasters gather enough insight to predict the near future market, and primarily compete on product performance and time to market.

Visionary Trendsetters search for a white space, creating demand for what customers did not know they needed, making the competition irrelevant.

Structured Ideation

This is the most creative and elusive step of the innovation, and generally, the source of the myth that you cannot teach innovation, or innovators are born. Ideation may not be science, but it is certainly not magic. It is probably an art, and sustained practice gets you to a state of mind that is continuously generating great ideas. Experience has shown that the ideas are not a random occurrence, but rather triggered by some form of an intellectual stimulus. This implies that we can create a stimulating environment or an exercise to generate hundreds of ideas. Often, an ideation session can lead to new markets, besides serving a specific pre-defined objective.

Structured ideation helps ask the right questions, bring together perspectives and strengths of the participating members, take steps beyond the obvious solutions and therefore increase the innovation potential of a solution, through volume and variety. The structure includes planning, facilitation, technique, triggers, data capture, and preliminary sorting or screening into themes.

Purposeful Qualification

After a couple of iterations between customer problem and solution ideas, you will get to the stage of assessment of their worth. At this point, you must ask these three questions before investing any resources.

Value Proposition: Does it add value to a customer/user/consumer? A good value proposition acts as a pain reliever and/or gain creator for a job to be done by a prospective customer.

Purpose & Ethics Check: Does it fit your self-defined purpose and self-imposed ethical standards, besides being legally compliant?

Concept Qualification: Can you deliver it profitably, to sustain or grow your own business? Is it dependable, scalable, sustainable, and whatever else as a part of your purpose in the short or the long run?

The steps will be iterative, more often than desired. It takes a bit of practice to get good at it. If you ever get it right the first time, then you are God or have already done something similar, it isn't innovation anymore.

I am not offended when people use the traditional term – *Business Case*; I just dislike it, from the perspective of a mindset. A business case subconsciously tends to diminish the purpose to just a financial drive.

Creative Execution

A qualified concept now needs to be converted into reality. Most companies have some form of project management, or phase-gate process to continuously reduce the execution and market risk. Depending on how far out your innovation is from existing knowledge and experience, you need to be prepared to iterate on its value proposition and execution options. The ability to work with others, learn, and adapt is still the key to successful innovation.

The simplified *ideation to monetization* innovation value chain, described here can be used routinely to address the growing needs of an organization or as a core execution engine in any of the innovation types discussed in Chapter-3.

Role of Human in the Value Chain

Market insight requires empathy, compassion, patience, and objective analysis. Human perception can easily skew the outcome and misguide investment.

Ideation is an intensive human exercise, although we have tried an AI agent GPT-3 (OpenAI) to expand the list of ideas, with some success.

Concept qualification step is where major investment decisions are made. Machines will help build objectivity, but in any innovation, since there are likely to be so many assumptions, machines can only help assess and mitigate risks. The decisions are still a human choice at this point.

Every innovation project works through a series of assumptions and requires continuous adapting to achieve a desired outcome. Machines are great a routine production, but when it must be done for the first time, like a prototype demonstrator, **execution** is again a serious human activity. *Truth is that doing anything truly innovative is still predominately a human activity assisted by machines, which are getting smarter by the day.*

Machine Assistance

To help humans in navigating this innovation value chain effectively and efficiently, we have created a cloud application – www.einstory.com. It provides a guided workflow to move step by step from idea to venture planning, covering everything in between.

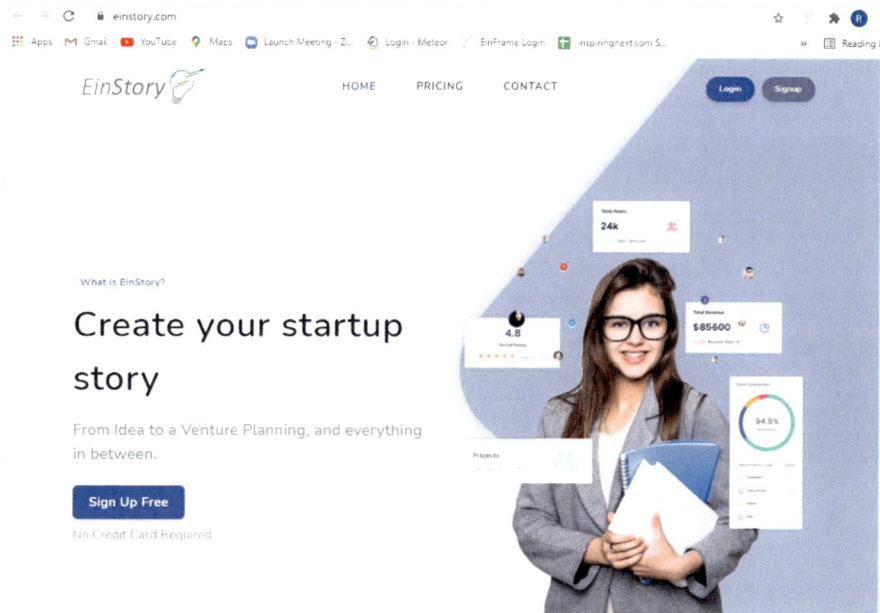

This application enables users to (a) Capture all the thoughts, ideas, suggestions at one place. Attach files if required, (b) Identify high level themes and group ideas into themes, (c) Identify the value proposition and qualify the concept to make sure that idea makes business sense, and (d) Check for purpose and ethics fit.

Let's Summarize

For many years, my innovation journey was a series of hits and misses. Then I came to corporate America, and was thrust into the world of process control, typically the lean six-sigma type. I could see both the value and the downside. The entire motivation to start my practice was to blend the concepts of structured process with creativity in a manner that makes innovation affordable, with managed risk. That led to integrating multiple tools and steps into the **Simple Innovation Value Chain** discussed herein which has now been applied at over a dozen clients. Most of the time people understand the individual pieces, however, the real joy becomes visible on their faces when they go through this to launch a new project.

Each of these steps and gates require serious decision making and humans are not perfect at that task. Similarly, at times the decision makers must make hard choices between options that are equally wrong, or their impact is not yet fully understood. We will discuss this more throughout the book.

> If you wish to go deeper into the models discussed here,
> Please refer to Volume-2 **Inspiring Next Innovation Value Chain**.

Let's Take a Selfie

I believe we are good at …

☐ Understanding the customer/market and assessment of the competition.
☐ Generating ideas.
☐ Screening and qualifying ideas.
☐ Making a business case.
☐ Executing a project.
☐ Working with humans.

Our typical ratio of funded projects to ideas generated is …

☐ One Project for ~ 2-5 ideas.
☐ One Project for ~ 6-20 ideas.
☐ One Project for ~ More than 20 ideas.
☐ Someone tells us what to do.
☐ Do not know.

This is what we do with unfunded ideas or failed projects.

☐ Trash/forget them.
☐ Capture them somewhere.
☐ Archive for future use in a database.
☐ Iterate a few times, archive in a searchable database, tagged with alerts.
☐ I am not sure.

I can see role of humans in the Innovation Value Chain.

☐ Totally driven and executed by humans, from ideation to execution.
☐ Driven by humans, assisted by machines.
☐ Driven by machines, corrected by humans
☐ … My view …

6.   *Innovation Pursuit: Human Decisions*

---

*TRULY SUCCESSFUL DECISION-MAKING RELIES ON A BALANCE
BETWEEN DELIBERATE AND INSTINCTIVE THINKING.*
— MALCOM GLADWELL

In early 2000s, while working as a technology manager, I had to take so many decisions with varying impact on the future of the organization. Fortunately, we had set up a robust process involving a diverse team, that provided a variety of check and balances. One particular year, my budget was oversubscribed by 4X. We got the project leaders together, cut the fat out down to 2X, removed redundancies and deferred low priority projects to next year. We were still needed another 25% budget to meet all the needs. I went to my executive asking for extra funds. I tried to plead and explain how *difficult* it is to cut any project out of the proposed portfolio. He gave me a lesson, "*One thing about leadership is to make a difficult decision and live with the outcome. If you are telling me that the choices are all equally important, it should not matter which one you drop. Go make a call on my behalf.*" Either he had more faith in my decision making than I had or the amount at stake was worth the experience and learning I will gain for the company. I assembled three of my peers in a room, used our gut feeling and judgment to identify two projects that will be put on hold until the funding situation changed. By the end of the year, it turned out to be the correct choice. We were all proud of the process. However, four years later, it proved to be a poor choice. I guess that is how we learn, by making decisions that are rarely perfect.

Innovation value chain discussed in the previous chapter, consumes serious investment resources in the project execution phase, which carries a degree of uncertainty and risk depending upon the '*scope of the leap*' in creating a novel solution. One reason projects and even businesses fail miserably or just drag along, is because human factors interfere with rational decision making. For decades, a stage-gate process has been in place helping project leaders decide on continued investments. This process is designed to manage and reduce risk in new product development. It has been successfully implemented by many government organizations and commercial companies. Yet many entities either cannot recognize or pay heed to the warning signs during the development and marketing stages; and keep pushing the project through until it is too late and too big to handle.

Having worked with major OEMs as technology leader and coach, I have had the good fortune of being a part of several reviews at various levels and disciplines – design, technology, component, system, product, manufacturing, process, program, business, and so on. There are well-documented practices which make the process successful and can be adopted by everyone. Yet the maturity of the process varies from organization to organization, mainly depending upon the cultural attributes and human factors, making it interesting. I am convinced that the value of review gates comes from the review team, more than the process. At times, the team can make a good decision despite insufficient input and significant uncertainty; whereas other times, it makes a poor choice despite clear evidence that might be contradictory.

Let's review the stage gate process and discuss which of the human factors makes it successful and what makes it interesting.

Stage-Gate Process Overview

A quick story to illustrate the point. After a nasty accident at an intersection, city authorities asked, *"Why do we not have a STOP sign here?"* The reply came, *"People were complaining about seconds lost due to 'stop and go' at an intersection with virtually no traffic. Since we have not had an accident here in a long time, we took the sign off, just yesterday."* There is a reason for a stop sign: *stop and look* for other traffic and de-risk.

The stage-gate process is just that—a momentary pause to become situationally aware of what is moving and may be on a collision course with your plan. It goes by various names – Phase-Gate, Stage-Gate, Stage-Kit, Passports, Toll Gate process.

Objective(s)

The primary purpose of a gated process is to align all stakeholders and reduce the risk of continued investments. It aims to improve innovation effectiveness by separating project leadership from resource decision making to avoid conflicts of interest; formalize points at which discontinuation decisions can be made; and nudge leadership to critically compare projects with other projects vying for the same set of resources.

For Business Objectives and Leaders: Annual or quarterly strategic reviews serve this purpose—to pause and look for where the competitor might come from. All it takes is a little time with the Board of Directors to properly re-position for success and mitigate business risk.

For Development Projects and Innovation Managers: Milestone-based progress reviews serve this purpose—to pause and look if it still makes sense to continue into the next major phase. All it takes is a little time with experts to properly assess readiness to move on and mitigate quality and development risk.

Typical Model

The Stage-Gate model takes the complex and chaotic process of converting an idea into value and breaks it down into smaller **Stages** (where the project team conducts activities) and **Gates** (where the review team makes a Go/No-Go decision). In its entirety, Stage-Gate incorporates the following three categories of tasks into one continuous robust process, graphically depicted here.

1. Pre-Development Activities,
2. Development Activities, and
3. Commercialization Activities.

Pre-development Activities

This includes all activities that help leadership decide if a particular project deserves serious investment or not; primarily data gathering, and analysis required to build a business case. The gates[21] may include:

- Strategic Foresight (What do we want to accomplish?).
- Market Insight (Do we understand the customer need or market gap?).
- Ideation (Do we have enough ideas to address a market need?).
- Value Proposition (Does the idea create value for a consumer?).
- Concept Qualification (Can a product/service be delivered profitably?).
- Funding Secured/Available (Project has been prioritized to start).

Development Activities

Generically, all qualified concepts become eligible for funding and should feed the pipeline for development activities. In a robust organization, there should be enough qualified concepts that leadership can choose from and build a portfolio of projects to maximize returns and manage the risk. The first gate would then be to get funded. That is not a gate for the project but for business to make a strategic investment decision. Once the project is funded, it may go through technical, marketing, and operational gates:

- Proof of Concept (Is it possible?).
- Product/service Design/Development (Do we have details to produce?).
- Prototype Testing, Verification, & Validation (Is it practical for users?).
- Production Process (Can we mass produce it for profit?).
- Regulatory and Certifications (Are we in compliance with regulations?).
- Repair and Service Readiness (Can we handle customer concerns?).

---

[21] Inspiring next Innovation Value Chain; Ripi Singh; Book, Outskirts Press; Sept 2020.

Depending upon complexity, confidence, and risk assessment, the project may have more or fewer gates. A simple study project may have an interim content review and final report and review. Complex product design may have a hierarchical gate structure such as component design gate(s) to support a system-level design gate. A very popular example of a gated process is the Technology Readiness Levels[22,23] used by DoD/NASA and many other commercial organizations. A similar one called Manufacturing Readiness Levels[24] is used by many organizations.

Commercialization Activities

Once the product has been market-tested, it is ready to create returns. The gates after this phase may include:

- Branding and Go-to-Market strategy (Do we know how to sell?).
- Back-office Sales Support (Are we ready to handle buyer calls?).
- Online Presence (Are we optimized for SEO?)
- Product Launch Plan (Do we know what the first steps to users are?).
- Early Market Capture (What have we learned from early customers?).
- Scale-up and market share growth (Do we know how to grow?).

Commercialization activities do not need to wait for all development activities to finish. It generally starts before beta users are engaged. Also, development activities may include steps to manage end-of-life, such as recycle or repurpose.

---

[22] Best Practices: Better Management of Technology Development Can Improve Weapon System Outcomes; s.l.: NSIAD-99-162, U.S. Government Accountability Office; July 1999.
[23] From NASA to EU: the evolution of the TRL scale in Public Sector Innovation; H. Mihaly; The Innovation Journal, Issue 22, p. 1–23; September 2017.
[24] Best Practices: Capturing Design and Manufacturing Knowledge Early Improves Acquisition Outcomes; s.l.: U.S. Government Accountability Office, GAO-02-701; July 2002.

Predevelopment Activities

| Strategic Foresight | Gate | Market Insight | Gate | Ideation | Gate | Value Proposition | Gate | Concept Qualification | Gate | Funding Secured | Gate |

Development Activities

| Proof of Concept | Gate | Design & Development | Gate | Prototype Testing, V&V | Gate | Production Process | Gate | Regulatory & Certifications | Gate | Repairs & Services | Gate |

Commercialization Activities

| Branding & Go To Market | Gate | Back Office Sales Support | Gate | Online Presence | Gate | Product Launch | Gate | Early Market Capture | Gate | Scale - up | Gate |

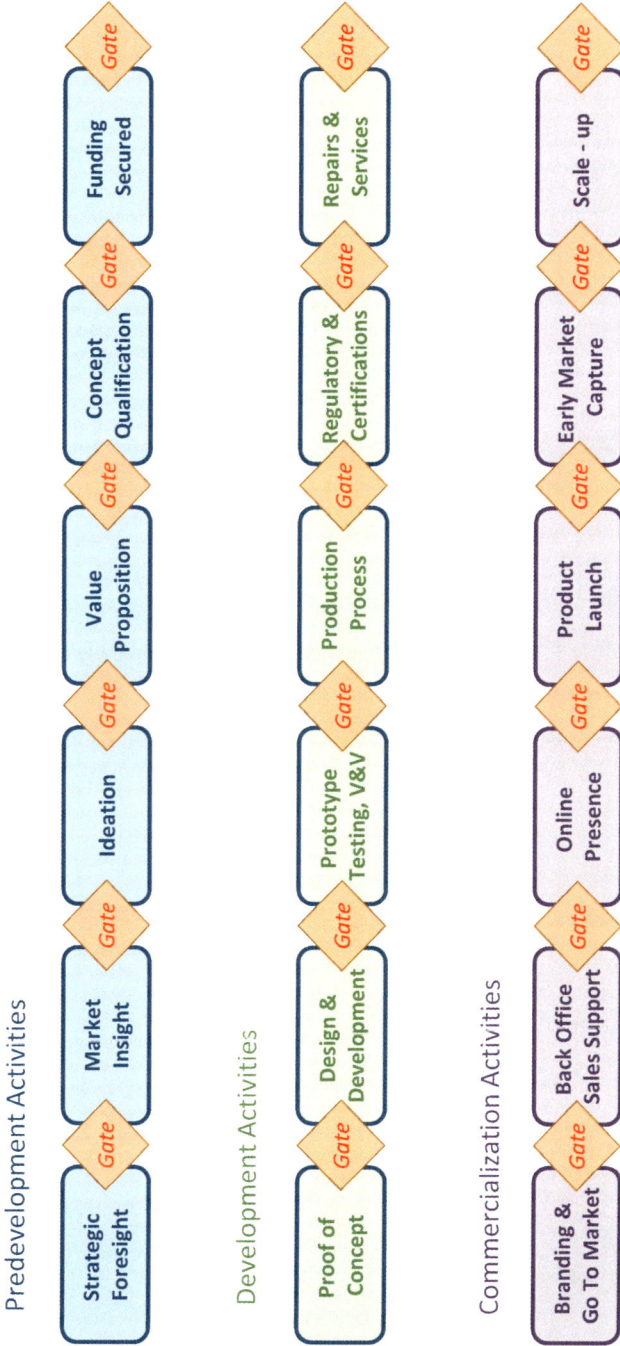

The model portrays all project activities as a visual pipeline where the Gates surface and prioritize the opportunities deserving of the company's scarce resources, acting like a filter.

Outcome(s)

The outcome of each review gate could be categorized under various classes:

GO: The team is approved to proceed to the next stage. There may be reviewer comments or recommendations for the next stage.

Conditional GO: The team is approved to proceed to the next stage, with very specific actions that must be completed by a specific date to the satisfaction of the review team, for it to be considered a GO.

NO-GO – RE-DO: The team is not approved to continue to the next stage at this point. They are assigned specific actions and asked to return for another review. This indicates a serious gap between project parameters and gate success criterion.

NO-GO – HOLD: The team is not approved to continue to the next stage at this point. There is a specific unmet criterion, or changed context, that requires a temporary hold on the project. The hold may last until the criterion is met or just a for a specific period, at which point it should be brought back for review again.

KILL: Completely abandon all effort forever and let the team move on to other activities.

A company can choose to have additional potential outcomes or have different names for these outcomes. There should be enough options to minimize both rework and schedule delays and avoid bigger cost implications later.

Implications of various outcomes

The purpose of a review gate is to reduce the risk, by ensuring continuation if the concept still qualifies. The review process is susceptible to human factors and the review team can make an error in judgment, despite all the available data and experience.

For the five potential outcomes defined above, there are five possible True outcomes and 20 possible False outcomes. Each outcome has a different impact. To reduce complexity, let us just limit ourselves to Go and NO-GO options. Figure below presents the implication of human error at the review gate.

Review Outcome	Given a **Re-DO**	Given a **GO**
Deserves a **GO**	**(False Negative)** Unnecessary rework. Demoralizes a good team. Improves communication	**(True Positive)** Ensures progress. Build confidence. Gets buy in.
Deserves a **Re-DO**	**(True Negative)** Improves learning. Saves bigger failure later. Builds stronger teams. Drives humility.	**(False Positive)** Increase losses. Exposes to a liability. Makes good learning stories. Drives process changes/policies.

True positive (GO when it should have been a GO) ensures progress, confidence, and team agreement.

True negative (RE-DO when it should have been a RE-DO) improves learning, saves failure later reducing losses, builds stronger teams, and drives humility.

False negative (RE-DO when it should have been a GO) leads to some unnecessary rework, schedule delays, and a demoralized team when they are confident. The positive that comes out is improved communication.

False positive (GO when it should have been a RE-DO or a NO-GO) will continue to accumulate losses and even an escape of a poor design to the market leading to liabilities. They usually make good learning stories, which drive process improvements, policies, and even regulations.

You can observe that there are both positive and negative implications to both correct and incorrect review outcomes. Most of us tend to miss out on positives that may come out of a poor decision.

Best Practices in a Stage-Gate Process

Thamhain[25] makes a case for careful integration of the stage-gate process with the various physical, informational, managerial, and psychological subsystems of the enterprise and its cultures and values, to be effective. I agree with many of his observations. An important one being that the team members must work in an environment conducive to mutual trust, respect, candor, and risk-sharing. Equally important, the work environment must foster effective communications, cross-functional linkages, and a business process conducive to interconnecting people, activities, and support functions.

The organization should facilitate certain practices to make the process effective and efficient. Let us look at these controllable factors first.

Success Criterion

Each gate must have a clearly defined set of criteria for a GO, based on the activities of the last stage. Meeting these criteria should essentially ensure successful completion of the project. The criteria must be agreed upon by all the stakeholders at the beginning of the project cycle, with specific metrics wherever possible. It should be transparent to the project team, and they must agree to it at the previous gate.

Review Team

The gate reviewers should be assigned early in the project life cycle and fully committed to the success of the organization and not biased towards the project. They must represent all disciplines appropriate for that gate. The suggested participation for the project review team under the phase-gate process includes the following roles:

- Funding sponsors, who are accountable for profit & loss,

---

[25] Applying stage-gate processes in concurrent engineering; H. Thamhain; Wescon/96, pp. 2-7; 1996.

- Product/service line heads, who will eventually own this innovation,
- New Business Development, which must sell the product/service,
- The project team, to defend the progress and learn from gate experience,
- Chiefs or subject experts, who are responsible for technical excellence,
- Optional invitees with wisdom. E.g., retirees, consultants, or customers,
- Representatives from the group of potential users (customers' hat), and
- Support functions such as legal and HR required for successful delivery.

Certain roles may skip certain gates, depending upon relevance, to keep the process efficient.

The members of the review team should not have any conflict of interest. The outcome of the gate review should not impact their professional or personal lives, in any way, shape, or form.

A review team must have a chair or primary gatekeeper. This can change as the project goes through various gates depending upon the primary success criterion. For example, the Detailed Design review may be chaired by a Chief Engineer, while the Go-to-Market strategy will be chaired by the Head of Business Development.

Stage Execution

In an innovation project, allow as much creativity during the stages in between gates as practical. Preference should be to keep the rigor to gates. This advice must be contrasted against the prevailing wisdom in manufacturing setups or for incremental design projects, where the gates are considered a quality assurance step and thus are viewed as a waste to be eliminated or reduced by putting rigor into the stages.

Professionally interesting and stimulating work appears to be one of the strongest contributors to a successful gate later. Project leaders should try to accommodate the professional interests and desires of their personnel whenever possible. It leads to increased involvement, better communications, lower conflict, and higher commitment. A good way to assure interesting work is for the manager to carefully match personal interests with the scope and needs of the tasks during the 'Signing on' of personnel to the task or project team. In addition, the manager should build a project image of importance and high visibility, which can elevate the desirability of participation and contribution. Such an environment helps to motivate people toward established goals, innovatively and creatively, in cooperation with stage-gate process.

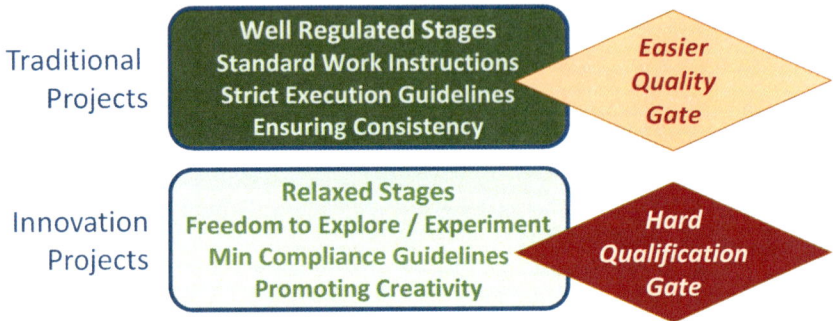

	Well Regulated Stages	
Traditional Projects	**Well Regulated Stages** **Standard Work Instructions** **Strict Execution Guidelines** **Ensuring Consistency**	*Easier Quality Gate*
Innovation Projects	**Relaxed Stages** **Freedom to Explore / Experiment** **Min Compliance Guidelines** **Promoting Creativity**	*Hard Qualification Gate*

Gate Execution

The first thing is that a gate review needs to be taken seriously. The project team must come prepared to present and discuss. A well-organized status summary, major actions, and closure from the previous gate, change announcement, or problem statement often requires detailed background work and considerable effort organizing the presentation or discussion. It sometimes happens that merely preparing for the gate review throws up concerns that the team must address to make the project successful.

Next, the review team must receive the presentation and data well in advance so that they have a chance to prepare as well. The review meeting should allow ample time to present, discuss, explore, and demonstrate that project meets the agreed-upon success criterion to the satisfaction of every review team member. Assign actions and follow-up. Publish major milestones and project objectives. This provides cross-functional visibility for the overall project and helps to unify the project team toward critical outcomes on schedule.

Meetings must be highly interactive and run on a mutual trust basis. Good review meetings are often noisy with plenty of candor and broad involvement. It is this dynamic that helps to discover minor problems at an early stage. The review team needs to maintain a healthy level of conflict and collaboration at the same time amongst various roles and disciplines. For example:

Marketing and development folks should collaborate throughout to work toward the same innovation and timeline.

Talent development manager and innovation chief should collaborate for proper talent acquisition and development.

Program manager and subject matter experts could have a perpetual conflict between product excellence and project cost/schedule performance.

Market domain experts and subject matter experts could either have a conflict or be collaborative depending upon customer push and pull for innovation.

Having seen so many reviews with passionate debates, leading to some exciting outcomes, we say *"conflict at the review gate is a good thing. How we choose to resolve that conflict during the review or afterwards – as an action, defines the gate experience and employee engagement with innovation."* The team ought to go into the gate review with an open mind, focused on the purpose, objectives, and ethics, and to educate each other.

> We must accept that both the project and the review teams
> are on the same side, addressing uncertainty.

A project should only move forward to the next stage when both the product or service development and business development teams feel that the concept still makes sense, and all the previous gated criteria have been successfully met. Any exception to the review gate or waiver of criteria or expectations should require a review team approval. The higher the uncertainty, the lower the first pass yield.

Biggest Challenge in a Stage-Gate Process – Humans!

Like any organizational system, the gated process does not always work as intended. It is a highly emotional event, irrespective of objectivity designed in the process, using all the above practices. Let us look at some of the human factors that make it interesting.

Applicability

A good friend Dr. Anukram Mishra of Genus Infrastructures asked an important question about the applicability of the Gate reviews to all projects. He questioned if there was a way to determine if a project is right for stage-gate process or not? Sethi and Iqbal[26] argue that Stage-Gate controls have the potential of restricting learning in a new product development project and thus hurting the performance of novel new products. They specifically observed through data, that control on new development exercised through rigorous gate review criteria, increases project inflexibility, which in turn leads to increased failure to learn.

For example, in some agile software development contexts for products with low failure impact, speed of execution and ease of deployment trumps rigor in gate reviews. This is probably because of the ability to pivot hard and pivot fast easily and to use the early adopter customer base as proxies for the gate review committees. An example may be an up-and-coming social media web application, that can directly track the quality, market capture, client engagement, and other business metrics in real-time; and can even run A/B testing in live environments with real users.

Success Metrics

Sometimes, the management chooses a metric around increasing the first pass yield of gated reviews. That is not a good practice. It drives many

---

[26] Stage-Gate Controls, Learning Failure, and Adverse Effect on Novel New Products; R. Sethi, & Z. Iqbal; Journal of Marketing, 72(1), pp. 118-134; Jan 2008.

wrong behaviors, such as (a) a tendency to pick low-risk ideas/projects to begin with, (b) to keep working to perfection; and (c) the review team's bias towards a GO outcome. That is all counter to innovation and the purpose of a gated review. You want to fail fast and learn fast. It is OK to track, but not to set a goal for yield. Another problem with this metric is that it assumes a balanced portfolio. A 95% first pass yield may mean that the top 5% of the innovative initiatives were all filtered out.

Schedule pressure creates a tendency to compromise marginal situations, and nudges towards making decisions with insufficient data or to under-estimate risk. And if there is a sense of urgency or a need to meet a specific performance metric, the entire interpretation of the data gets skewed.

Cognitive Human Biases that Affect Gate Review Outcomes

Decision making at the gate review is affected by bias from various directions. The reviewers can get emotionally vested with the idea and progress based on watching it develop with their input at previous gates.

Biases and conflicts of interest affect gate review performance by influencing the interpretation of data and the selection of criteria for success and failure. Existing bias in the review team can affect the project gate review outcomes by biasing their interpretations of the findings. This may lead to situations where objective assessment is almost impossible, and the review just manifests predetermined outcomes. In other words, they can look for information that will support their existing bias or what they believe about the project, instead of seeking information that will give them new insights. Individual biases[27] (Pohl, 2004) also play a role in team dynamics if the review team chair is unable to handle conflict.

---

[27] Cognitive Illusions: a handbook on fallacies and biases in thinking, judgement and memory; R F Pohl; 1st ed. s.l.:Psychology Press; 2014.

Delicate Engagement

This is an even more serious problem when the review team members are the same people who developed the project plan or have been somehow involved in project execution. Continuous engagement of the review team with the project, even when limited to reviews, leads to a 2-way entanglement. The project team learns how the review team thinks and develops ways to influence the outcome of the gate review. The review team gets empathically attached to the project (and team) and develop a bias towards their earlier feedback. Since the gate committee is not a machine devoid of emotions and biases (yet), they will find it incredibly hard to stop or kill a project in line with the changing marketplace environment. It is thus important to bring back a higher authority into the review mix at later stage gates, where those who were involved in the original approval of the project can look objectively at the project against the original success criterion.

HiPPO Effect

The most dangerous voice in a review meeting is the HiPPO: (Highest Paid Person's Opinion). The person with the biggest salary or title can crush diversity of thought and more, if not careful. Trying to keep the big boss happy can sway decisions in one direction. Opinions of certain well-recognized individuals carry more weight than data-based evidence. Status disparities can fuel conformity and group-think. When you need diversity in thinking, ask everyone else to share their views before turning to the HiPPO.

Personal Insecurity

A gated process often comes across as a threat to career progression or job security. Managers feel uncomfortable at the idea of a NoGo outcome. Management must foster a project team environment of mutual trust and cooperation, an environment that is low in personal conflict, power struggles, surprises, unrealistic demands, and threats to personal and professional integrity. Aftereffects should not include unnecessary inferences to performance appraisals, tight supervision, restriction of personal freedom and autonomy, and overhead requirements.

Anchoring and Adjustment

Anchoring and adjustment are a cognitive bias that describes the common human tendency to rely too heavily on the first piece of information offered (the 'anchor') when making decisions. Anchoring entails that the review team's decision making is clouded by irrelevant information. When the discussion is about the project plan, the team will bring in factors such as the number of man-months for a project task. This can be an inadvertent action because of the order in which the project team presents the project progress. It can even be a nefariously planted step to fixate the review team's attention to trivial aspects rather than on some aspects where the project team may be uncomfortable. Experience creates an anchor bias to previous success stories and traditional ways of doing things.

Stereotyping, Recency Bias, and Availability Heuristics

Stereotyping occurs when one applies a mental shortcut to a problem, by using generalizations. This can lead to overconfidence, especially when information is scarce. Typically, in high risk or technologically complex project reviews, the review team has a tendency to fall back onto simpler explanations and drawing parallels to their own experiences, especially recent ones. (Recency bias is the tendency to weigh recent events more heavily in memory than earlier events of the same kind.) While this thick slicing may be useful, it can lead to the review team's disregard for the nuances of the current projects in favor of – potentially – irrelevant factors. This problem can be exacerbated by another cognitive bias called the Availability heuristic, which is the tendency to judge the frequency or likelihood of an event by the ease with which relevant instances come to mind. For example, in judging how likely an event is, one might ask, "*How easily can I recall examples?*" This results in 'registered' impressions from recent projects being given more weight than the more relevant ones from further in the past.

Confirmation Bias

Confirmation bias is the tendency to search for or interpret information in a way that confirms one's preconceptions, leading to statistical errors. Confirmation bias occurs when people focus on information that supports their beliefs, while discounting other information. This phenomenon can be harmful to project gate reviews, as project managers are likely to present their proposals in a way that is most likely to be supported by the people reviewing them. Also, the review team will hear what they want to hear, not what is being presented. This may mean that project managers, being wary of being rejected without due consideration, are less likely to present the more difficult problems they knew existed with their proposals. As a result, these problems may not be surfaced until it is too late to make any changes.

Probability Neglect

Project gate reviews should be completed to ensure that the project is on the right track and to identify any potential risks. Risk identification is often not done well because of risk neglect cognitive bias and because of uncertainty about the probability of the risk. This can cut both ways. The review team can overplay a risk with low likelihood and downplay a risk with high likelihood. The review team can also underplay a risk with high likelihood and not pay attention to a risk with low likelihood. The project gate reviews should be completed by a review team with individuals who are not on the project. This would ensure an unbiased evaluation of the probability of the risks.

Framing Effects

Framing effects occur when the same issue can be seen in different ways, leading to different choices being made. There are two framing effects that can affect the effectiveness of project gate reviews. The first effect is that people are more likely to reject a new idea when it is framed negatively. For example, when they are told that the new idea will cost more than the old one. The second effect is that people are more likely to accept a new idea when it is framed positively. For example, when they are told that the new idea will have a higher probability of success. To avoid these effects, project gate reviews should be framed neutrally, with all aspects clearly represented, and a predetermined qualification criteria so that the decision is data driven. We have also seen cases where the salespeople (good at framing) get away with substandard ideas being funded to support their initiatives as compared to ideas that may be more valuable to the company.

There is an anecdote about a frustrated Ph.D. student that illustrates this effect. The student was frustrated by the advisor's incessant and repeated requests for major revisions on each review. On one occasion, he injected a few major spelling and grammar snafus in the opening paragraph of the paper. The advisor latched on to those and spent his entire time identifying more such errors, completely forgoing the criticism of the content.

Sunk-cost Fallacy

Sunk-cost fallacy is the tendency to continue an endeavor based on cumulative prior investment, despite new evidence suggesting that the investment is likely to be wasted. Sunk-cost fallacy causes the review team to keep a project going that may not be worth the time and effort required to finish it based on the time and effort that has already been spent on it. This can lead to a project review that does not make any viable recommendations for the project to continue, even if there are more viable options. Basically, the project review is not objective to the data. The decision is heavily influenced by what has already been spent to produce the project.

The way the project review teams can avoid falling in this trap is to look at the project from a global perspective. The review team should look at the alternatives available to them and ask themselves whether the project will produce adequate results to justify the time and effort already spent in the project, besides the time and effort still required to bring it to market.

Social Influence and Compliance

The need for social influence and compliance has an important role in project gate reviews. Within reviews these can be seen as a pressure, which may inhibit the honesty and transparency within reviews. The perception of this pressure may differ from person to person and could cause a different outcome of the project gate reviews. This can lead to the review team being risk-averse and opting for decisions that are mainstream. This can lead to a Groupthink bias where reviewers develop an identity as a group, focused on a mission, and reinforced by rewards. There is pressure to conform, as well as a fear of dissent.

Other Human Biases

There are a few more cognitive biases that can affect gate reviews adversely if the participants are not vigilant at recognizing them and keeping them at bay.

Hindsight bias is the inclination, after learning an outcome is true, to see it as having been predictable.

Optimism bias is the tendency to be overconfident and believe that good things are more likely to happen to them than to others.

Self-serving bias is the tendency to claim more responsibility for successes than failures.

Egocentric bias is the tendency to over-emphasize our own attributes and to under-emphasize the role of external factors.

Outcome bias is the tendency to judge a decision by its eventual outcome instead of based on the quality of the decision at the time it was made.

Choice-supportive bias is the tendency to remember one's choices as better than they were.

Good-job bias is the tendency to evaluate a task by the ease with which it is performed, rather than by the objective quality of the results.

Illusion of control is the tendency to believe we can control or at least influence outcomes that we clearly cannot.

Illusion of external agency is the tendency to ascribe one's actions to other forces.

Overconfidence effect is the tendency to overestimate one's own abilities in a given field, relative to others.

Violation of the expectation effect is the tendency to expect a given outcome based on previous experience, despite new evidence suggesting that the outcome is no longer likely.

Backfire effect is when, given evidence against their beliefs, people can reject the new evidence and believe even more strongly, thus maintaining or strengthening their initial belief.

Attraction effect is the tendency to overvalue what one already has.

Less-is-better effect is the tendency to prefer a smaller set to a larger set with a higher probability of success when the costs of the sets are the same.

Focusing effect is the tendency to place too much importance on one aspect of an event or a decision.

Contrast effect is the tendency to see a comparison as more extreme when it is made against an extreme reference point.

Representativeness heuristic is the tendency to judge the likelihood of an event by how well its characteristics match those of a typical event.

Unwarranted certainty is the tendency to decide without the information.

Duration neglect is the tendency to neglect the duration of an episode compared to its other properties.

Memory distortion occurs when reconstructions of reality get filtered through people's minds and are not perfect snapshots of actual events.

Word of Caution

I have been learning from new product developments for decades now and have seen many variations of the stage-gate process. Simple ones may have as few as two to three gates. Complex systems have multiple parallel streams, with nesting and cross-dependencies. They have seen the process from every angle—leader/member of the project under review, chair/member of the review team, neutral observer/learner, process improvement champion. This experience never seizes to bring new learning. There is simply no limit to how creative individuals in the process can affect the outcome, and there is always room for improvement.

Re-thinking the Stage-Gate Process

In light of the discussion above, the Stage-Gate process requires a critical reappraisal. This is useful for existing practitioners to improve the effectiveness, as well as for new practitioners to get a strong start. The gate review should become an integral part of the business process. Particular attention should be paid to the workability of the tools and techniques for task integration and technology transfer across organizational lines. When implementing a new gate review procedure, build on existing tools and systems whenever possible. If possible, the new gate review process should be consistent with established project review procedures and management practices within an organization.

Overall project success depends on cross-functional integration via teamwork. Each task team should clearly understand the transfer mechanism and the interfaces for their work, be encouraged to seek out cooperation, and to check out early feasibility and integration. At times it is important to include into these interfaces support organizations such as purchasing, product assurance and legal services, as well as outside contractors and suppliers, especially if there are work interdependencies or issues affecting the project integration.

When introducing the stage-gate procedure, project leaders should anticipate anxieties and conflicts among their team members. These negative biases come from uncertainties associated with new working conditions and requirements. They range from personal discomfort with skill requirements to anxieties over the impact of a new tool on the work processes and personal performance evaluations. This requires open communication and leadership trust.

Pilot Process

When revising or introducing a new management tool or process such as a stage-gate, try it first with a small project and with an experienced, high-performing team, and even an external experienced review chair. Asking such a team to test, evaluate, and fine-tune the gate review process for the company is often seen as an honor and professional challenge. Further, it usually starts the implementation with a positive attitude and creates an environment of open communications and candor.

Once proven, it should be documented and made a standard practice. Provisions must be made for updating and fine-tuning the stage-gate process on an ongoing basis to sustain relevancy. Like any other management tool, stage-gate processes require top-down support to succeed. Managers can influence the attitude and commitment of their people toward gate reviews as a project control tool by their own actions. Concern for project team members, help with the use of the tool, and enthusiasm for the project and its administrative support systems, can be inspiring. It can create a climate of high motivation, increasing employee engagement, build trust, open up communications, and willingness to cooperate with the changing requirements.

Some Helpful Tips

One possibility to avoid subjectivity and bias is that the success and failure criteria of a project is custom tailored, formalized, and held inviolate in the custody of some entity, like the IRB in some research institutions. Data from the project is evaluated against those metrics at each gate review and the same is used to de-bias the decision process. The gate committee's human instinct to go against the data should be documented and analyzed to "calibrate the gut" once the results are in. A caveat and key step must be to pivot hard on the criteria to correct misestimations.

It is easier to refine project-return estimations as a project nears launch. The unfortunate reality at many companies is that, near launch, attention shifts to delivery – and few like to disrupt execution. As a result, project managers rarely bother with updating business cases with the latest insights. Even if it is late in the game, discontinuation remains hugely important, considering that most projects consume most their development resources in those later stages as things move toward mass production. (Refer to the sunk-cost fallacy above.) A single late-stage project can prevent dozens of alternative early-stage ideas from being funded. Failing to update business cases near launch, and thus missing signals of failure, ends up disproportionately expensive. Once again, a senior level person, not emotionally attached to the project should seek clarifications, and be willing to kill the project.

Ronald Klingebiel[28] a professor of strategy at the Frankfurt School of Finance and Management in Germany, recommends having the role of business case sleuth. Such detectives could go after changes to business case assumptions when others have lost interest in evaluation and instead focus on getting across the finish line. Independent sleuths allow decision makers to build on new information about technological advancements, customer preferences, competitors' moves, or other factors with bearing on project business cases when these have the greatest resource implications. Averting one expensive fail stands to more than pay for the extra business case detective on your team.

The heightened attention to bad projects would be better placed on more promising alternatives. There is also the question of how much better a flagging business case can become, even if you look at it long and hard. Such attentional inertia can be reduced by minimizing the scope for interpretation and discussion. Setting clear discontinuation criteria beforehand ensures swifter, more automatic responses, preserving stage-

---

[28] How to get better at killing bad projects? R Klingebiel; https://hbr.org/2021/04/research-how-to-get-better-at-killing-bad-projects, April 2021.

gate decision-makers' emotional energy for worthier pursuits. If needed, split the review teams into two and play it like a mock court with defense and prosecutor to bring out hidden nuggets.

Finally, do not let decision paralysis set in when performance lags. Selective project progression is key in markets where investment occurs prior to knowing, and where learning during development determines the chances of success.

Let's Summarize

Effective management of the stage-gate process and review meetings involves an entire spectrum of critical factors: clear direction and guidance; ability to plan and elicit commitments; communication skills; dealing effectively with managers and support personnel across functional lines, often with little or no formal authority; information-processing skills; the ability to collect and filter relevant data valid for decision making in a dynamic environment; and the ability to integrate individual demands, requirements, and limitations into decisions that benefit the overall project. It further involves the project leader's ability to resolve intergroup conflicts and to build multifunctional teams. Several practices described in this chapter have been derived from the broader context of this field study to help both project leaders and their managers understand the complex interaction of organizational behaviors involved in innovation.

The stage-gate process is designed to minimize cost and risk of innovation projects through synergy and the alignment of expectations. A well-defined and well-controlled process:

- Identifies the makeup of a review team and the decision criteria upfront,
- Provides a forum and timing to discuss and approve any scope changes,
- Uses a common language,
- Maintains a nonthreatening atmosphere,
- Clarifies and adapts the roles and responsibilities during execution,

- Identifies intellectual property and other business protection needs, and
- Facilitates informed decision making for the continuation of the project based on the availability of resources, business case, and risk analysis.

However, for the process to deliver on its promise effectively, the organization must deliberately create an environment of healthy conflict at gate reviews. The review team must be:

Competent to make the right decisions, despite any emotional attachment,
Objective to minimize bias and emotional interference, and
Empowered to judge and stop/redirect a project, despite business concerns.

Good gate reviews are a work of art and science.

> If we fail to fail an innovation, we send it to market
> — Paul Misener, Amazon
> During Innovation Roundtable 2021

Special Acknowledgement

Part of this chapter is a collaborative work with Vaibhav Garg and an AI agent GPT-3. Some details on human-machine collaboration are discussed in the Appendix. In July 2021, this work was submitted for publication to International Journal of Innovation Science, titled *"Human Factors and Best Practices in Stage-Gate Process."* Its application to inspection industry was published in Volume 40 as Article # 71 in a special issue of Journal of NDE on NDE 4.0, titled *"Human Factors in NDE 4.0 Development Decisions."*

Did you notice?

The shadows of the heart, brain, and bulb on the cover page are as if the light source is overhead. It was technically correct until I decided to turn the light 'ON' during cover page review. Then the artist forgot to change the shadow pattern and I missed it during my final OK. The consequence – we have a real-life example of human factors at gate reviews, to quote here. 😊

Let's Take a Selfie

 # I believe we have a robust stage-gate process, because …

- ☐ Lot of check lists at each stage and each gate.
- ☐ Diverse and empowered review team.
- ☐ Executives attend every conversation.
- ☐ All decisions are data-based.
- ☐ There are ample funds to verify all assumptions.

 # Our review team has the following attributes

- ☐ Listening, learning, and mentoring.
- ☐ Full spectrum of discipline knowledge, market knowledge, and more.
- ☐ Sense of urgency and discipline.
- ☐ Ability to address bias, illusions, conflicts, and other human traits.
- ☐ Ability to harness assistance from intelligent systems.
- ☐ Reviews are isolated from traditional business metrics.
- ☐ Tough and success oriented.
- ☐ Pragmatic and success oriented.
- ☐ Bias towards failure at the gates.

 # Our review Stage-gate process has the following attributes

- ☐ Loosely defined stages   and loosely structured gates.
- ☐ Well-defined stages   and loosely structured gates.
- ☐ Loosely defined stages   and well-structured gates.
- ☐ Well-defined stages   and well-structured gates.
- ☐ I don't know

 # Bias Concerns – Please go back to the section and mark them if you have not already done.

7.   *Innovation Framework: Human Control*

---

*YOU DON'T HAVE TO BE A GENIUS OR A VISIONARY OR A GRADUATE,
YOU JUST NEED A FRAMEWORK AND A DREAM
— MICHAEL DELL*

For years, people have been made to believe that innovation is a privilege of the gifted few. Well, the gifted folks do it naturally, and for the rest of us, it comes with training, ambiance, and some method to the madness. In my early days of innovation coaching practice, I had a matrix of exactly 25 processes and tools to *Enable organizations to build a culture of Robust Innovation and Productivity Improvement* (my original mission statement in 2014). Like many entrepreneurs, I had ventured into the market with little market insight and some appreciation of the innovation value chain. At one conference, I bumped into a former colleague Dr. Gopi Katragadda, who had just taken over as Chief Technology Officer for the Tata Group, a $110 billion conglomerate. He asked, if I could help him use my toolset for his 90 business units that span from Tea to Automobiles. My quick response was *"I am a butterfly; I should not go out on a date with an elephant."* He laughed out loud and probably thought '*What if the elephant wants to go on a date with the butterfly?*' He still left me with an open-ended offer to get back to him when I think I was ready. Although I was convinced that they should work with McKinsey or Accenture and not Ripi Singh, I looked at redefining the matrix, to drive consistency and confidence across diverse business units of a global entity. The +4π **Innovation Framework** was born, for use by any organization. I got back to the Tata Group, but it was too late. By then, that elephant had gone on a date with a bumblebee. You see, the beauty in engaging with leaders like Gopi, is they leave you with inspiring questions and confidence that even a butterfly can date an elephant! Their early feedback validated the concept.

Coming back to the evolution of innovation; for the last three centuries, we have seen many entrepreneurs convert their inventions to products of value and change the lifestyle. Nowadays, innovative products result from multidisciplinary engagement, and entrepreneurship requires serious business and marketing skills. Large corporations struggle to innovate faster, cheaper, better. So many books hit the market on the topic, each addressing some elements of value. Still, the leaders struggle. The books provide the ingredients; you need a recipe that helps create a dish to your taste. Where does that come from?

On one side, the business schools will teach you the need for vision, objectives, planning, IP management, knowledge augmentation, strategy, etc., and they all appear to be jumbled up in real life. Management Professors and consultants tout that their tools and approach is the best one, because they believe in them, just like me. On the other hand, every organization leader, chartered to innovate, is driven by his/her competencies and management objectives, essentially their taste preference. That creates a real challenge – *'How to lead innovation for excellence in outcome?'*

The +4π Innovation Framework Layout

The +4π Framework addresses the need. It is a structured matrix of five *Innovation Profiles* and four synergistic *Activity Tracks*, as laid out in the graphic below. It provides a structure to the application of various tools and processes and identifies areas that are human intensive. Enterprise-level excellence emerges through synergy, continuity, and connectivity of the best practices and practitioners; use of the same language, measures, and monitoring. This holistic approach is often missing in organizations despite their focus on process optimization. In fact, I would say, a belief that process control is the answer to all miseries is a fallacy. Human connection across processes is where things breakdown, particularly when processes are also subject to continuous improvement. Most organizations realize it when they try to automate a value stream of several processes that looks good on paper.

The Five Innovation Profiles

The innovation profiles as defined earlier in Chapter-2, are

1. *Just Aware:* Have successfully innovated once and **know** how to,
2. *Agile Follower:* Innovate profitably in **response** to market demand,
3. *Smart Forecaster:* Innovate in **anticipation** of market demand,
4. *Visionary Trendsetter:* Innovate and **create** a market demand, and
5. *Robust & Resilient:* Visionary Trendsetters **immune** to market changes.

This definition is simplistic. It helps create a starting point, but you need a bit more to self-assess and a lot more to improve your profile. Over the years, many more characteristics have emerged that define the profile and organization behavior, or culture, or attitude towards innovation.

The Four Activity Tracks

The synergistic activity tracks are

1. *Innovation Strategy* provides direction,
2. *Innovation Capital* addresses resources,
3. *Innovative Activity* is for effective execution, and
4. *Lean Innovation* makes it efficient.

Inspiring next Innovation Framework[29] defines the $+4\pi$ Innovation Framework model along with several profile characteristics. It also compares the proposed Framework with some of the well-established models from McKinsey, Booz & Company, Boston Consulting Group, as well as ISO. Most of them seem to either discuss outcomes (equivalent to profiles) or efforts (equivalent to tracks). The $+4\pi$ Framework is the only one with a full matrix style, making it easier to use as an actionable set of tools.

---

[29] Inspiring Next Innovation Framework; Ripi Singh; Book Outskirts Press, 2020.

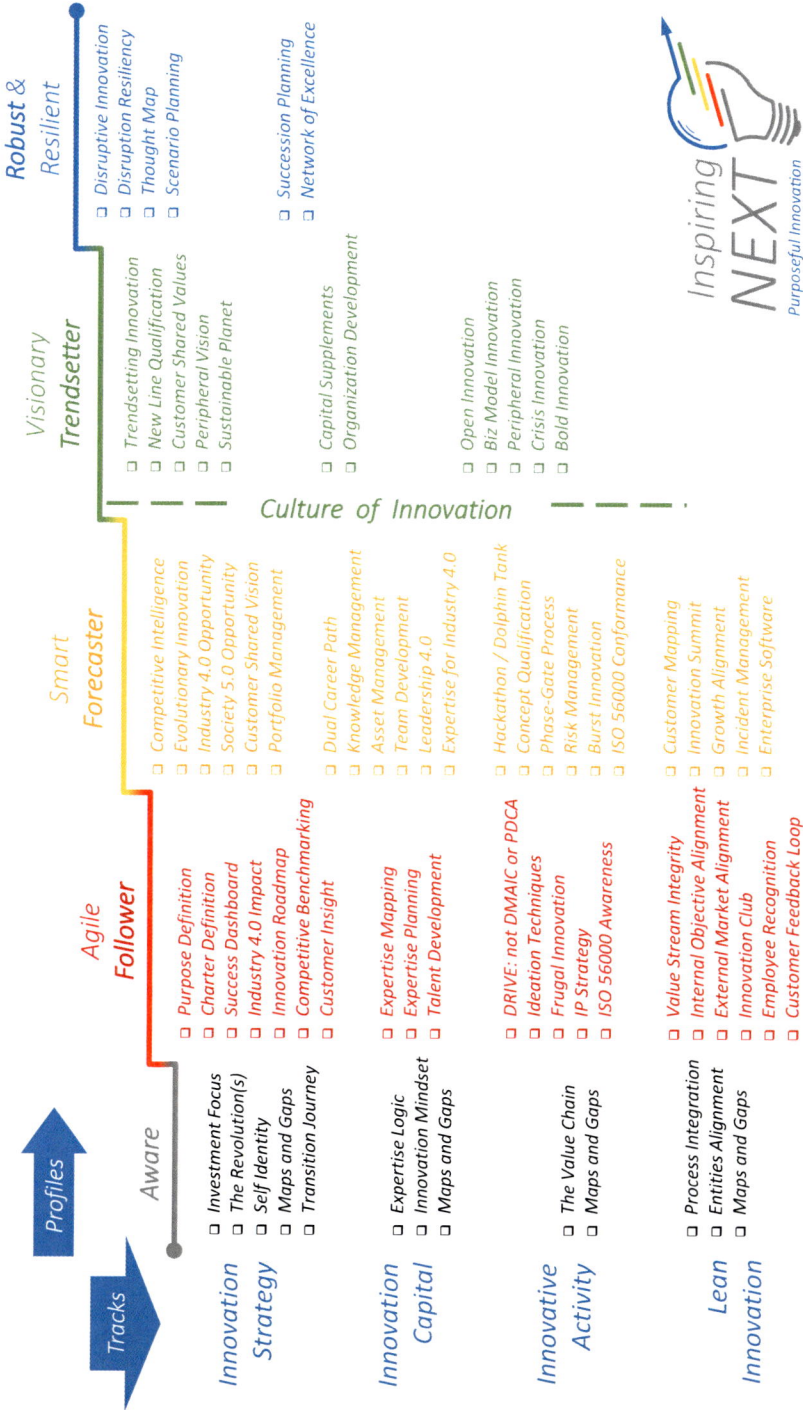

Profiles (→): Aware · Agile Follower · Smart Forecaster · Visionary Trendsetter · Robust & Resilient

Tracks (→): Innovation Strategy · Innovation Capital · Innovative Activity · Lean Innovation

Culture of Innovation

Innovation Strategy

- **Aware**
  - Investment Focus
  - The Revolution(s)
  - Self Identity
  - Maps and Gaps
  - Transition Journey
- **Agile Follower**
  - Purpose Definition
  - Charter Definition
  - Success Dashboard
  - Industry 4.0 Impact
  - Innovation Roadmap
  - Competitive Benchmarking
  - Customer Insight
- **Smart Forecaster**
  - Competitive Intelligence
  - Evolutionary Innovation
  - Industry 4.0 Opportunity
  - Society 5.0 Opportunity
  - Customer Shared Vision
  - Portfolio Management
- **Visionary Trendsetter**
  - Trendsetting Innovation
  - New Line Qualification
  - Customer Shared Values
  - Peripheral Vision
  - Sustainable Planet
- **Robust & Resilient**
  - Disruptive Innovation
  - Disruption Resiliency
  - Thought Map
  - Scenario Planning

Innovation Capital

- **Aware**
  - Expertise Logic
  - Innovation Mindset
  - Maps and Gaps
- **Agile Follower**
  - Expertise Mapping
  - Expertise Planning
  - Talent Development
- **Smart Forecaster**
  - Dual Career Path
  - Knowledge Management
  - Asset Management
  - Team Development
  - Leadership 4.0
  - Expertise for Industry 4.0
- **Visionary Trendsetter**
  - Capital Supplements
  - Organization Development
- **Robust & Resilient**
  - Succession Planning
  - Network of Excellence

Innovative Activity

- **Aware**
  - The Value Chain
  - Maps and Gaps
- **Agile Follower**
  - DRIVE: not DMAIC or PDCA
  - Ideation Techniques
  - Frugal Innovation
  - IP Strategy
  - ISO 56000 Awareness
- **Smart Forecaster**
  - Hackathon / Dolphin Tank
  - Concept Qualification
  - Phase-Gate Process
  - Risk Management
  - Burst Innovation
  - ISO 56000 Conformance
- **Visionary Trendsetter**
  - Open Innovation
  - Biz Model Innovation
  - Peripheral Innovation
  - Crisis Innovation
  - Bold Innovation

Lean Innovation

- **Aware**
  - Process Integration
  - Entities Alignment
  - Maps and Gaps
- **Agile Follower**
  - Value Stream Integrity
  - Internal Objective Alignment
  - External Market Alignment
  - Innovation Club
  - Employee Recognition
  - Customer Feedback Loop
- **Smart Forecaster**
  - Customer Mapping
  - Innovation Summit
  - Growth Alignment
  - Incident Management
  - Enterprise Software

Inspiring NEXT — Purposeful Innovation

Framework Design

Let us look at the Framework, one track at a time, and see how various tools buildup the profile.

Track – Innovation Strategy

This track defines the strategic roadmap – the products and services a company would develop along with a timeline to capture the market share. Most of us have some form of a roadmap. It may be a simple list of things to do in a sequence; or a full up graphic representation of projects linked to markets and resources along with timelines. The important things are the quality of data used to create the roadmap, how far ahead are you looking, and how much uncertainty you are prepared to handle. All these are explicitly connected with and determine your innovation profile.

This track contains methods to understand the marketplace for building a strategic innovation roadmap. The set of tools in this track progressively adds rigor to the roadmap through deeper customer insight, competitive intelligence, technology trends and forecasting, investment management, and uncertainty management.

A strategic roadmap is like the GPS for your car that guides you through the fastest or shortest route to your destination.

Track – Innovation Capital

This track includes developing and managing critical resources to support the Innovation Strategy and build a competitive advantage in today's knowledge economy. Most of us think that the funding is a primary resource, popularly referred to as 'Cash is King.' But today, 'Talent is King' and 'Cash is Queen.' Talents and its ability to create new knowledge, apply existing knowhow, secure IP is a differentiator. The approach to capital development is also profile dependent.

This track progressively develops the innovation capital to build a sustainable organization, have strong partnerships, and even support a healthy eco-system. Set of tools guide subject matter expertise & leadership development, high-performance team building, knowledge augmentation, leveraging networks, succession planning; all using novel visual maps.

Innovation capital is like the power under the hood of your car that will enable you to reach your destination.

Track – Innovative Activity

This track defines the process to systematically develop new products, reducing risk and cost. This guides the team through an innovation value chain which begins with a white space or a market demand and ends with an emotionally engaged customer. The basic value chain outlined in Chapter-5 can be adapted to any type of innovation identified in chapter-2.

Innovation activity is like traveling in your car.

Track – Lean Innovation

This track aligns products, processes, employees, customers, and business metrics, to continuously improve the efficiency and productivity of the innovation. Most of us have lean initiatives and they often stifle creativity. This track is designed to work specifically with the three tracks above to remain creative.

This track provides guidance to assure effectiveness and efficiency through (a) continuity of processes (b) alignment with customers and markets, (c) alignment across roadmap, employees, and suppliers, and (d) cloud-based information management platform, based on the Framework. These things all help reduce the execution friction. This set of tools guides the employee morale and customer engagement from management objectives, providing synergistic benefits making the whole greater than the sum of individual pieces.

This is like the 4-wheel alignment & balancing to run the car smoothly.

Framework Application

If you look closely, you will notice the 3rd track – *Innovative Activity* only goes up to *Trendsetter* profile. This is so because to become *Robust and Resilient* you only need a sound strategy and capital. On similar lines, the 4th track of *Lean Innovation* only goes up to *Forecaster*. The premise being, you need to get all your processes aligned and effective by the time you become a Forecaster and should not be thinking of efficiencies from alignment while being a *Trendsetter*.

According to this Framework, if your company can reach the level of *Smart Forecaster* you can claim to have built a culture of innovation. This may be a suitable position for many; because the risk goes up sharply as you move to be a *Trendsetter,* and everyone does not need to get there.

If you do a quick self-check, you will likely discover that you do not belong to one vertical column. Most of the companies are like that. Also, you may not be consistent in your behavior to stay in one column all the time. That is a good thing. It goes to show your capability, which is always higher than typical performance; and gaps across various rows where you need to change to move the profile. Once you figure out your current innovation profile and your desired state, the framework will help you build the processes and prepare you to reset the mindset discussed in the next chapter.

This Framework is continuously growing; you can get the latest copy by reaching out to the author.

Digitalization of Innovation Framework

A major problem during implementation of such a framework is managing data, as it changes from day to day. Most common and a terrible situation is when companies keep it all in meetings, in the executive's heads, or personal notebooks. It gets a little better when it moves into the digital form of common electronic files. Problem is that they are scattered all over the company, particularly many versions so of it, in so many files, Word,

PowerPoint, Excel, and emails, not easily accessible. It gets much better with platforms like OneNote or SharePoint, because of version control and a single page for everyone.

Best is to digitalize it. Have an enterprise information management system, so there is a single page of truth for everyone. The data, information, knowledge, and workflow can be managed and controlled. Applications such as Sales*f*orce for Customer Relationship Management, SAP for Enterprise Resource Planning, and Siemens NX for Product Lifecycle Management are examples that have all shown enormous benefits to companies committed to implement.

There are a few ideation tools in the market. But really nothing that can help build the profile of your company like explained in Volume-3 or briefed here. Based on demand for innovation, a Framework for implementation, and a desire to make it efficient and effective, I partnered with one of my customers and we converted the **+4π Framework** into a cloud-based application 'EinFrame.'

Your Innovation Partner from Purpose to Success

EinFrame enables three major value streams in an intertwined manner that helps put innovation into the culture of an organization.

EinFrame: Three fully connected value streams enabling Innovation Culture

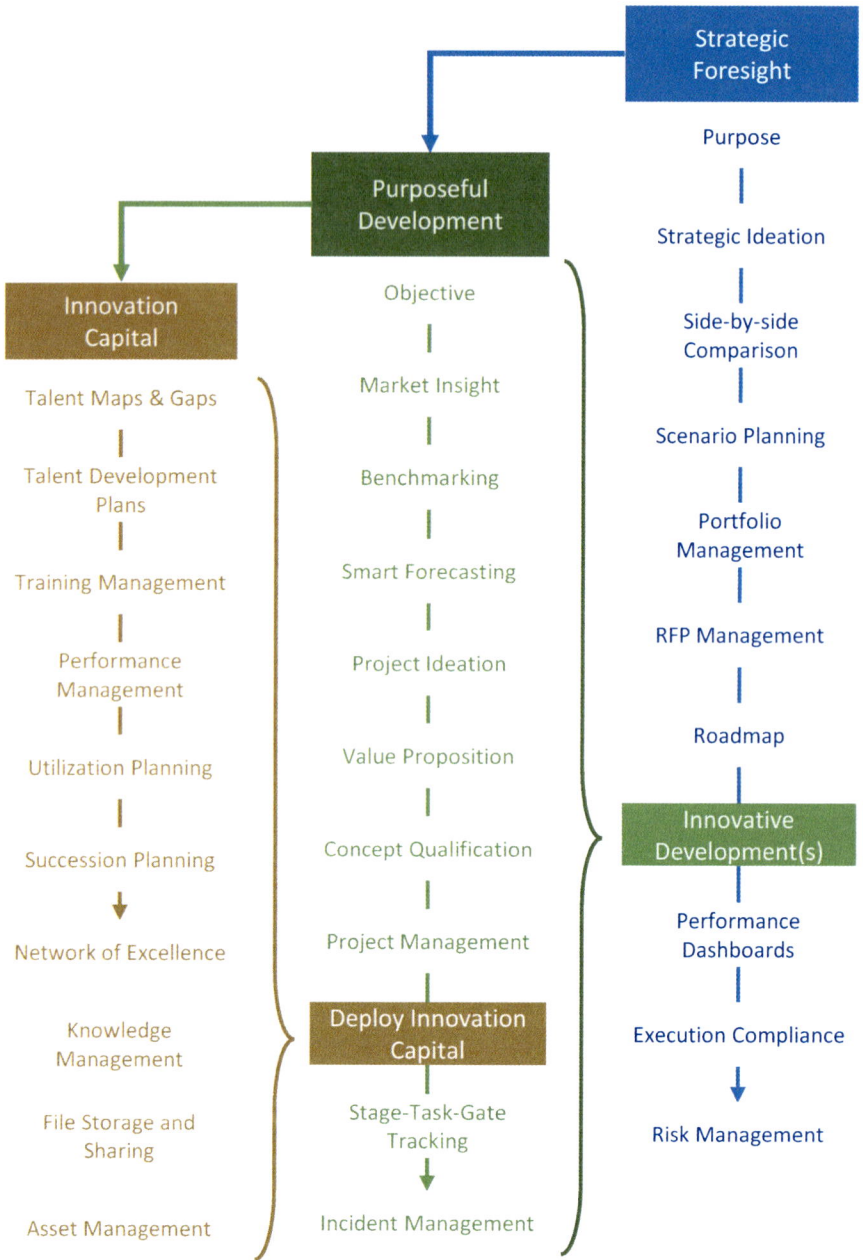

Role of Human in the Framework

The 5x4 framework has 74 processes as of Aug 2021. They fall under three broad types – creative activities, analysis, and decision making. Other than analysis that can be handled by a machine, creative and decision making is all a human endeavor. And that makes one organization better than others. Although we have digitalized a major portion of this framework in EinFrame, it does not take the human competency away, as of now. It just makes data handling efficient and effective. In the future, we will have advanced analytics to **help** with decision making.

Let's Summarize

An organization's ability to innovate is a key factor for sustained growth, economic viability, increased well-being, and the development of society. An innovation management system guides the organization from the purpose to valuable intended outcomes through proper use of tools, processes, best practices, and development of an innovation mindset.

The +4π Innovation Framework empowers leaders with a holistic view of innovation management – purposeful and sustainable.

This is how we defined an innovation management framework. My mentor used to say, "*You manage process, you lead people.*" So, the human element, an important piece of the innovation equation is all built-in the innovation mindset from leadership down to practitioners. A mindset that identifies target innovation profile, that puts roadmap, talent, and knowledge development ahead of projects; a mindset that accepts certain failure as a part of learning and growth; and a mindset that is open in every direction, all the time.

> If you wish to go deeper into the models discussed here,
> Please refer to Volume-3 **Inspiring Next Innovation Framework**.

Let's Take a Selfie

 # I can see some of these symptoms in my organization …

- ☐ Developing products in response to market need.
- ☐ Generally competing on cost.
- ☐ Market share is declining.
- ☐ Business is stable, yet stagnant.
- ☐ Projects are running late or over budget, or missing expectations.
- ☐ Quality is being compromised to be profitable.
- ☐ Customer complaints are increasing.
- ☐ Top talent is walking out.
- ☐ … any more alarms

 # I am familiar with the following innovation management models …

- ☐ McKinsey's – 3 horizons.
- ☐ Booz & Co – 3 strategies.
- ☐ Boston Consulting Group – 6 types.
- ☐ Johns Hopkins Applied Physics Laboratory.
- ☐ Innovation 360.
- ☐ Others such as …

 # Action: Please go back to the page of the Framework graphic and 'x' mark the processes you need to improve or create afresh.

8.   *Innovation Mindset: Human Behavior*

As a coach, I once worked for a company that had been highly focused on operations for a long time, with innovation being sidelined even in the engineering department. I was a little surprised. Is it possible to have many engineers and yet no innovation in the department? Deeper discovery revealed that several creative types were doing high-tech projects in their basement or at local incubator on stuff completely unrelated to their job; no conflict of interest; nothing illegal; they just needed to flex their innovation muscle. But why couldn't they do it at the workplace that may even have a business need for them to do so? My contract did not last long.

Interestingly, most of my customers and prospects want it, without having to change themselves.

By now, I have probably heard every excuse, why companies cannot innovate. Every time, I hear a very genuine concern or a legitimate reason, the above quote rings in my ear. Innovation appears to be a priority, yet even the successful leadership struggles to innovate consistently. Are they trapped in the very system that they created to help them grow?[30]. Some companies have added the word **'innovation'** to their mission, vision, or value statements **without making it clear** to the organization what exactly it means to them. They need a program and an action plan, to follow through.

---

[30] The Innovators' Dilemma; Clayton M. Christensen; Book; May 2002.

Struggle to Innovate

There are several reasons holding executives back from taking steps to create innovation-driven differentiation to change their destiny. Some highly visible aspects include leadership mindset – quarter to quarter performance, incentives, risk-averse style, too much familiarity with the market, etc.

Then there are the human minds at play, which are statistically distributed and only about 16% are innovators or early adapters. The organizations show a basic physical phenomenon:

- **Friction**: Opposing force resisting relative motion,
- **Inertia**: Tendency to do nothing or to remain unchanged,
- **Energy**: The capacity for doing work, and
- **Momentum**: Impetus gained by a moving object.

It is possible to overcome inertia/friction and build momentum through infusion of energy – a systematic transformation exercise for behavioral change and a STRONG leadership commitment.

Building the Innovation Muscle

Just like physical muscle, building of a mental muscle requires consistent sustained effort over a long period, starting with getting rid of the fat. A simple model is depicted below.

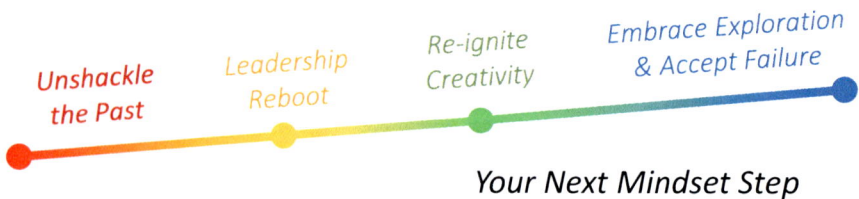

Unshackle
the Past

Leadership
Reboot

Re-ignite
Creativity

Embrace Exploration
& Accept Failure

Your Next Mindset Step

Unshackle the Past

Most of us are tied down by various success formulas, such as formal education, brand name consulting practices, management bestsellers, and other proven tools of the trade. Innovation requires that we question these, but failure can be career limiting. This fear is like a dead weight (inertia). We need to challenge the accepted wisdom and, wherever appropriate, should break free from these shackles.

Initiatives such as six-sigma which add value to repeatable activities such as manufacturing, are not suited for new product development. Lean helps with productivity, and perhaps innovation at the process level, not so much at ideation for content or creative outcomes. A Fortune article stated that 'Out of 58 large companies that have announced six-sigma programs, 91% have trailed the S&P 500 since.' The article summarizes that six-sigma is effective at what it is intended to do, but it is narrowly designed to fix an existing process and does not help in coming up with new products or disruptive technologies. Innovation and six-sigma need not be combatants. They should act as compatriots. Executives need to deploy them in the right balance, when and where appropriate.

> When people say, innovation is unaffordable;
> I ask *"Do you know the cost of not innovating?*

In the famous TV serial 'Survivor', in every round of the game, one individual gets to win get an immunity necklace, and that guarantees them a place in the next round. In the industrial revolution, there is no immunity. Do you see any business out there today that is running without email? Such will be the case with AI, Robotics, VR, ... a few years from now. Great ideas seldom occur in isolation. If someone in your company has come up with a fantastic idea that consumers love, eventually, a bright spark employed by one of your competitors will also dream up a similar idea. How much will it cost you then, when you are forced to respond, rather than forcing your competitors to respond to your great ideas?

Reboot Leadership

According to Linda Hill[31], innovation leadership is about creating a space, where people are willing and able to work hard, share, and combine talent and passion to innovatively solve a problem. Some of their characteristics include:

- Open to rapid continuous change,
- Open-minded and willing to take risks,
- Usually take the customer-first perspective,
- Embrace the iterative nature of Innovation,
- Align innovation strategy with overall business purpose,
- Stay out of the way of people innovating,
- Defer judgment, focus on success criteria,
- Accept failure, even on unapproved tasks, and
- Build communities that enjoy experiments.

Leaders understand that ultimately, innovation is more about mindset than skill set. They are not fooled into thinking that innovation is easy. They are prepared to roll up their sleeves and play to learn and then win.

Peter Drucker says, *"In innovation, there is talent, there is ingenuity, and there is knowledge. But when it is said and done, what innovation requires is hard, focused, purposeful work [human]."*

Employee mindset exhibits normal distribution, with innovators (2.5%), early adopters (13.5%), early majority (34%), late majority (34%), laggards (13.5%) and CAVE[32] people (2.5%) based on Rogers[33] in 1962. There is a good possibility that the executives are neither innovators nor laggards. If

---

[31] How to Manage for Collective Creativity; Linda Hill; Ted Talk; https://www.ted.com/talks/linda_hill_how_to_manage_for_collective_creativity; Mar 13, 2015.
[32] CAVE – Consistently Against Virtually Everything; Learned from Prof Jack Weber of Darden School, Possibility Thinking Training, 2006.
[33] Diffusion of Innovations; Everett Rogers; Book; 1962.

the executive is an early adopter, then management behavior will be biased towards accepting the change and promoting the culture of exploration. The system will encourage ideation, learning, and innovation activities. The innovators in the team will be respected for their contributions and provided space to play.

If the executive is in the late majority group, then management behavior will be biased towards resisting change and discouraging exploration. The system will prefer a known path with low risk. The innovators will be treated like a problem child, to be placed in a corner, and early adopters will always be under stress.

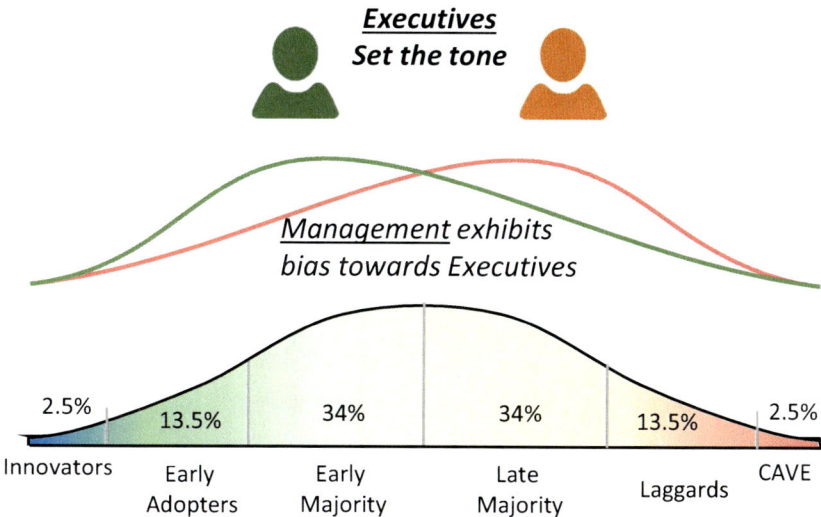

Employee engagement depends upon Management support

The leadership is best served with a role of Chief Innovation Officer and Chief of Subject Matter with an early adopter mindset.

Re-ignite Creativity

If we agree that innovation is a mental muscle, then we accept it needs a daily workout. And periodic health check. Or as Simon Sinek says, dental hygiene requires daily brushing of the teeth and a bi-annual cleaning to keep them healthy. To re-ignite creativity across the organization, you need to make a conscious effort on several activities that over some time can build the mental muscle, such as …

- Inspiring language through use of terms that promote exploration,
- Weekly innovation minute in staff meetings to discuss anything new,
- Quarterly Dolphin Tank type open ideation competition,
- Annual Innovation Summit or open day to showcase,
- Couple of hackathons a year, and
- Gamification of innovation.

The model proposed by Hienrich for industrial safety during second industrial revolution to build a 'safety mindset' can be adapted for 'innovation mindset' as well. For us to get one disruptive innovation, we need to get a few breakthroughs and trendsetters, many evolutionary innovations, and a continuous improvement in business processes, all supported by widespread workbench innovation.

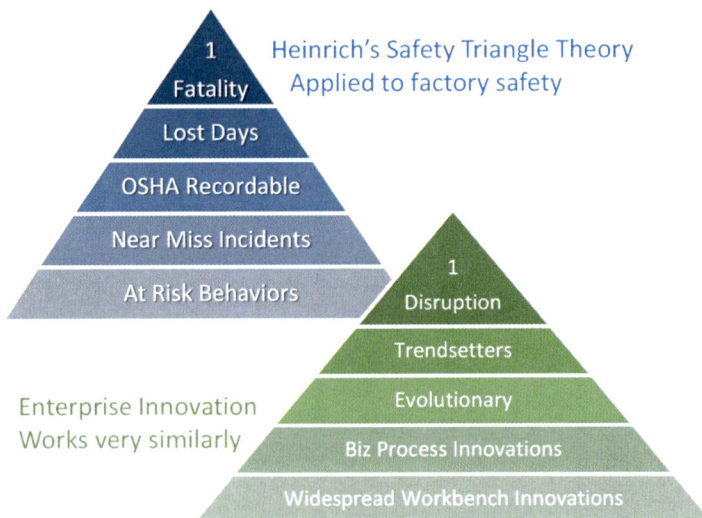

In some sense, companies like 3M and Google are where they are today because of this very fundamental cultural aspect. They encourage a widespread innovation mindset. Almost everybody is encouraged to engage in novel value creation most of the time. Multiple things listed above can go into building a mindset, including recruitment and career management.

Hiring an innovator is trickier than we think. A typical hiring process, which is designed to quickly eliminate potential low performers, also ends up identifying an innovator as a misfit. In so many instances, I am sorry to say that HR kills their first chance to spot an innovator, by making a specific size and shape of the "keyhole" for the candidate to apply through.

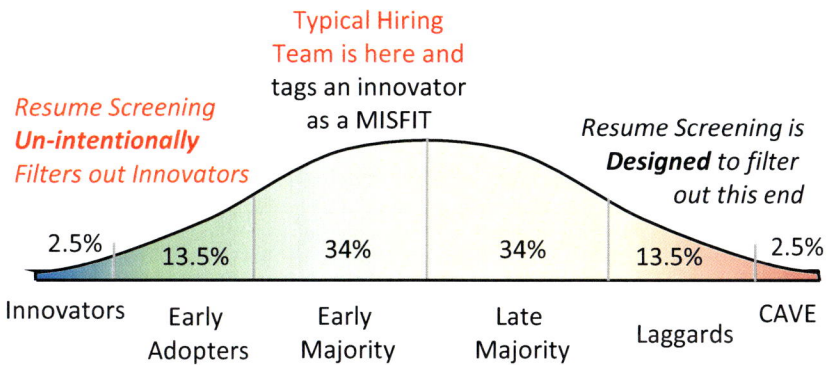

True innovators are hard to contain. They are always questioning, itching to do something different, something new, and most companies do not have an endless supply of such opportunities. To add insult to the injury, most companies have some standard performance appraisal systems, which rarely reward innovation. Repeatedly, I have seen firefighters grow rather rapidly as compared to those who creatively avoid fires. Employees bringing instant cost savings to the department get better annual reviews than those who invest in the department's growth. So many innovators put their personal energy and passion into something which has long-term value and most of their managers cannot see the contributions or the potential thereof if it does not line up with their annual objectives. Early adopters become manager's favorite, while innovators move from job to job searching for space to play, or to start an activity in their garage.

Embrace Exploration and Accept Failures

We can attempt to learn by strategically producing failures, through systematic experimentation[34]. Researchers in basic science know that a large percentage of experiments will fail. First, they know that failure is not optional in their work; it is a part of being at the leading-edge of scientific discovery. Second, far more than most of us, they understand that every failure conveys valuable information, and they are eager to get it before the competition does.

On the other side, the corporate managers, vary of failure, typically do whatever they can to make sure that the test is perfect right out from the start. They design optimal conditions rather than representative ones, leading to a successful demonstration and a failed project later. That is why I am very concerned when my clients boast of the success rate in their product review process. Recall we discussed it in Chapter-6.

Exceptional organizations are those that go beyond detecting and analyzing failures and try to generate intelligent ones for learning and innovating. It is not that managers in these organizations enjoy failure. But they recognize it as a necessary by-product of experimentation. They also realize that they do not have to do big experiments with large budgets. Often a small pilot, a dry-run of a new technique, or a simulation will suffice.

The courage to confront our own and others' imperfections is crucial to solving the apparent contradiction of wanting neither to discourage the reporting of problems, nor to create an environment in which anything is acceptable. This means that managers must ask employees to be brave and speak up—and must not respond by expressing anger or strong disapproval of what may at first appear to be incompetence. More often than we realize, complex systems are at work behind organizational failures, and their

---

[34] Strategies for Learning from Failure; Amy Edmondson; HBR https://hbr.org/2011/04/strategies-for-learning-from-failure; April 2011.

lessons and improvement opportunities are lost when the conversation is stifled.

Failures are a significant contributor to building a strong character, confidence, and a believable personality. I have a hard time working with those, who claim they have never failed. Either the claim is false, or the explorer in them is non-existent. Besides Subject Matter Learning, failure breaks down our egos, and promotes team bonding and integrity. Building of the innovation muscle through industry 4.0 requires a distinct style of leadership.

Leadership 4.0

This new style of leadership can tackle the issues surrounding human in *human-machine integration.* These leaders are digitally competent who can take responsibility for the human side of this massive change, providing a clear direction and management in a transparent, human-centric environment. They build the employee mindset, develop talent, and overcome human inertia and friction to change. They lead the pack by transforming themselves first.

Brian Bacon[35], Chairperson and founder of the Oxford Leadership states, *"Leadership in the 4th Industrial Revolution will be defined by the ability to rapidly align & engage empowered, networked teams with clarity of purpose & fierce resolve to win."* Effective digital leaders in industry will be responsible for continuously changing interaction between technologies, machines, and human, while nurturing ongoing knowledge-sharing, competency development, collaboration, and innovation. They will need to mirror the technology of Industry 4.0 and IoT in that connectivity is at its core. Some call is 'Connected Leadership' for that very reason.

---

[35] Redefining leadership for the fourth industrial revolution;
https://www.oxfordleadership.com/leadership-4-0/ Accessed Aug 2021.

Industry 4.0 has brought about a business opportunity for a lot of technology solution developers, who may not yet fully appreciate the method, purpose, and intricacies. These solution providers are motivated to force fit what they sell to any customer they can have access to. As an organization leader, you will get approached by different technology vendors and service providers with so many diverse options, you need an appreciation of what is a better fit and when. Lack of awareness around the digital technology, uncertainty associated with continuous change, and levels of funding required make it extremely hard for management to decide where to invest. Leaders need process and criterion to down select, validate, and embrace new technologies, accepting a certain risk of obsolescence even before the investment has paid off.

The fourth revolution is about agility. Workforces, especially the technical, digital, and engineering teams, will need to analyze data and respond fast with their predictions and decisions across the business. Teams will not be fixed but formed from the competencies required for that cross-functional project. This will require exceptional organizational and delegation skills from digital leaders who understand where those talents are and how to distribute tasks according to competencies.

Since Industry 4.0 is often spoken with fear that many jobs will be replaced by technology, the leadership 4.0 can play a big and important part of how digital transformation is integrated into a new working life. Leadership 4.0 fosters a transparent, creative culture that can bend and move as change and situations dictate. This new work environment will be a big and possibly uncomfortable move for many who are used to closed and rigid project management within traditional manufacturing environments.

Purposeful leaders bring their partners along with them. They hire, train, set expectations, reward employees who support the purpose. They engage with suppliers who understand and customers who appreciate their purpose. Their innovation programs develop new offerings, deploy business models, use materials and processes that promote their purpose. They step up to provide counsel to regulatory bodies and policy makers, wherever appropriate.

Some of the business leaders are responding to the revolutionary change, some others are in a wait and watch mode, and some have decided to lead this. Leaders who wish to pursue excellence in developing new technologies must include relevant elements of Industry 4.0 in their purpose and roadmap. Those who have chosen not to do so must at least monitor it so they can act before it is too late. This revolution is an unprecedented opportunity for those who can see it and is a grave threat to those who deny it or cannot seem to accept the need to innovate.

Competitive forces are unpredictable. Technology is transforming. Communication needs to be real-time. This means the hierarchical organization structures are detrimental to digital transformation and leaders need to free up the decision-making process. Peripheral vision and leadership agility, transparency, and connectivity is important to thrive in this era of Volatility, Uncertainty, Complexity and Ambiguity (VUCA). We routinely witness the death of companies that flourished prior to digitization and were slow to adapt. Self-awareness and mindfulness are key for leadership from now on. A good fraction will likely fail the test of time.

Mindful leaders: The most recent Innovation Summit (2021) included topics on meditation and mindfulness. Scott Shute, Head of Mindfulness and Compassion Programs at LinkedIn, leads the programs to serve the employees, building characteristics like emotional intelligence, resilience, and a better sense of well-being. LinkedIn appears to be convinced that it ultimately translates to a better experience for their employees and customers. It revealed an interesting parallel. Physical exercise requires a physical warm up. Mental exercise could benefit from a mental warm up. So often, we tend to keep strategic planning or ideation session first thing in the morning. And then we open the sessions with some kind of ice-breakers. So, meditation could be considered as a valuable tool to trigger the human mind to innovate, particularly in corporate settings. A former colleague Dr. Prabha Srinivasan supports the hypothesis, and I am exploring now.

Overcoming Intrinsic Barriers

Innovation appears to be a priority for so many leaders seeking growth, yet they struggle to innovate consistently. They need to recognize the trap they may have fallen in and create an action plan to break free.

Leadership Development Programs: Management consultants who lead change initiatives and business school professors who publish bestsellers based on large amounts of data analytics generally provide valuable insight into successful companies; unfortunately, all in hindsight. The book Good to Great[36] became very popular in early 2000. Yet the growth model in 21st century has been quite different, which is now captured in the book – The Four[37]. And I bet the formulas given by Scott Galloway used by Amazon and Google will not work on startups of today. Perhaps, management books should have an expiration date or carry a statutory warning, "Past performance is no guarantee of future results."

On so many occasions, leaders with decades of experience in a particular area cannot see major shifts happening outside their organizations and industries. Revolutions have been unforgiving to many of these well-known names in the history. Leadership must evaluate the applicability of proven success formulas to their current situation before adopting. Appendix on Perceptions Unfolded has a long list of such predictions from experts compiled through internet research.

Management Incentive: Annual bonus programs promote data-driven incremental improvements. Initiatives such as six-sigma and Lean, which help with productivity and quality, have stifled creativity for many

---

[36] Good to Great: Why Some Companies Make the Leap…and Others Don't; Jim Collins; Harper Collins book; 2011.
[37] The Four: The Hidden DNA of Amazon, Apple, Facebook, and Google; Scott Galloway; Portfolio/Penguin Books, 2017.

companies. An article published in Fortune magazine[38] stated that out of 58 large companies that announced Six Sigma programs, 91% trailed the S&P 500. Research shows how the top innovators outperform the S&P 500 through integration[39]. The promise of predictable near-term profit is a trap that so many leaders still fall in, trading off larger intangible gains in the future for marginal visible gains in the here and now. Leadership must establish proper innovation metrics and incentive programs around short-term and long-terms growth.

Risk Capacity: Companies are excessively risk-averse, rightly so. They focus a lot of energy on "*what*" (metrics) and "*how*" (process), and more recently, "*why*" (purpose). Organizational consultant and writer Simon Sinek puts these in the so-called Golden Circle[40] of Why-What-How. However, innovation requires a little unique twist to the golden circle. Innovators start with "*Why not?*" and go on to "*How about?*" and "*What if?*"

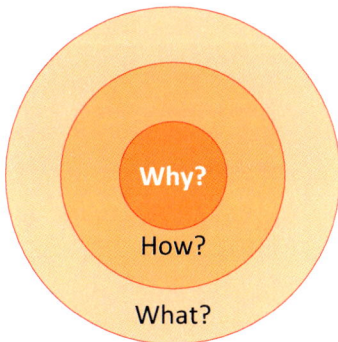

Simon Sinek's
Golden Circle
(For Exploitation)

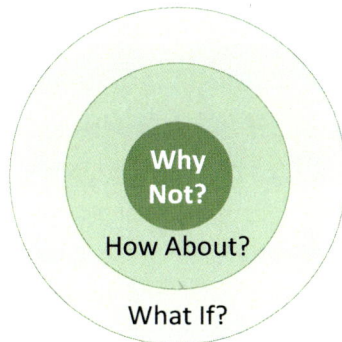

Innovator's
Golden Circle
(For Exploration)

---

[38] New Rule: Look Out, Not In; Betsy Morris, Fortune, July 11, 2006.
http://archive.fortune.com/2006/07/10/magazines/fortune/rule4.fortune/index.htm
[39] Ten Types of Innovation: The Discipline of Building Breakthroughs; L Keeley, W Helen, Ryan Pikkel, and Brian Quinn; Wiley Book, 2013.
[40] Start with Why: How Great Leaders Inspire Everyone to Take Action; Sinek, Simon; Portfolio/Penguin Book; 2009.

During a revolution, risk of not exploring is greater than the risk of exploring. The leadership must accept a certain failure rate at portfolio level and not hold individual project managers for outcome of their activities if they were to encourage and embrace innovation. If you do not bet on small projects every day, one day you will have to bet your company.

Building a Dream-Team

Innovation is a contact sport and is played in the marketplace with mostly unwritten rules and shifting goal post. It is also a team sport simply because no single individual has all the skills required today to go from concept to cash. Why some companies are more successful than others, depends upon how the team works. Google launched Project Aristotle to study this. Abeer Dubey, Google's director of people analytics, put together a team of statisticians, organizational psychologists, sociologists, engineers, and researchers to help solve the riddle.

Over 2 years they studied 180 Google teams, conducted 200-plus interviews, and analyzed over 250 different team attributes. There was no clear pattern of characteristics that could be plugged into a dream-team generating algorithm. Things began to fall into place when Google started considering intangible group norms – the traditions, behavioral standards, and unwritten rules that govern how teams' function when they gather. The intangible norms may be unspoken or openly acknowledged, but their influence could be often profound.

With a new lens and some added direction from a research study on collective intelligence (abilities that emerge out of collaboration) by a group of psychologists from Carnegie Mellon, MIT, and Union College, Project Aristotle's researchers went back to the data looking for unspoken customs. Specifically, any team behaviors that magnified the collective intelligence of the group. Through Google's Re:Work[41] website, a resource that shares

---

[41] re:Work https://rework.withgoogle.com/print/guides/5721312655835136/

Google's research, ideas, and practices on people operations, Rozovsky outlined the five key characteristics of enhanced teams.

Psychological safety: In a team with high psychological safety, teammates feel safe to take risks around their team members. They feel confident that no one on the team will embarrass or punish anyone else for admitting a mistake, asking a question, or offering a new idea.

Dependability: On dependable teams, members reliably complete quality work on time (vs the opposite – shirking responsibilities).

Structure and clarity: An individual's understanding of job expectations, the process for fulfilling these expectations, and the consequences of one's performance are important for team effectiveness.

Meaning: Finding a sense of purpose in either the work itself or the output is important for team effectiveness. The meaning of work is personal and can vary, financial security, supporting family, helping the team succeed, or self-expression for everyone, for example.

Impact: The subjective judgment that your work is making a difference, is important for teams. Seeing that one's work is contributing to the organization's goals can help reveal impact.

Engineering the perfect team is more subjective than we would like but focusing on these five psychological components increases the likelihood that you will build a dream-team, less likely to leave, more likely to harness the power of diversity, and ultimately, succeed.

Organizations need to periodically rediscover and reinvent themselves. Learning and innovative organization grow, particularly during revolutions. Leader's role today is to build a learning organization, where dream-teams happen serendipitously.

Learning Organization: To create a learning organization, leadership must insist on human resource department to maintain a well-structured competency development plan for all employees in sync with their innovation profile. Here are a few actions to become a learning organization and thrive through digital transformation:

- Clearly define and communicate your business purpose,
- Identify market opportunities for industry 4.0 in your eco-system,
- Hire people not for what they know, but how quick they are at learning,
- Maintain a bidirectional outreach with academia (teach and learn),
- Provide a safe space (projects/time/money) for employees to explore,
- Sponsor toastmasters style learning around new skills, and
- Deploy a proven innovation framework or ISO 56000 guidance.

Leadership for Society 5.0

If we go with the premise that the purpose of Industry 4.0 is to enable Society 5.0; then the discussion around leadership 4.0 is the starting point. Beyond that leadership needs to also ask the questions – What social issues can/should we resolve, and what we may create? Leadership 5.0 is perhaps leadership 4.0 with a clear human-centric purpose besides business purpose using industry 4.0 technologies.

Building Momentum

In the last chapter, we discussed 4 tracks of activities to build an innovation profile. Consistent execution will help build the momentum. Leadership needs to think of the following steps as a wheel

1. Be clear about the **Innovation Purpose**, and the vision of success.
2. Create, communicate, and use the two sheets of music, the **Innovation Strategy** (Roadmap), and the Dashboard to track the progress.
3. Build the **Innovation Capital**, by investing in talent and knowhow.
4. Inspire talent to engage in **Innovation Activity** to realize the roadmap.
5. Keep **Innovation Lean** by aligning people, products, and markets.
6. **Recognize** and reward teams for performance and learnings.
7. Update the roadmap and dashboard annually and go back to step 2.

Keep rotating this flywheel and build a momentum that would be hard to stop. Purpose, strategy, and rewards provide the willingness to innovate. Capital and activities build the capability. Lean reduces internal friction. Collectively, they build the culture of innovation, over a few years. It is a mental muscle. Just like a few workout sessions at the local gym won't build your body muscle, a few successful projects won't build the mental muscle of your organization. You will have to go through many projects, over the years, and slowly change the basic behavior. I often get into conversations with senior leaders who think that a 2-day workshop on ideation or innovation is all they need, and after that, it will happen on its own. A 2-day workshop is just like taking a tour of the gym.

Building Momentum

Developing People

Besides a shift in leadership mindset, the digital transformation of an organization also needs a whole new skill set. Skills around Information and Communication Technologies (ICT not just IT), co-working with intelligent systems, and willingness to accept that what you know today will likely be obsolete before you can establish yourself as an expert. The need and speed for learning through any revolution is an order of magnitude larger than continuous evolution, and even faster than the previous revolution.

Employers and employees both need to take the learning and development as shared continual investment. While all employees will need training on technology, the managers need to get on top of the processes, and leadership ought to explore new business models. Let us look at the human factors associated with this personal development.

The Fear Factor

"Will industry 4.0 kill our jobs?" This is the most popular question in our panel discussions on this topic. Answer is *"NO. But it will make your skill set obsolete."*

History shows that all previous industrial revolutions have created new economies all together, around new skills, with higher-paying jobs, and reduced working hours, improved productivity, and prosperity. People who were worried about jobs, and companies that were slow to adapt to the change, paid the enormous price. We have come down from a 7-day workweek before the first industrial revolution to 5-days. I can foresee a 4-day workweek by the time we are all digitally transformed.

Many of us grew up through the 3rd revolution. My freshman engineering was using log tables, I got a calculator in sophomore year, and touched the computer for the first time as a senior in 1985. When computers came to India, we had serious nationwide social protests against the Prime Minister's move to bring the technology. It was perceived as a job-killer. Today the economy of many countries runs on IT skills.

It is not a jobs question. It is a competency question. Your skills will go obsolete. You need to reskill, you need to retool, you need to relearn. To confidently try new things and new ways of doing something is the most important trait. So, employees should not worry about the jobs. There will be plenty more. We need to worry about developing the competencies and knowledge for the jobs that will be available.

Job Descriptions are dying. If you can describe your job in sufficient detail, it will soon be replaced by a robot or by automation software. Leadership needs to focus on talent that can bring intellectual capability and adaptability to meet *Job Expectations*. Employees need to focus on continuous skill development to sustain the current job and prepare for the next one.

> The most important skill is to pick up any new skill, quickly.

Skills for Digital Transformation

Traditional trade skills will have to embrace the entry of **new digital skills** – some multidisciplinary blend of digitalization, networking, data science, automation, cyber security, human-machine interface, machine learning, machine communication, additive manufacturing, and new ones every few years. The role of data scientist has already picked up. These are specialists who will extract and prepare data, conduct advanced statistical analysis, and apply their findings to improve products or production.

Traditional soft skills will have a higher focus on complex problem-solving (identification), **creativity**, open mind, critical thinking, teamwork and transparency, psychology, decision making under uncertainty, robotics supervision, and more. We can see a role for a full-time fictioneer, ideation facilitator, concept artist, … Creativity can be learned, it is a practiced art. An entire library of 'How to' books has already been written on the theme. Some books are better than others, but they all focus on a couple of central ideas – be open to new things, ask questions, doodle around, and create 'firsts.'

Agility at workplace has become an important trait. Simple tasks are being taken over by robots or by automation software and shop floors are getting digital. According to the BCG[42] employees will need to shift their focus to the things machines so far cannot do. They will have to be more open to change, possess greater agility and flexibility to accept new roles and working environments, and become accustomed to continuous inter-disciplinary learning. Humans now need to oversee humans and cobots together. Perhaps we will see robots supervising other robots and then humans, sooner than we think. And let us add artificial intelligence or intelligence augmentation to the mix. We now need to understand a whole

---

[42] Man and Machine in Industry 4.0; M Lorenz, R Strack, K Lueth, & M Bolle; BCG Report; https://www.bcg.com/publications/2015/technology-business-transformation-engineered-products-infrastructure-man-machine-industry-4.aspx ; Sept 28, 2015.

new set of psychological challenges associated with talented machines in the mix at workplace.

The global pandemic demonstrated the need for **resiliency** skills. Businesses surviving such a tough time are those where the organizations are flexible, adaptive, and agile; constantly analyzing and adjusting. Employers might look for such skills as a requirement soon. These skills are hard to teach or learn.

If you consider digital technologies, their applications, and business models; the universities will have a hard time adjusting to the market demand for talent. In one of our recent conversations with a University Dean, we asked her how they will adapt when their curriculum revision cycle is 3-year, because soon the application and business model content obsolescence period will be shorter than three years.

In the USA, focus is also shifting from graduate-level college degrees to rapid certification and creating relevant competency just in time and in place. From an industry perspective, HR may not be able to handle the retraining, because of scope and content. Chief Talent Officer (CTO) may have to take this one on. There will be room for new types of colleges and academies to develop talent for the digital requirements.

Let's Summarize

Given the challenges and opportunities, the digital transformation demands that leadership keep an open mind while capturing market insight, developing talent, managing risk, exploring business models. They need to be selective in acquiring new digital technologies as well as adopting proven business practices. The mindset shift across the organization requires a serious, sustained leadership effort. It is a matter of choice.

Innovation can be learned, and profiles can be transformed with leadership commitment, competency, and agility. And that translates into the talent development activity. This building of a mental muscle requires breaking away from the past and stick to the exercise routine with patience. It takes many activities, language, commitment, consistency, over a long period and the progress is invisible mostly, until one day, you just feel very different. It is just like you keep dating for a while and one day you suddenly feel you are in love.

The inertia and friction associated with digital transformation from the fear of job loss needs to be pushed aside. The revolution is coming, and like all previous revolutions, it will create more high-paying jobs but for a fresh set of skills.

From an organization perspective, this includes Leadership 4.0 skills, Industry 4.0 skills, as well as an open mindset, which strikes a balance across exploration and exploitation. Individual talent development plans need to support the technology awareness and adoption roadmap. There are several open online courses and university certification programs that can be leveraged. Talent development needs to be viewed as a shared investment by employee and employer to make it work for both parties.

Learning to innovate is an art and science. You can pick up the science quickly, but the artistic side needs practice. It can be learned. It is not a pure gift.

The breadth of trade skills and soft competencies required for innovation, needs acceptance of diverse team members, to innovate in this global economy and connect with diverse customers.

If you wish to go deeper into the models discussed here,
Please refer to Volume-4 **Inspiring Next Innovation Mindset**.

Let's Take a Selfie

I think the following reasons are holding us back from innovating …

☐ We believe our customers are not ready for this.
☐ To the best of our knowledge, our primary competitors are not doing it.
☐ We have had desired growth for so many years; why disturb it now.
☐ We are already very innovative.
☐ … Any more
☐ …

I think the right questions to ask are …

☐ How much should I spend on innovation?
☐ How much should I invest in Innovation?
☐ How much will it cost me if I choose not to innovate?
☐ … Any more
☐ …

The following roles exist in our Company …

☐ Chief Innovation Officer.
☐ Chief Engineer/Architect/Scientist/Artist/Actuary/…
☐ Chief of Talent, or Knowledge Chief, or Delivery Chief.
☐ Customer Experience Chief.
☐ Chief of Products and Services.

We have the following in our organization …

☐ A designated space, free to capture and experiment with ideas.
☐ A campaign to discourage the use of certain common language.
☐ Conversation around innovations in other industries in staff meetings.
☐ Ideation or hackathon type competitive events.
☐ Annual meeting around innovation with senior staff.
☐ Sponsorship of innovation events outside the company.
☐ … Any more
☐

I can accept a failure in …

- ☐ Process deviation – Deliberate.
- ☐ Process deviation – Unintentional.
- ☐ Lack of ability.
- ☐ Process inadequacy.
- ☐ Challenging task.
- ☐ Process complexity.
- ☐ Dealing with uncertainty.
- ☐ Hypothesis testing.
- ☐ Exploratory study.
- ☐ … Any more
- ☐ …
- ☐
- ☐

We value following skills in our business …

- ☐ Digital technology development and integration.
- ☐ Data science.
- ☐ Complex problem-solving (identification).
- ☐ **Creativity** and critical thinking.
- ☐ Decision making under uncertainty.
- ☐ Robotics supervision.
- ☐ Fictioneer.
- ☐ Ideation facilitator.
- ☐ Concept architect.

We value following traits in our business …

- ☐ Teamwork.
- ☐ Transparency.
- ☐ Psychological safety.
- ☐ Promoting and building on other's ideas.

9.   *Innovation & Diversity: Human Inclusion*

One fine day in Feb 2019, I got a call from Fernanda Ave in Vancouver. She asked me if I would be willing to give a talk on Women in Industry 4.0. I asked how she found me. The answer was LinkedIn, which surprised me because my profile picture leaves no doubt that I am a man. She assured me she would like to hear a male perspective and there are 3 other women presenters. They were willing to fully sponsor my visit, so I accepted the invite. My wife joked, '*so now you have to study what women can do.*' Well, I have worked for women managers, and my experience has been quite positive. That was not enough. I did my research for four weeks and concluded that women would make better leaders through the next revolution. They will also be a big part of supporting digital transformation. Covid proved it. My trip was successful. It further opened my eyes to many new topics in technology.

This chapter is intended to highlight roles that women can and likely will play in shaping the future of Industry 4.0, from execution to leadership levels and from development to transformation activities. We will then delve into other forms of diversity as well. Digital transformation faces multiple challenges such as technology standardization, talent and skills shortfall, massive transformation, and regulatory requirements. Many of these challenges are better addressed with a proper mix of gender in responsible teams. Women in STEM (science, technology, engineering, and mathematics) fields are a source of talent that can be harnessed as digitalization becomes a major part of every sector.

According to a Forbes article[43], traits like listening and empathy serve women well in "change leadership," which is the ability to influence and inspire action in others and respond with vision and agility during periods of growth, disruption, or uncertainty to bring about the needed change. While driving innovation value chain (Chapter-5), emotional intelligence makes women better suited to capturing marketplace insight and easing friction in technology adoption, and a balance of gender in a team makes for more productive ideation sessions for effective problem-solving and objective execution. Let us first look at how the gender divide started and how closing the gap can effectively reduce the pain and speed up the digital transformation for social good.

Gender Gap[44] – Perception of Reality?

Historic Evolution

Equality in the gender roles of men and women in the workforce and household has changed throughout the industrial revolutions, especially in the United States. Prior to the first industrial revolution, people lived in rural areas. Farming was the most common occupation for most families, as it was a reliable source of income. However, once industrialization occurred, many more job opportunities opened for people. Naturally, families moved to where the better jobs were and where the money was, which was primarily in urban centers.

While working on the farm, both men and women shared the responsibilities of the work fairly equally. Yes, they had different jobs; however, these duties were often intertwined, and the work women did on

---

[43] Why women are Natural Born leaders; N Lipkin; Forbes; Nov 19, 2019; https://www.forbes.com/sites/nicolelipkin/2019/11/19/why-women-are-natural-born-leaders.

[44] I am aware that gender is nonbinary; however, for the purposes of this research chapter, the scope is limited to traditional biological XX/XY groups.

the farm was valued just as much as men's work. However, after the first industrial revolution, the jobs of men and women diverged, both in function and in value. In the cities, men would go out and work tedious jobs, while the women typically stayed home with the children and took care of them, as well as cooked and cleaned. Though there are notable exceptions to this, such as the "Lowell girls" who were employed in Lowell factories because they could pay young women less than men, as machinery became larger and more capable, the industry shifted toward male employment.

The first industrial revolution also brought about poor working conditions: dark, overcrowded factories; machines that covered workers in soot; and little focus on safety[45]. This led to accidents and disease. Whereas initially employers hired women because they thought they would be less likely to protest poor working conditions, they found this to be not true, and many women helped lead protests and movements to protect workers and child laborers. Female workers formed both the Women's Trade Union League and the Women's Bureau, which fought for shorter workdays and more safety measures[46]. Unfortunately, this helped spur a trend of employers hiring fewer and fewer women. Certain industries, such as textiles, continued to employ women as workers, but most factory and other urban-center jobs shifted toward male-centric roles.

The second industrial revolution further reinforced these stereotypes except for the period during World War II. When the men returned home, post-war America enjoyed a thriving economy which allowed many families to thrive on one salary. Women were encouraged through the media and social norms to stay in the home and provide a safe place to raise a

---

[45] The Change in Male and Female Spheres of Work and Equality; D Zabbatino; Social Change and the Future https://socialchangecourse.wordpress.com/2014/10/04/the-change-in-male-and-female-spheres-of-work-and-equality/; Oct 4, 2014.

[46] Women in Industrializing America, in The Gilded Age: S A Cordery; Essays on the Origins of Modern America, edited by C.W. Calhoun, Wilmington, DE: Scholarly Resources; 1996.

family[47]. Unfortunately, this period started some trends that still affect us today, for example, unequal wages. Men and women became seen as separate entities, and a man's work was considered to be more valuable to a boss than a woman's, as she was paid much less. What began here has only grown into a bigger problem with time as women are still fighting for equal pay and respect.

The third industrial revolution, however, brought a bit of women's strength back into the workplace with computers and the ability to work flexible hours and work from home. Additionally, the struggles of the middle-class in the 1970s and 1980s caused many middle-class 'homemakers' to look for paid work outside the home. This trend continued, as the middle and lower classes continued to require two incomes to provide for their families. As more and more women entered the workforce, more infrastructure was put into place to better facilitate the two-income family structure.

The fourth industrial revolution can dismantle gender stereotypes altogether. Joyce Burnette[48] showed that market forces—not discrimination, as it is now—were the largest driver in gender differences in occupations and wages during the second revolution.

In the first industrial revolution, craftworkers who were valued for their ingenuity and creativity were replaced by workers who were valued for their physical strength and quick acquisition of skills. Today, they are being replaced more and more by machines (particularly AI and robotics) that can handle repetitive tasks and do the heavy lifting in our factories. The fourth industrial revolution is therefore poised to eliminate the gender stereotypes created by the first, putting the emphasis back on human talent (ingenuity and creativity), and not on traditional masculine skills.

---

[47] Women and Work After World War II; PBS, n.d., Tupperware! (blog), American Experience PBS, https://www.pbs.org/wgbh/americanexperience/features/tupperware-work/ accessed 1 February 2021.
[48] Gender, Work and Wages in Industrial Revolution Britain; J Burnette; Cambridge University; 2008.

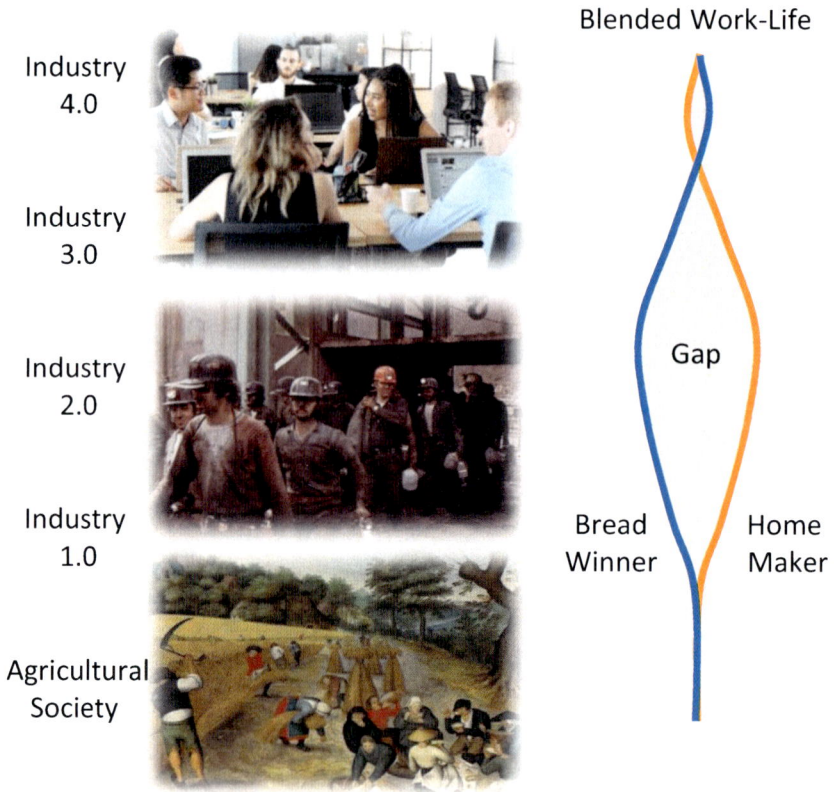

Industry 4.0

Industry 3.0

Industry 2.0

Industry 1.0

Agricultural Society

Blended Work-Life

Gap

Bread Winner

Home Maker

In the fourth industrial revolution, success is found in the on-demand production of customized things, and talent is becoming the most valuable asset. This may well be the antithesis of the first industrial revolution, where the mass production of uniform things drove success, and therefore physical strength was more highly valued than human ingenuity. In an economy based more on talent and less on capital, women are more likely to be treated as equals to foster an environment where there are fewer obstacles to hiring the right talent.

And as people become the new competitive advantage, organizations will need to stop reinforcing gender roles to fuel an unprecedented race for the best talent. The most successful companies in the future may be those that truly eliminate gender stereotypes in favor of innovation and growth[49].

The Labor Force Today

According to the B.A. Women's Alliance[50], women in the USA have made incredible strides in achieving equal representation in education and the workplace over the last five decades. Today, women earn 57% of all bachelor's degrees and make up 48% of the labor force. Certain fields, however, have not seen the same growth as others. In particular, women are less present within STEM sectors. Only 12% of women's bachelor's degrees are in STEM fields, compared to 19% for men. Even more worrisome, after college, women in STEM leave the workforce in much higher numbers than their male counterparts: only 5% of college-educated women are working in STEM two years after graduation, and only 3% after 10 years. This phenomenon has been called the "leaky pipeline," a metaphor that suggests women "leak" through various cracks along the professional development path from education to advanced careers. The B.A. Rudolph Foundation's white paper[51] discusses the current state of women in STEM, identifies five critical points in which women tend to diverge from STEM fields, describes the factors that push and pull women out of STEM, highlights unique opportunities these fields represent, and provides recommendations for getting women to stay.

Research into the experience of women has found that women working in occupations traditionally considered to be masculine domains confront barriers that contribute to poor experience and to premature departure. Many of these barriers are associated with masculine organizational cultures that

---

[49] The Fourth Industrial Revolution Will Eliminate the Gender Stereotypes Created by the First; R Funna; Quartz, https://qz.com/1177843/the-fourth-industrial-revolution-will-eliminate-the-gender-stereotypes-created-by-the-first/ Jan 12, 2018.

[50] www.bawomensalliance.org/womeninstem/

[51] Solving for XX: Challenges and Opportunities for Women in STEM; E Schaub; B.A. Rudolph Foundation, https://pub.lucidpress.com/womeninstem/; Nov 2017.

do not offer flexibility, do not value female attributes, and associate females with having less ability or skill than males. Such belief systems, values, and resultant organizational practices have been linked to social exclusion, isolation, and gender management, which are hard for women to endure. Other significant problems women encounter come from the lack of 'critical mass' (a certain minimum percentage) needed to provide support, mentoring, role models, and leadership. It has also been found that women who enter environments considered to be "hyper masculine" are confronted with discrimination, harassment, and violence. Therefore, it is vital to question how women negotiate these barriers[52].

Female representation is not just a problem at the top of the company hierarchy. It remains an issue at each stage of the corporate hierarchy, with the odds stacked particularly high against Asian, Black, and Latina women, as well as other women of color.

Early efforts by companies to improve female leadership focused on appointing more female board members. Yet McKinsey research[53] quickly established that addressing women's absence at the top could only occur by looking at their career progression. It turns out that the underrepresentation of women is already a factor at the outset of their careers, and their representation diminishes with further progression along their careers. The odds of progression differ by industry. Some industries, such as technology, are particularly poor at hiring women in the first place. In others, women tend to get stuck at middle- or senior-management level. The overall picture is nevertheless clear. The 2017 research on women in the workplace, which looked at 222 companies in the United States employing more than

---

[52] Women in Masculine Jobs: Understanding Resilience and Social and Cultural Capital; D Bridges, B. Krivokapic-Skoko, L. Bamberry, and S. Jenkins; Gender, Work and Organisation; 10th Biennial International Interdisciplinary Conference, Sydney, Australia; 2018.

[53] Still Looking for Room at the Top: Ten Years of Research on Women in the Workplace; S Devillard, V. Hunt, and L. Yee; McKinsey Quarterly (blog), McKinsey & Company; Mar 8, 2018. https://www.mckinsey.com/featured-insights/gender-equality/still-looking-for-room-at-the-top-ten-years-of-research-on-women-in-the-workplace

12 million people found that, on average, women held just 22% of senior vice president roles. No wonder the odds of reaching the very top are so slim. Women of color fare even worse.

Anatomy Diversity

Sex differences in human behavior show adaptive complementarity: research[54] shows, males generally have better motor and spatial abilities, whereas females have superior memory and social cognition skills. Many social studies show sex differences in human brains but do not explain this complementarity. Ingalhalikar et.al. modeled the structural connectome using diffusion tensor imaging in a sample of 949 youths (aged 8 to 22 years; 428 males and 521 females) and discovered unique sex differences in brain connectivity during development. Connection-wise statistical analysis, as well as an analysis of regional and global network measures, presented a comprehensive description of network characteristics. In all supratentorial regions, males had greater within-hemispheric connectivity, as well as enhanced modularity and transitivity, whereas between-hemispheric connectivity and cross-module participation predominated in females. However, this effect was reversed in the cerebellar connections. An analysis of these changes developmentally demonstrated differences in trajectory between males and females mainly in adolescence and in adulthood.

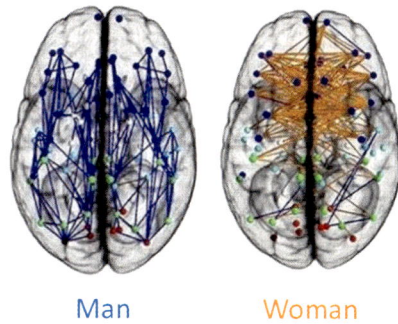

Man   Woman

Overall, the results suggest male brains are structured to facilitate connectivity between perception and coordinated action, whereas female

----

[54] Sex Differences in the Structural Connectome of the Human Brain; M Ingalhalikar, A Smith, D Parker, T D Satterthwaite, M A Elliott, K Ruparel, H Hakonarson, R E Gur, R C Gur, and R Verma; Proceedings of the National Academy of Sciences, Vol. 111, No. 2, pp. 823–828; 2014.

brains facilitate communication between analytical and intuitive processing modes. The left brain is used more for logical thinking while the right brain is for more intuitive thinking. Industry 4.0 needs both logical and intuitive thinking. Does that make female brains better suited to lead in Industry 4.0?

Role of Gender in Industry 4.0

At the Leadership Level

Barbara Trautlein[55] asserts that every change agent has a certain basic tendency to lead with their heart, head, hands, or some combination thereof. Leaders who lead mainly from

- the heart, connect with people emotionally (I want it!),
- the head, connect with people cognitively (I get it!), and
- the hands, connect with people behaviorally (I can do it!).

Her research shows that men tend to lead change more with the head and women primarily with the heart, and that for women, hands are a strong secondary style. Said another way, almost half of the men surveyed led change by focusing on vision, mission, and strategy (head strengths). Almost half of the women, conversely, placed a premium on engaging, communicating, and collaborating (heart strengths), and almost a third of the women emphasized planning, tactics, and execution (hands strengths). Most men had their radars tuned to purpose, and women on people and process.

Note that it is not inherently better or worse to focus on heart or head or hands; the most effective change incorporates all three. The point is not for leaders of change—men or women—to change their natural style. The point, instead, is an awareness of our styles and the ability to adapt our behavior

---

[55] Do Men and Women Lead Change Differently? B Trautlein; LinkedIn, Jan 19, 2016; https://www.linkedin.com/pulse/do-men-women-lead-change-differently-barbara-trautlein/

to incorporate other approaches to be optimally impactful across a variety of people and situations. According to Trautlein, when leading through change, men tend to display behaviors traditionally associated with strategic executives, concentrating on future vision and new business horizons. Conversely, women tend to center on supporting their teams to work together and to develop a detailed road map to achieve a change objective, functioning more like supportive coaches.

The uncertainty of Industry 4.0, the need to collaborate for technology integration, and changing workforce dynamics require leading by heart and hands. The research cited previously shows that, women will likely have an edge in leading through digital transformation in this era of the innovator.

As an example, an organized response to COVID-19 required significant innovation and resiliency. The success of female leaders of different nations demonstrated this value in leading diverse teams to tackle intense challenges[56] and I believe that this offers a good parallel to the challenges of Industry 4.0, where there will be many "failures" before success. Additionally, where the resilience of systems will help to justify the incorporations of Industry 4.0 into corporate processes and business continuity planning, women in traditionally male careers have been shown to exhibit the trait of resilience in order to prosper in their chosen field. Bridges et al.[57] also pointed out that for women to succeed in engineering fields, their success depends on four aspects, including personal traits and ability, and also social and cultural conditions.

An economist from Carnegie Mellon found that teams that included at least one female member had a collectively higher IQ than teams that

---

[56] What Do Countries with the Best Coronavirus Responses have in Common? Women Leaders; A Wittenberg-Cox; https://www.forbes.com/sites/avivahwittenbergcox/2020/04/13/what-do-countries-with-the-best-coronavirus-reponses-have-in-common-women-leaders/ Forbes, April 13, 2020.
[57] Women in Masculine Jobs: Understanding Resilience and Social and Cultural Capital; D Bridges, B. Krivokapic-Skoko, L. Bamberry, and S. Jenkins; Gender, Work and Organisation; 10th Biennial International Interdisciplinary Conference, Sydney, Australia; 2018.

included only men. When Fortune 500 companies had at least three female directors, several key factors increased: the return on invested capital jumped over 66%, return on sales went up 42%, and return on equity increased by 53%. Gallup[58,59] found that companies with more diversity on staff had a 22% lower turnover rate, and if an organization had a more inclusive culture that embraced women, it was easier to recruit a more diverse staff.

In the Innovation Value Chain

The innovation value chain described in Chapter-5 has four major steps. The first two steps focus on marketplace insight and ideation, which require heart skills (emotional intelligence and teamwork) better suited to traditional female thinking processes; while the second two steps (qualification and execution) require head skills, better suited for traditional male thinking processes. A well-balanced team could help speed up the entire innovation value chain.

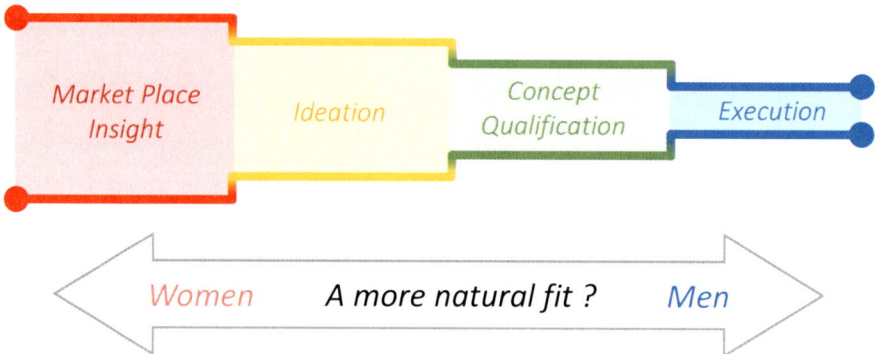

---

[58] How Leadership Presence is Different for Women; C K Goman; Ladders-Fast on Your Feet, https://www.theladders.com/career-advice/how-leadership-presence-is-different-for-women. Sept 18, 2019.
[59] Innovation by Design: The Case for Investing in Women; Anita Borg Institute, report, available at https://anitab.org/resources/case-studies-and-whitepapers ; 2014.

A 2012 study[60] on women's participation in IT patents found that patents with mixed-gender teams were cited 30% to 40% more than similar patents with all-male teams. A London Business School survey of 850 individuals in 17 countries, in different industries, found that across the board, having a larger number of women on a team accounted for greater psychological safety, team confidence, group experimentation, and team efficiency. We discussed some of these traits earlier in dream-team. These are optimal when women are from 50% to 60% of the team.

As per a report from PwC[61], more and more CEOs regard talent diversity and inclusion as vital to their organization's ability to drive innovation and gain a competitive advantage. As businesses across the world inject greater urgency into their gender diversity efforts, there is an intensifying focus on hiring female talent. In fact, 78% of large organizations are actively seeking to hire more women, especially into more experienced and senior level positions.

According to McKinsey research[62], gender diversity on executive teams is strongly correlated with profitability and value creation.

All these reports point out that innovation thrives better with gender diversity. Thus, this industrial revolution will evolve faster and better with the inclusion of both genders in appropriate proportions. Within Industry 4.0, three out of the four guiding principles require a significant amount of emotional intelligence, soft skills, and resilience, thus providing a natural advantage to women.

---

[60] Women in the Workplace; D.H. Recruitment Services, http://datum-recruitment.com/blog/2018/03/08/women-in-the-workplace/ Mar 8, 2018.

[61] Winning the Fight for Female Talent: How to Gain the Diversity Edge through Inclusive Recruitment; A Flood; PwC report, March 2017, https://www.pwc.com/gx/en/about/diversity/iwd/iwd-female-talent-report-web.pdf

[62] Delivering through Diversity; V Hunt, L. Yee, S. Prince, and S. Dixon-Fyle; McKinsey & Company, https://www.mckinsey.com/business-functions/organization/our-insights/delivering-through-diversity Jan 18, 2018.

How to Inspire Gender Neutrality

Gender-Neutral Education at Early Age

Studies[63] have shown that parents start reinforcing gender stereotypes when their children are just two years old. As an example, parents take their kids to gender-specific lanes for toys. Boys are exposed to cars, play guns, and other toys that promote competition, excitement, danger, and spatial and math skills. The girls' toy lane has dolls, dollhouses, and dress-ups that generate nurturing, domesticity, physical attractiveness, and verbal skills. And this continues for many years until the brains are wired. We as parents may not appreciate the psychological studies that suggest most children develop the ability to label gender groups and to use gender labels in their speech between 18 and 24 months. This knowledge of basic gender information was related to increased play with strongly stereotyped toys.

Mattel's '*You Can Be Anything*' campaign targeted to girls offers doll accessories such as safety goggles, laptops, and humanoid robots. Debbie Sterling, founder and CEO of GoldieBlox, is on a mission to inspire girls to love STEM with her line of toys designed to develop an early interest in engineering and confidence in problem-solving. Lego advocated gender equality in toys in 1974 with a letter to parents[64], saying that the most important thing is to 'put the right materials into children's hands and let them create whatever appeals to them: a bed or a truck, a doll house or a spaceship.' Qubits construction sets are another good example of gender-neutral STEM toys.

Innovation needs diversity, and we ought to build those skills for all ages: preschool, school, early social, college, and then the workplace. Roles

---

[63] Patterns of Gender Development; C L Martin, and D.N. Ruble; Annual Review of Psychology, Vol. 61, pp. 353–381, 2010.

[64] Lego Letter from the 1970s Still Offers a Powerful Message to Parents 40 Years Later; A Withnall; The Independent, https://www.independent.co.uk/news/lego-letter-1970s-still-offers-powerful-message-parents-40-years-later-9878303.html; Nov 23, 2014.

at home and in the workplace should be tied to skills and interests in a gender-neutral manner to make the best use of the talent pool.

Gender Acceptance in the Workplace

For companies to hire more women in top management, they need to create a culture of open and constructive feedback; invite women leaders to review and revamp processes and systems; and acknowledge the unique qualities both genders bring to the workplace.

Due to their resilience and the physical attributes of their brain function, women are well-suited to lead us into and through the fourth industrial revolution. While getting more women into STEM needs to start at childhood, Industry 4.0 cannot wait for the next generation to grow up. A conscious effort must be made now to take advantage of the skill sets in the talent pool in a gender-neutral manner.

Pull is coming from market forces—there is just not enough talent pool to choose from, and leadership needs to open their minds and accept that women can do the job.

Push must come from company policies on gender diversity, retraining, intentional innovation groups, and focus on resiliency, justifying a move toward Industry 4.0.

Gender-neutral Language

Now that we have established the need for female leadership and participation in innovation, we should also reinforce it in our daily language.

George Bernard Shaw said, "The reasonable man adapts himself to the world; the unreasonable one persists in trying to adapt the world to himself. Therefore, all progress depends on the unreasonable man." The gender-neutral statement would say "person" instead of "man." Gender-neutral language takes conscious effort. Consider this recent example from SpaceX, which uses "**crewed**" instead of "**manned**": "*The dummy is part of a full* *suite of sensors aboard the uncrewed mission, which will produce data that SpaceX and NASA will rely on for future, crewed missions."* [65]

Value of Human Diversity in Innovation

Besides gender, there are so many other forms of diversity, discussed in a workplace. There are three broad categories[66,67].

Legacy or Demographic Diversity includes attributes such as social constructs, race, age, religion, ethnicity, gender, physical abilities, and sexual orientation. It is tied to our identities of origin – characteristics that classify us at birth and that we will carry around for the rest of our lives.

Experiential Diversity includes attributes such as physical and social identities, based on our education, life histories experiences, hobbies, affinities, and even socio-economic status. It is based on life experiences that shape our emotional universe and influences identities of growth.

Cognitive or Thought Diversity defines how our neural makeup, experiences, and hard wiring, impact our ability to solve problems and create new insights. This one makes us look for other minds to complement our thinking: identities of aspiration.

Although demographic diversity of more visible and can be easily measured, experiential and thought diversity bring tremendous value to an organization from an innovation perspective. The reality is all three types are correlated. They collectively bring new perspectives for better problem

---

[65] Meet Ripley, SpaceX's Dummy Astronaut Riding on Crew Dragon Test Flight; M Bartels; https://www.space.com/spacex-crew-dragon-dummy-called-ripley.html; Mar 1, 2019.
[66] Diversity of thought and the future of the workforce; A Diaz-Uda, C Medina, B Schill; https://www2.deloitte.com/us/en/insights/topics/talent/diversitys-new-frontier.html; Jul 2, 2013.
[67] The 3 Types of Diversity That Shape Our Identities; Celia de Anca and Salvador Aragón; https://hbr.org/2018/05/the-3-types-of-diversity-that-shape-our-identities; May 24, 2018.

solving leading to innovation, offers a wider talent pool to meet the demands of industry 4.0; improve performance and profits. Deloitte study also points out three clear benefits –

- Eliminate group-think and expert arrogance with thinker's diversity,
- Identify individuals most fit to solve the most complex problems, and
- Increase volumes of new insights through crowdsourcing of ideas.

There are many studies[68] that show diverse teams simply perform better and, as a result, bring in more profits. A 2015 McKinsey report on 366 public companies found that those in the top quartile for ethnic and racial diversity in management were 35% more likely to have financial returns above their industry mean. Additionally, those in the top quartile for gender diversity were 15% more likely to have returns above the industry mean. Another McKinsey study found that U.S. public companies with diverse executive boards have a 95% higher return on equity than those with homogeneous boards. Yet another study by the Boston Consulting Group found that increasing the diversity of leadership teams leads to improved financial performance. Clearly, diversity pays off. One of the BCG reports[69] talks about 6 key dimensions – education, age, gender, career path, industry, and nation of origin.

Brian Chesky of Airbnb remarked, "As a founder, I think we were late to this issue. ...When we designed the platform, three white guys, there were a lot of things we didn't think about." I agree with Brian. I have observed this with many of my clients who have a dominant workforce on one type.

---

[68] Benefits of diversity in the workplace; Sophia Lee; https://www.cultureamp.com/blog/benefits-of-diversity-in-the-workplace; Date written unknown.

[69] Rocio Lorenzo and Martin Reeves, How and Where Diversity Drives Financial Performance https://www.bcg.com/publications/2018/how-diverse-leadership-teams-boost-innovation.aspx; Jan 23, 2018.

Collective Intelligence

Collective intelligence (CI) is shared or group intelligence that emerges from the collaboration, collective efforts, and competition of many individuals and appears in consensus decision making. The term appears in sociobiology, political science and in the context of mass peer review and crowdsourcing applications. It is about understanding that every point of view adds something important to the process of change, even if that something is "how not to do it."

To create the best collaboration in a work group[70], organizations should strike the right balance of three different cognitive styles among the participants which describe how the people receive and analyze information:

Verbalizers, such as Journalists and lawyers,
Spatial visualizers who think analytically, such as engineers and people in math-driven professions, and
Object visualizers who tend to think about the bigger picture such as artists.

Those who straddle two of these categories tend to be group facilitators. To harness collective intelligence, within your organization:

- Make space for collaboration amongst diverse individuals, and a way to appreciate the difference,
- Find ways of listening to people at all levels, regardless of diversity in thought or appearance, and
- Recognize the long-term value, finding ways to start small and continue to adjust over time to improve and refine.

---

[70] The Impact of Cognitive Style Diversity on Implicit Learning in Teams; I Aggarwal, A W Woolley, C F Chabris and T W Malone; Front. Psychol., Feb 07, 2019.

Religion

The Center for Religious Studies of the Fondazione Bruno Kessler (FBK-ISR, https://isr.fbk.eu/en/) in Italy is engaged in an ongoing study of the relationship between religion and innovation[71]. As they consider this connection, they see it from three perspectives.

Innovation In Religion: How is innovation being understood, experienced, and practiced within religious traditions and communities of faith or belief?

Religion In Innovation: How do religious traditions and communities of faith or belief contribute to innovation in the areas of culture and society, science and technology, politics, and the law?

Religion Of Innovation: Has the vocabulary of innovation itself become a rhetorical vehicle for quasi-religious discourses? Has innovation itself turned into a belief system and become a sort of religion?

They make the following 11 recommendations for research and action in religion and innovation:

1. Avoid looking at religion as a friend or foe of innovation and vice versa.
2. Take the context into account to avoid unwarranted generalizations.
3. **Value diversity and freedom of religion or belief.**
4. Go beyond the "from the lab to the market" model of innovation.
5. Value collective agency and responsibility with focus on users and providers in innovation processes.
6. Pursue multi- and inter-disciplinary research and combine qualitative and quantitative methodologies.
7. Engage with innovation in politics and the law.
8. Engage with different value systems and ways in which they are challenged by scientific and technological novelties.

---

[71] Religion and Innovation, https://religiousfreedomandbusiness.org/2/post/2020/06/religion-and-innovation.html; Jun 23, 2020.

9. Think of scientific, technological, social, and cultural innovation as interrelated processes.
10. Employ an inclusive and dialogical approach in the identification of problems and challenges.
11. Listen carefully to opponents of innovation and to opponents of religion.

#3 is a good one. Which is described as, "Do not think of religion as a simple, homogeneous, and easily describable phenomenon, but rather think of it as a diachronically and synchronically diversified phenomenon that resists essentialist definitions. Trying to think of and approach religious diversity as a resource rather than (just) as a problem may improve the effectiveness and inclusiveness of innovation processes in society, culture, science, and technology. For this to be possible, value and protect freedom of religion or belief for all."

A good example of #9 is a turban for Sikh motorcyclists which is also a protective helmet, thanks to incredible material innovation developed by creative agency Zulu Alpha Kilo in collaboration with Pfaff Harley-Davidson. Tough Turban's chain-mail-like design features bulletproof laminate and a foam that hardens on impact. My brother who owns a bike dealership and an array of bikes loves this solution.

Ethnic Background and Values

A McKinsey study[72] found that the companies with high ethnic diversity within the senior-management level were 30% more likely to outperform the national industry median. Ethnic diversity has a larger impact than gender.

Ramasamy and Yeung[73] evaluate the effects of two main types of diversity on the innovation performance of a country. They used well-

---

[72] Diversity Matters; V Hunt, D Layton, and S Prince; McKinsey & Co.; 2014.
[73] Ethnic Diversity, Values Diversity And Innovation: A Cross-Country Analysis; B Ramasamy, M Yeung; Perspectives of Innovations, Economics & Business; Volume 18, Issue 3, 2018.

known measures of ethnic, religious, and linguistic diversity within a country as well as a purpose-built values diversity measure to evaluate the impact of innovation performance. First, they consider the effect of outward diversity, namely ethnic, religious, and linguistic diversities. They ask if such outward diversities do indeed contribute towards creativity and innovation, or whether these diversities lead to greater conflicts that harm innovative efforts. Second, they consider the effect of values diversity on innovation output. Values are those inner principles that influence one's outer attitude and behavior. Thus, diversity in values may reflect those inner differences that transcend the color of the skin and language. A nation may comprise either or both type of diversities, thus, they also consider the joint effect of these diversities on innovation. The sample size of 61 countries provides a very dependable analysis. They find that ethnic diversity has a negative effect on innovation while other types of diversities, particularly values diversity, positively contribute to innovation. In both cases however, the effect is mainly indirect, in that diversity influences the determinants of innovation.

Their findings have important policy implications, particularly on immigration policies.

Age

We discuss a lot about various generations and how difficult it is to have them all in one team. When I was doing my prior research on Gender and Industry 4.0 for Vancouver talk, I made a conscious effort to engage multiple perspectives. I did a dry-run of my pitch with my 26-year-old son and wife. They gave me a lot of input to digest. I took the simple ones immediately and resisted a little on the major shifts suggested in the first round. But next day morning, they began to make sense. I accepted. Interestingly millennial managers are beginning to appreciate seasoned staff members for their expertise and stability.

A study conducted by Institute for Employment Research provides evidence on the relevance of different aspects of the age composition to companies' innovativeness. They[74] find indications to support these three hypotheses: (1) Companies with older workforces (on average) are less innovative, (2) Companies with more diverse workforces are more innovative, and (3) Companies need to exceed a minimal threshold of age diversity to realize innovation potentials. However, the positive effect of age diversity again decreases above a certain level. A robust relation between a uniform age distribution and innovation was not found.

Mothe et al. explored[75] the linkage between age diversity and innovation and studies the moderating effect of human resource practices on such relationships. Based on a linked dataset that contains cross-sectional survey data and longitudinal employer–employee data from Luxembourg, they show that the effect of age diversity on innovation depends on the age distribution pattern of employees. This observation resonates with my experience from corporate America and working with several small businesses. The correlation is positive for firms characterized by heterogeneous age groups (variety), and negative for those dominated by polarized age groups (polarization). HR practices such as information sharing mitigate the adverse effects of age polarization on innovation. Practices enhancing development such as training are found to play a significant and negative role in moderating the relationship between age diversity and innovation. I have observed that a formal mentoring program across age groups is a powerful way of developing mutual appreciation.

Heather Tinsley[76] reports that mixed-age teams fuel innovation and are also more productive. This is partially because diversity in general increases innovation and boosts organizational outcomes. But age diversity in particular appears to boost productivity at the team level, likely because of

---

[74] Age Diversity and Innovation; A Hammermann, M Niendorf, J Schmidt; IAB-discussion paper, http://doku.iab.de/discussionpapers/2019/dp0419.pdf; April 2019

[75] Does age diversity boost technological innovation? Exploring the moderating role of HR practices; C Mothe, T U Nguyen-Thi; European Management Journal; Available online Jan 29, 2021.

[76] 3 Reasons You Should Hire an Age-Diverse Workforce; Heather Tinsley-Fix; AARP, https://www.aarp.org/work/employers/info-2020/age-diversity-value.html; Aug 20, 2020.

"knowledge spillover" – team members share knowledge gained from past experiences, which in turn sparks new solutions to problems while avoiding costly mistakes. This combination of tacit knowledge – for example, a nuanced understanding of the regulatory environment, or the anticipation of unforeseen roadblocks — with new ideas and approaches often results in a quicker path to success. Perhaps this is why Information Technology & Innovation Foundation found that the average age of innovators across a range of industries at the time of their innovation is 47. Unfortunately, outdated beliefs about aging often persist in ways that diminish the impact an age-diverse workforce. Organizations perform best when workers of all ages are included and empowered to contribute their unique skills and perspectives. The important message here is roles assignment to match the skills, knowledge, energy, and interest.

Veterans

In 2005-06, during our business school, we had a team member, Nancy Lansing, an ER nurse retired from US Navy. We were a cohort for all home-work assignments. Every time we started, there was a vast difference in pace of execution around tasks taken by each of us. Being a researcher, I would want to define the problem, investigate options, take steps, evaluate, draft, refine, finalize. Whereas Nancy, to her every task was like a patient about to die. She would dive straight in, gather whatever data is available, and use her experience to make a call. Interestingly, most of the times, we were both right. For most exercises, even on outcome side I had a bias towards an all-encompassing solution, she had bias towards speed without compromising the requirements. I learned some valuable techniques in innovative problem-solving. Together we made a great team.

In every business there are days of crisis, in every project there are moments of crisis, because nothing really goes as planned. Guys like me, sweat and breakdown under that type of pressure. My veteran friends are trained to be creative under crisis. So, they have a very important role to play. I do not imply that they are not creative during normal operations.

Earlier in 1999-2002, working on a USAF project as program manager, I reported to a retired colonel and my Technician was a retired master-sergeant. The pace of their decision making, emotional intelligence, ability to stick to a process, proactively do things that were repetitive in nature, ability to anticipate competitor moves were some strengths that my engineering brain was not fully prepared for, then.

Experiential Diversity

This by far I believe is the most significant contributor to innovation. I think it is also well-recognized that innovation happens at the intersection of scientific, social, technical, business disciplines. Every time we build a team, we look for all the different skills to come together.

Intelligent Machine

Co-working with machines brings in an interesting form of diversity to the table. Recently, while working on a research topic, my partner Vaibhav Garg brought beta version of GPT-3 (OpenAI.com) into the mix. We worked with it to generate ideas and draft an outline for an essay. Then refined it, researched the content on human biases, and submitted our work for publication in an international journal. Appendix has the details of the case study. It was quite unnerving to see several options coming from the machine, which made sense. Despite all the knowledge we have about these learning machines, we were amazed at first, skeptical next, and scared a week later at the power of this thing. Even though it may be developed and trained by the most ethical engineers and linguists, overuse by good guys, and fear of misuse by bad guys bothers us. But before we even get there, the entire experience of this machine rapid firing relevant content at us was just uncomfortable at first. We are likely to get used to it, but by the time we get there, we will have our next uncomfortable situation with technology. At some point, the machines may develop variants faster than we can comprehend.

The Unreasonable Me!

I was born to a Sikh family in India with colored skin. That continues to define my demographic diversity.

I grew up in India, a third world country at that time, with scarcity of everything – scheduled rolling power outages, 4 hours of water supply every day, 3-5 years of waiting period to get a gas/phone connection or even purchase an automobile. Everything must be repaired or repurposed until it completely dies out. That made us creative with whatever little resources we could access.

When I left my home State of Punjab in Northern India and went to the top graduate school in Bangalore, South India, I had to work hard to accept so many cultures that blend there from all over India. I am sure, others had difficulty accepting me as well. It took me about a year to learn one song in every official Indian language (about 14 in total) and make friends from every state. That helped with acceptance, and I still have some of them as friends. When I moved to Georgia tech, this scope of acceptance reached global level with the making of friends from Korea, Europe, Africa, Middle east. It takes effort to learn and understand different perspectives and open your mind that other perspective may be equally correct. I am still working on it.

Over the last four decades, I have worked and learned in India, Germany, and now USA, which allows me to blend multiple cultural attributes to anything I work with. This added experiential diversity. Being a religious minority with an appearance that makes many people uncomfortable, I can easily relate and connect to any other minority.

Psychological Innovation Profile[77] reflects I am an Artist, and all my training has been in Engineering, which allows me to blend art and science

---

[77] The Innovation Code; Jeff DeGraff and Stanley DeGraff; Book, 2017.

– a delightful combination to be an innovator. Having been a Professor and a Corporate Executive, I can relate to short-term business goals as well deep thinking and blend them as needed.

Based on the models discussed so far and decades of diverse experience, I fall in the categories of spatial and object visualizers, legacy experiential, and thought diversity, on top of demographic minority. Very few people can see the value of so much diversity in one person. Invariably my resume is interpreted as a 'confused guy.' In 2006 during an Emerging Leadership Development Course at UTC, the industrial psychologists could not fit me in any of the popular profiles. They expressed that my diversity will be an **enormous strength** or *baggage* under different situations, depending upon how I perceive the situation, portray my position, and choose to connect with people. I have since then learned to live enjoy and work with it. I am ready to jump into anything new, fearlessly, because somewhere in there I will find a comfort level just ripe for innovation.

Perhaps this drives and enables me to study the subject of innovation from so many angles and keep sharing it with you through a series of books. Maybe this makes me sound unreasonable in so many conversations. Someday, I will sit and write about my zig-zag personal journey.

Diversity Challenges

Accepting diversity is difficult. It has to go through the challenges of awareness and acceptance. Within an organization, it needs to start from the top. Leadership and board must include individuals with diverse backgrounds. Then they need to identify a champion, who defines diversity practices in sync with organizational goals. This champion needs resources to bring training and awareness, run social activities and games, create a psychological safe space to help humans overcome bias and internal resistance. There are many books and consultants on the topic. None of them are perfect. This is a work in progress.

Being a diverse individual myself and usually the only one in the workplace or a conference with a head gear, I must make a special effort to get accepted. My approach is being open, transparent, and welcoming. Over the years, 6th sense has developed to a level, where it only takes me a few minutes of conversation and an eye contact to gauge an individual's position on my personal inclusivity scale; however, it takes many conversations to move them one or two steps upwards.

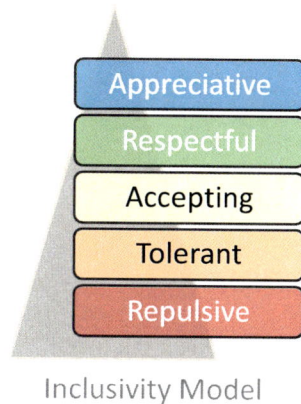

Appreciative

Respectful

Accepting

Tolerant

Repulsive

Inclusivity Model

> Inclusion is a 2-way street.
> Both the majority and minority must actively work at it.

Diversity also needs to be optimized. When not enough diversity exists within a group, it stagnates, while too much diversity can create gaps that participants cannot bridge.

Let's Summarize

Digital Transformation is taking place all around us. It is a serious confluence of digital and physical technologies and innovative business models are changing every aspect of our existence – home, work, school, health, mobility, entertainment, security, finance, and even mental health. It will change technology, applications, and business models. It requires a new set of trade skills, a blend of a logical-emotional mindset, and an agile leadership. All of this makes gender balance critical to successfully go through the massive transformation associated with the fourth industrial revolution. It requires a commitment from leadership in the near future and parental involvement for a long-term sustainable solution. It also presents a genuine opportunity for every industry to harness the resources and talents of traditionally underrepresented groups, which have learned the importance of resilience in their careers and how to translate that to systems and company resilience to better adapt to volatile environments.

The well-established research cited in this chapter shows that women are well-suited (perhaps even better suited) for leadership roles through the next industrial revolution(s). These women leaders must not suppress their innate abilities to "fit in" in a male-dominated field but use them to transform the company and industry culture to value those attributes and show how they contribute to innovation, resiliency, and overall company success.

Special Acknowledgement

This work was initially presented in March 2019 at the BC-Tech Summit in Vancouver on invitation from Fernanda Ave. Then highlighted at a panel discussion on leadership during ASNT Annual conference in Nov 2020, and later published by ASNT.

Reference: Role of Women in Pursuit of NDE 4.0; Marybeth Miceli and Ripi Singh; Mater. Eval Vol 79, pp 273-284, 2021.

Disclaimer

The research and viewpoints included here are not intended to diminish or promote any demographic. They are simply presented to make a case for a proper blend and balance of diversity in working teams as the right thing to do to create business value and build an equitable social structure.
The fourth industrial revolution needs it.
The fifth social revolution is inclusive by design.

Let's Take a Selfie

Our position on Diversity policy is ...

☐ I do not know if we have a policy.
☐ We have a policy, but I am not sure if employees understand it.
☐ We have a policy, and we work hard to enforce it.
☐ We have a policy, and its implementation is showing value.
☐ We practice inclusion of diversity so much that we do not need it.

I can see a correlation between innovation and diversity in ...

☐ Age.
☐ Gender.
☐ Military experience.
☐ Race, Religion, and ethnicity.
☐ Presence of an intelligent machine.

Our organization is more focused on

☐ Demographic diversity.
☐ Experiential diversity.
☐ Cognitive diversity.
☐ Photo ops and PR.
☐ Cash is King.
☐ None.

10. Ethics in Innovation: Human Dilemma

In 2017, a local firm hired me to help them build and optimize the value stream for growth. We did the process mapping, took out the fat, re-purposed assets, re-aligned employees, and deployed a gamut of lean tools. We then set up a small team for innovation to increase market penetration. For 60 days it was going great. Then one Monday morning, the admin at the entrance gate gave me quite an unwelcome look. I presumed she had an awful weekend, gave her a courtesy greeting and went to the conf room. The meeting was very unusual, tense, low energy engagement, no information sharing, and now I was concerned. During coffee break, I bumped into a supporter, and she shared her perception. Apparently, I was responsible for 3 people laid off on the previous Friday. I fulfilled my role for the day and while walking out, I checked with front desk if we lost any staff members. She looks me in the eye and said, "*you tell me… I was told they were your pick*!" I could not sleep that night. Next morning, I consulted my mentor and pulled out of my engagement with this client. I cannot work with people who would mis-represent me like that.

Looking back in my 30 years of learning, with various organizations, I have generally been fortunate to work with ethical professionals. But now and then, the human greed drives someone to act in a manner that may be legal, but not necessarily the right thing to do or the right way to do. How will this situation manifest when machines are optimized to maximize an objective function, without total awareness of collateral implications, and learn from a mixed bag of diverse inputs? **It can be scary.**

Emerging Reality

One aspect of any revolution is that innovation happens faster than laws and regulations needed to keep the business drivers in check, and particularly where there is no precedence to provide initial guidance. Figure below depicts that dangerous zone, where no one is looking out in the interest of public.

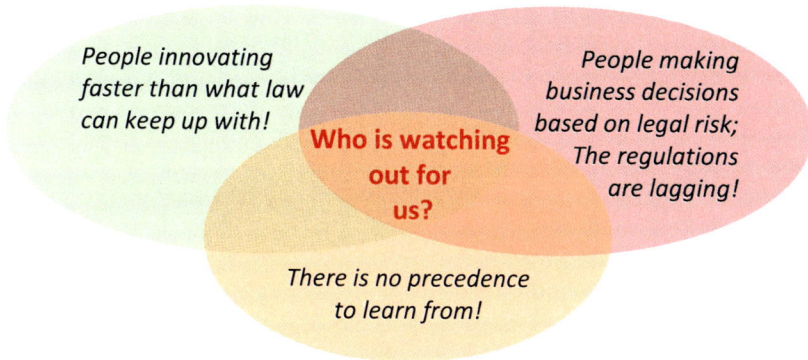

People innovating faster than what law can keep up with!

People making business decisions based on legal risk; The regulations are lagging!

Who is watching out for us?

There is no precedence to learn from!

Ethics help us navigate the gray area between absolute right and morally wrong. They provide the structure that helps us decide and be proud of it. Without ethics, society would be reduced to the type of animal behavior that is seen in nature. The Markkula Center for Applied Ethics at Santa Clara University says that the term refers to well-founded standards of right and wrong that prescribe what humans ought to do, and the study and development of one's ethical standards. We cannot provide perfectly correct or incorrect answers or a common list of 'dos and don'ts.' We need a conversation.

There are serious questions about programming machines to replace human activity. Greg Satell[78] says that when businesses gain access to

---

[78] These are the 4 Biggest Innovation Challenges We Must Solve Over the Next Decade – Ultimately, it's about humans rather than technology; Greg Satell; Inc.; https://www.inc.com/greg-satell/these-are-4-biggest-innovation-challenges-we-must-solve-over-next-decade.html; Aug 25, 2018.

advanced technologies like artificial intelligence and gene editing, the managers will be thrown into an unusual position. Should a self-driving car risk killing its passenger to save a pedestrian? Do decisions made by robots require greater transparency than those made by humans? Who gets to decide which factors are encoded into AI systems that make decisions about our education, whether we get hired or if we go to jail? How will these systems be trained? We all worry about who is educating our kids, who is teaching our algorithms? What is striking about the moral and ethical issues of both artificial intelligence and genomics is that they have no precedence. We are in a totally uncharted territory. Nevertheless, we must develop a consensus about what principles should be applied, in what contexts, and for what purposes.

Some Illustrative Examples

There are too many unknowns around the development and adoption of industry 4.0, that it needs a hard conversation around ethics. The situation becomes alarming as decision making shifts from humans to machines that can learn to act autonomously, without fear of penalty. It is unreasonable for us to expect such machines to be 'ethically neutral.' Gartner notes that 85% of all AI will be biased in 2022[79]. The technology development community needs guidance and controls. All the ethical considerations that have evolved through the third revolution are still valid. So, the additional ethical principles for handling this next revolution should build on existing ethics framework in use, within the organization and longstanding norms and values in individual companies, industrial sectors, cultures, and countries.

---

[79] Gartner Says Nearly Half of CIOs Are Planning to Deploy Artificial Intelligence
https://www.gartner.com/en/newsroom/press-releases/2018-02-13-gartner-says-nearly-half-of-cios-are-planning-to-deploy-artificial-intelligence; Feb 13, 2018.

Most of us are already using Artificial Intelligence (AI) in some form or the other without even realizing it[80] through our devices (phones, TV, computer, appliance, etc.) And so many of us are on the receiving end of targeted advertisements and market campaigns based on analytics performed by retailers. Is that right? Let us set a context with a few known cases around machine learning.

The pricing algorithms in e-commerce have become ubiquitous in online retail. They have moved from rule-based programs to reinforcement-learning ones, where the logic of deciding a product's price is no longer within a human's control. Calvano et al.[81] suggest that these systems could pose a huge problem: *"They quickly learn to collude, purely by trial and error, with no prior knowledge of the environment in which they operate, and without being specifically designed or instructed to collude."* This leads to a risk of driving up the price of goods and ultimately harming consumers. Is this the case of post pandemic widespread inflation in 2021? I am not sure.

Your profile and social data on Facebook and LinkedIn are your partial digital twin. We know how it has created ethical situations arising out of access, analytics, and privacy concerns. We go back and forth on rights, exposure, exploitation in the name of the connectivity and communication service business. Facebook paid over $20B to acquire Whatsapp[82] in 2014, with revenue of $15M and losses of over $200M. With over 2 billion free users of the app, Facebook is monetizing something somewhere, legally. Some days we wonder if the legislation has caught up to *'protect the rights of data owners from data dealers.'*

---

[80] Most Americans Already Using Artificial Intelligence Products; RJ Reinhart; Gallup, https://news.gallup.com/poll/228497/americans-already-using-artificial-intelligence-products.aspx; Mar 6, 2018.

[81] Artificial intelligence, algorithmic pricing, and collusion; E Calvano, G Calzolari, V Denicolò, and S Pastorello; https://voxeu.org/article/artificial-intelligence-algorithmic-pricing-and-collusion; Feb 2019.

[82] WhatsApp: The Best Facebook Purchase Ever? A L. Deutsch; Investopedia; Mar 18, 2020.

Algorithms have become a key element underpinning crucial services and infrastructures of information societies. Individuals interact with a recommending algorithm that makes suggestions about what a user may like on a given day, be it to choose a song, a movie, a product or even a friend. At the same time, schools and hospitals, financial institutions, courts, local and national governments, all increasingly rely on algorithms to make significant decisions. The potential for algorithms to improve individual and social welfare comes with significant ethical risks since the algorithms are not ethically neutral as discussed extensively by Tsamados[83] et al. Learning algorithms do not seem to care about morality or preventing discrimination. In the single-minded pursuit of their tasks, they align themselves with the ideological, racial and gender biases of their creators and society at large[84]. Social media platforms such as YouTube, which benefit from engaging a consumer, use algorithms that select more and more sensationalizing content that keeps users hooked on watching[85].

Amazon[86] experimented with building a computer program in 2014 to review job applicants' resumes to mechanize the search for top talent. It used artificial intelligence to give job candidates scores ranging from one to five stars – much like shoppers rate products on Amazon. By 2015, the company realized its new system was not rating candidates for software developer jobs and other technical posts in a gender-neutral way. That is because Amazon's computer models were trained to vet applicants by observing patterns in resumes submitted to the company over a 10-year period. Most came from men, a reflection of male dominance across the tech

---

[83] The ethics of algorithms: key problems and solutions; A Tsamados, N Aggarwal, J Cowls, J Morley, H Roberts, M Taddeo, and L Floridi; AI & Society; Jan 2021.

[84] Power Business with AI: Augmented Intelligence; M J. Barrenechea; CEO white paper OpenText, https://www.opentext.com/info/augmented-intelligence-ceo-white-paper

[85] Study of YouTube comments finds evidence of radicalization effect; N Lomas; Jan 28, 2020 https://techcrunch.com/2020/01/28/study-of-youtube-comments-finds-evidence-of-radicalization-effect/.

[86] Amazon scraps secret AI recruiting tool that showed bias against women; J Dastin; https://www.reuters.com/article/us-amazon-com-jobs-automation-insight/amazon-scraps-secret-ai-recruiting-tool-that-showed-bias-against-women-idUSKCN1MK08G; Oct 10, 2018.

industry. In effect, Amazon's system taught itself that male candidates were preferable. It penalized resumes that included the word 'women's,' as in 'women's chess club captain.' And it downgraded graduates of two all-women's colleges. Amazon edited the programs to make them neutral to these particular terms. But that was no guarantee that the machines would not devise other ways of sorting candidates that could prove discriminatory. The Seattle company ultimately disbanded the team in 2017. Amazon's recruiters looked at the recommendations generated by the tool when searching for new hires, but never relied solely on those rankings. In a sense, using machines to augment human intelligence rather than independent intelligent actor.

A good friend David Gilbert (UK) shared these ethical concerns in relation to robotics and automation. Many robots use Artificial Intelligence and Machine Learning, which does not, of itself, create ethical issues. It can introduce ethical problems, from the redistribution of risk, where actions may have positive and negative effects on multiple individuals at the same time. The ability to oversee, or govern a robot is an ethical issue, as operators should be able to understand and manage the behavior of systems for which they are responsible. When the decisions are not transparent, i.e., open to scrutiny, there is a possibility that they are both unfair (unjust) and not open to correction. Robots might have a bias in their decision making (based on their learning). Robots may contain, and be able to provide to third parties, data that could violate an individual's right to privacy. Robots present the risk, especially to vulnerable users, of emotional attachment or dependency.

Ethics and Digital Transformation

The topic of ethics in context of digitalization is likely to be a long-drawn out debate, with continuously developing perspectives from successful technology disruptors with equally plausible opposing perspectives. The best we can do is discuss multiple perspectives, raise a few questions, throw in a few possibilities, with an intent to continuously adapt as we collectively learn more.

Defining a New Ethic for Technology

Michael Sandel of Harvard[87] has a series of lectures on YouTube, some of the best on ethics and morals. They show how the human mind thinks, thinking differently under seemingly similar situations, can justify a decision with a slight change in perspective. It is difficult to capture and summarize their content, but the experience of listening to them makes you realize the dilemma you must resolve. Prof Sandel has now turned his attention to technology[88]. Some of the key questions are:

- Whether decision-making based on algorithms is fair and whether robots will make work obsolete?
- Whether smart machines can out-think us and, if they can, whether we should worry about this?
- Are our traditional notions of privacy compatible with new technologies and with big data, or do we need to reconsider these conceptions? and
- Whether the age of big data and social media is friendly to democracy or corrosive of it?

"These are among the most fundamental ethical questions we face, prompted by our new technological powers. Often technology is a tool for the achievement of human purposes and to promote the common good, but today there's a fear that it will become a force that will redefine how we live and relate to one another." says Sandel.

So where do we start?

---

[87] What's the right thing to do, https://justiceharvard.org/ and the lecture playlist https://youtube.com/playlist?list=PL30C13C91CFFEFEA6
[88] Defining a new ethic for technology; Rae Ritchie; https://www.i-cio.com/management/insight/item/a-new-ethic-for-technology; May 2019.

Current State

Most mature organizations and professional bodies have created specific ethical codes for their respective fields. It is a set of rules that are drafted to ensure members/employees stay out of trouble and act in a way that brings credit to the profession/company.

When you review them, you discover that these are all variations or subset of normative ethics discussed above. They assume all judgements and decisions are made by humans and organizations capable of learning. They apply very well for systems where humans are in complete control of machines. However, when the machines start to learn and decide, we would still want the outcome to be morally right and ethically correct. The big question then becomes how do we build algorithms that can interpret and follow the Code of Ethics?

During the 3rd revolution, the Software Engineering Code of Ethics and Professional Practice was created for computer related professionals who are not required to be certified or licensed as compared to an attorney or physician. But as examined in the textbook[89], those who work with computers can, through inadequate education, insufficient practical training, or bad choices, cause a great deal of harm to members of the public. In this respect, the responsibility of computer "professionals" can be similar to that held by members of "fully developed professions." Even as recognized from within the profession, ethics in computer programming and engineering is essential but not necessarily designed into the programming professional. A few data science societies are now putting out a code of ethics, such ADaSci[90] and DSA[91] geared towards the fourth revolution.

---

[89] Ethics for the Information Age; 7th Edition; Michael Quinn: ePub; Pearson; Online publication date February 2016.

[90] Guidelines and Ethical Standards for Data Scientists; https://www.adasci.org/ethics-in-data-science/

[91] Data Science Code of Professional Conduct; Data Science Association; https://www.datascienceassn.org/code-of-conduct.html; Accessed Aug 2021.

Helping Resolve Existing Ethical Concerns

Despite organizational Code of Ethics and regular trainings on ethics, we are subject to situations that we wish were not there in the first place. Industry 4.0 technologies with automation, robotics, data traceability, workflows can help reduce many of the existing concerns and human factors that create difficult situations.

We can expect higher levels of integrity in design, manufacturing, operations, and services. Human factors such as fatigue, schedule pressure, uncomfortable environment, mental distractions, that push an honest individual to succumb, and compromise are reduced. Robots will be consistent, and you cannot hurry them up as easily.

Business pressures from management or customer to influence the outcome are reduced by virtue of trust in automation and traceability of reported data. Over a period, the reduced false calls will drive towards a more ethical system. Traceability can deter fraud/counterfeit replacement parts.

Many of these benefits will be easier to derive in a routine work amenable to predictable automation such as production shop floor environment, quality assurance, supply chain, consumption, and logistics. The important thing to understand is all the automation needs to have a human over-ride for reasons of safety and control. Which means that if a human still wants to be unethical, he or she can be. It will likely be more difficult and certainly traceable.

There are certain other benefits that we cannot identify until we put these systems in practice.

Raising New Ethical Concerns

Some of the Industry 4.0 technologies, such as AI/ML (Artificial Intelligence and Machine Learning) will require some additions to the existing Code of Ethics. Machine learning through neural networks is advancing rapidly for many reasons – increase in the size of data sets, an increase in computing power, improvement in ML algorithms, and more human talent to write them. Learning machines are likely to inherit biases in data and incompetencies of the trainers, just like learning from a human instructor. We need something soon.

Prof Keng Siau[92,93] of the Missouri University of Science and Technology defines the concern like this. The business and technology oriented ethical forces of Industry 4.0 exert their influence throughout the value chain activities – from design, development, production, to in-service application and maintenance. Tracing the ethical responsibility and decision making of each stakeholder associated with value chain activities is important and poses a major challenge. AI and autonomous systems make the tracing of ethical responsibility more pressing because some of those functions may be performed without human intervention. A lack of ethical and moral standards in those autonomous agents and decision-making software is a problem, and a lack of experience and guidance in formulating ethical and moral standards in Industry 4.0 exacerbate the problem.

Assigning responsibility to intelligent agents is contentious. Critics believe that designers and developers should take responsibility for the decisions of intelligent agents. However, Artificial Intelligence and Machine Learning (ML) present new challenges. While designers and developers may build the base model, the system will continue to learn and evolve. During the learning and evolution, the intelligent system may pick up poor examples and produce erroneous outcomes. Of course, there are ways to reduce this by regulated models and deliberate training on poor examples. Thus, some argue that intelligent systems may need to be assigned responsibility. Not assigning responsibility to intelligent agents

---

[92] Industry 4.0: Ethical and Moral Predicaments; W Wang and K Siau; Cutter Business Technology Journal, Vol 32, No 6, pp 36-45, 2019.
[93] Artificial Intelligence (AI) Ethics: Ethics of AI and Ethical AI; W Wang and K Siau; Journal of Database Management, Volume 31(2), pp74-86, 2020.

may create a hazardous policy and ethics vacuum with unforeseeable negative consequences. Furthermore, developers may be reluctant to develop advanced technology if they fear being assigned responsibility for the poor decisions intelligent agents make. Such reluctance would seriously hinder technological progress.

Beyond adding a responsibility component to AI/ML models or their developers, we may need surveillance of the system itself. They cannot just be created and let free to run. There is potential for bias to creep into a model over iterations of learning and model may drift over time. In both situations, the outcome of the model will become pointless, leading to errors and a bad outcome.

Various perspectives are emerging as we collectively learn the consequences of data management and digital technology development. Let us look at a few and see what can be done in that context.

Face of Ethical Issues with Data Application

There can be multiple issues with outcome from a machine that processes data using an algorithm.

- Machine Learning model can go wrong. It can have bugs.
- Machine is presented with data that it has not seen before and behaves in an unexpected way.
- Machine may not be able to raise an alarm when fed with bad data or data is inadequate.
- Machine could work exactly as designed but be used for something that we would much prefer it were never, ever used for.

Rachel Thomas[94] the co-founder of fast.ai and founding director of the Center for Applied Data Ethics at the University of San Francisco has extensively discussed multiple ethical issues with data handling. Let us examine some of those.

Recourse and Accountability

In a complex system, it is easy for no one person to feel responsible for outcomes. While this is understandable, it does not lead to good results. NYU Professor Danah Boyd described this phenomenon: "*Bureaucracy has often been used to shift or evade responsibility. Today's algorithmic systems are extending bureaucracy.*" An additional reason a recourse is so necessary is because data often contains errors. Mechanisms for audits and error correction are crucial.

In an unforeseen situation, with no recourse for correction, system can reward or punish incorrectly. A good accountability question to ask is who is the ultimate authority making these decisions? Are the right individuals accountable? Is it all placed onto the programmer? Where are the ethics requirements designed into the AI or neural network? What say does the customer get regarding accountability? Who is fired, fined, or put in jail when a failure occurs?

Bias and Fairness

Bias in AI entrenches and magnifies existing injustice. Therefore, any discussion of using AI for the good must start with eliminating AI bias and building responsible, accountable and transparent algorithms. One of the MIT researchers, Joy Buolamwini, warned: "*We have entered the age of automation over-confident yet under-prepared. If we fail to make ethical and inclusive artificial intelligence, we risk losing gains made in civil rights and gender equity under the guise of machine neutrality.*"

---

[94] https://github.com/fastai/fastbook/blob/master/03_ethics.ipynb Data Ethics. Accessed Aug 2021.

Bias in machine-based decision making comes in various forms.

Historical bias comes from the fact that people are biased, processes are biased, and society is biased.

Measurement bias occurs when our models make mistakes because we are measuring the wrong thing, or measuring it in the wrong way, or incorporating that measurement into the model inappropriately.

Aggregation bias occurs when models do not aggregate data in a way that incorporates all the appropriate factors, or when a model does not include the interaction terms, nonlinearities, and so forth.

Representation bias occurs when there is some clear, easy-to-see underlying relationship, a simple model will often simply assume that this relationship holds all the time.

Different types of bias require different approaches for mitigation. All datasets contain bias. There is no such thing as a **completely de-biased dataset**. Many researchers in the field have been converging on a set of proposals to enable better documentation of the decisions, context, and specifics about how and why a particular dataset was created, what scenarios it is appropriate to use in, and what the limitations are. This way, those using a particular dataset will not be surprised by its biases and limitations.

Diverse data input is an aspect strongly supported by many, but not so easy to accomplish. In such case programmers may have to use techniques that can eliminate or reduce the effects of intrinsic bias in a data set. It is a step that can be easily overlooked and must be built into the review process.

The important thing to keep in mind is that machine learning algorithms are different from humans.

- Machine learning can create feedback loops (Small amounts of bias can rapidly increase exponentially because of feedback loops).
- Machine learning can amplify bias (Human bias can lead to larger amounts of machine learning bias).

- Algorithms & humans are used differently (Human decision makers and algorithmic decision makers are not used in a plug-and-play interchangeable way in practice).
- Technology is power and with that comes responsibility.

Algorithms are used differently.

- People are more likely to assume algorithms are objective or error-free (even if they are given the option of a human over-ride).
- Algorithms are more likely to be implemented with no appeals process in place.
- Algorithms are often used at scale.
- Algorithmic systems are cheap.

The question is – how much can, and should we human depend upon algorithms and machine learning?

We should accept that measurement, aggregate, and representation bias can creep into the automated systems. Developers need to be aware and consciously work to address it to the extent known and continuously reduce it. Developers should search for ways to periodically validate, compensate, and eliminate bias. For example, Pymetrics.ai uses control through periodic audits of algorithms in their automated inspection machines.

When bias leads to an adverse event, it should be made transparent and discussed as a learning opportunity rather than an oversight or coverup of incompetency. It is a new subject, and we are all learning. Perhaps there is even hope that we could build an AI algorithm that will remove bias from other AI algorithms[95].

---

[95] A New Algorithm Trains AI to Erase its Biases; Dan Robitzski; Futurism, https://futurism.com/algorithm-trains-ai-to-erase-biases; Jan 29, 2019.

Feedback Loops

If a machine recommends an action based on certain data, and that action produces more data of the same type, the system can get out of control.

In an inspection, if a robot is pre-dispositioned to inspect certain regions based on historical data, then over time the findings in that region will continue to increase and eventually robot will ignore inspecting other regions, increasing risk to asset owners.

Information Integrity

This is the human side of data input tied with the intent.

Misinformation: Information that is false, but not created with an intention to cause harm (e.g., someone posting an article containing now out-of-date information but not realizing it).

Disinformation: Information that is false and deliberately created to harm a person, social group, organization, or country (e.g., a competitor purposely posting false statistics about your organization with an intent to discredit you).

Mal-information: Information that is based on reality, used to inflict harm on a person, organization, or country. E.g., someone using a picture of a dead child refugee without context in an effort to ignite hatred of a particular ethnic group they are against.

One possible approach is to develop some form of digital signature, to implement it seamlessly, and to create norms we should only trust content that has been verified. Several other approaches are feasible including the creation of validation mechanisms of information sources that range from simple logical tests to more sophisticated protocols and algorithms, such as the one used in banking operations, it may also include the use of cross-human validation for critical information.

Privacy and Surveillance

The two can be related in a variety of empirical and ethical configurations[96]. Privacy is often justified as a value because of what it is presumed to do for individuals. In contrast, surveillance is too often criticized for what it is presumed to do for more powerful groups such as government relative to the individual. Just as privacy can support the dignity and freedom to act of the person, surveillance can protect the integrity and independence of groups vital to a pluralistic democratic society. It can offer protection to individuals, whether for the dependent such as children and the sick, or to those who like clean water and industrial safety and do not want their precious liberties destroyed by enemies. Surveillance, like privacy, can be made good for the individual and for the society, but like privacy it can also have negative consequences for both.

They need to be seen as elements within a broader sociology of information control framework. They both are about the control of information – in one case as discovery, in the other as protection. At the most basic level, surveillance is a way of accessing data. Surveillance implies an agent who accesses (whether through discovery tools, rules, or physical/logistical settings) personal data. Privacy, in contrast, involves a subject who restricts access to personal data through the same means. Surveillance is not necessarily the dark side of the social dimension of privacy. There are four basic empirical connections between privacy and surveillance.

- Privacy may serve to nullify surveillance (e.g., encryption, whispering, and disguises).
- Privacy may serve to protect surveillance (e.g., undercover).

---

[96] Coming to Terms: The Kaleidoscope of Privacy and Surveillance; Gary T. Marx; In 'The Social Dimensions of Privacy' by B. Roessler and D. Mokrosinska; Cambridge University Press; https://web.mit.edu/gtmarx/www/thekaleidoscopeof.html; 2015.

- Surveillance may serve to nullify privacy (e.g., big data, night vision video cameras).
- Surveillance may serve to protect privacy (e.g., biometric identification and audit trails).

Language and Training

In an article by Falk Hendemann[97], he states, "*Researchers found that human language is not suitable for training AI, as cultural prejudices otherwise manifest themselves.*" What is there in the human language, from the context of how we communicate about NDE, which could introduce ethical dilemmas from a programming or training perspective?

Data Projects

Rachel Thomas[98] also compiled a few questions that provide guidance when working with data projects. You can start by asking if you have:

- ☐ Listed how this technology can be attacked or abused?
- ☐ Tested your training data to ensure that it is fair and representative?
- ☐ Studied and understood possible sources of bias in your data?
- ☐ Included diversity of opinions, backgrounds, and kinds of thought?
- ☐ Set up a mechanism for gathering consent from users?
- ☐ Set up a mechanism for redress if people are harmed by the results?
- ☐ Created a safe shut down mechanism when it is misbehaving?
- ☐ Tested for fairness with respect to different user groups?
- ☐ Tested for disparate error rates among different user groups?
- ☐ Ways to monitor for model drift and ensure fairness over time?
- ☐ …

---

[97] AI Ethics II: Why we need quality control; Falk Henemann; DMEXCO; https://dmexco.com/stories/ai-ethics-ii-why-we-need-quality-control/ Jan 23, 2019.
[98] 16 Things You Can Do to Make Tech More Ethical; Rachel Thomas; fast.ai; https://www.fast.ai/2019/04/22/ethics-action-1/; Apr 22, 2019.

Data Regulation

Just like clean air and water are nearly impossible to protect through individual decisions and require a coordinated regulatory action, data will need a pollution control when Industrial Internet of Things (IIoT) becomes widespread. Many of the harms resulting from unintended consequences of misuses of technology involve public goods, such as a polluted information environment or deteriorated ambient privacy. Too often privacy is framed as an individual right, yet there are societal impacts to widespread surveillance (which would still be the case even if it were possible for a few individuals to opt out).

We need both regulatory and legal changes, and the ethical behavior of individuals. Individual behavior change cannot address misaligned profit incentives, externalities (where corporations reap large profits while offloading their costs and harms to the broader society), or systemic failures. However, the law will never cover all edge cases, and it is important that individual software developers and data scientists are equipped to make ethical decisions in practice.

Information Transparency

Transparency helps promote ethical and moral behavior. Transparency of systems can clarify responsibility and make outcomes understandable. Users can better understand the underlying processes the system used to arrive at an outcome and use that knowledge to make correct decisions. Without transparency, it is much easier to maliciously use and control systems. Moreover, insufficient transparency may jeopardize human trust in autonomous systems[99]. Transparency without validation mechanisms is insufficient and susceptible to manipulation.

---

[99] Building Trust in Artificial Intelligence, Machine Learning, and Robotics; K Siau, and Weiyu Wang; Cutter Business Technology Journal, Vol. 31, No. 2, 47-53, 2018.

This is where the subject of AI needs to go a notch up to XAI – Explainable AI which refers to methods and techniques in the application of artificial intelligence such that the results of the solution can be understood by humans. It contrasts with the concept of the 'black box' in machine learning where even its designers cannot explain why an AI arrived at a specific decision.

Trust

Another important aspect is trust. Many people will put more trust in algorithmic (technology) decisions than they might in human decisions. While the researchers designing the algorithms may have a good grasp on probability and confidence intervals, often the public using them will not. Even if people are given the power to over-ride algorithmic decisions, it is crucial to understand if they will feel comfortable doing so in practice.

According to Sandel, trust has been a casualty of some technological developments as demonstrated by a couple of trends. First, people are losing trust in large technology companies, visible from use of personal data for monetization by some of the major social media companies. Most of us were unaware of its use in hacking into political campaigns or in disrupting the democratic process. Second, it is affecting the trust we have in one another that is necessary for communities to flourish. Trust is needed for a healthy social life, for a sense of community and for democracy. There must be a certain trust across society among citizens from different backgrounds and walks of life. But the technology has the tendency to separate us and divide us into narrow bubbles of opinion, which generates a kind of polarization that erodes social trust and damages communities.

Nevertheless, we are moving into a decade where trust and reputation will be a potent force that will shape the economy[100]. All this because in a

---

[100] What is trust in technology? Conceptual bases, common pitfalls and the contribution of trust research; Frens Kroeger; https://www.trusttech.cam.ac.uk/perspectives/technology-humanity-society-democracy/what-trust-technology-conceptual-bases-common; date unknown.

fundamental sense, all technology depends on trust. What makes technology 'technology' is precisely the fact that most users do not know – and do not need to know – how it works; instead, they hold the confident positive expectation that a mechanism which is ultimately opaque to them will bring about the desired outcome.

Need for an Ethical Debate

As we move forward in Industry 4.0, we need to give serious thought to the responsibility matrix. Who is responsible for the decisions a machine makes – developer, owner, trainer, regulator, user, or the machine? What should guide those decisions? What recourse should those affected by a machine's decision have? These are no longer theoretical debates, but practical problems that need to be solved. This is where the notion of Society 5.0[101] should be integrated into technology development, as the purpose of Industry 4.0.

Responsible technology companies need to discuss, think, and debate about respect for privacy as connected to the trust that we will ultimately have as consumers and citizens in the companies and in the technologies they produced. We need to resist the notion that technology is an independent force that we simply must adapt to. We must remind ourselves that technology is a set of tools, becoming more and more powerful, for a purpose. We must govern the technology with ethical considerations of the common good. Technology companies should think of themselves as responsible for shaping technology towards the common good so that these powers contribute to human flourishing and a sense of community, rather than pose a threat to privacy, communication, and democracy.

This requires a public debate, because technology companies cannot do it on their own, even if they truly mean to do so. This requires the opening

---

[101] Japan Cabinet Office, https://www8.cao.go.jp/cstp/english/society5_0/index.html since 2016.

of discourse between the creators of impactful technologies — its direction and uses — and the people affected by those technologies. The ethical use of technologies, particularly the emerging digital technologies around thinking machines, should not be judged only by robotics engineers and AI developer, but also by behavioral scientists and other practitioners of human-centered areas of knowledge, including philosophers.

"The most responsible technology companies will be those that welcome and encourage a broader public debate about how technology, rather than being disempowering, can be a force for the common good," says Sandel.

Many of us are eager for technical or design fixes to solve ethical concerns, (e.g., design guidelines for making technology less addictive). While such measures can be useful, they will not be sufficient to address the underlying problems that have led to our current state. If it is incredibly profitable to create addictive technology, companies will continue to do so, regardless of whether this has the side effect of promoting conspiracy theories and polluting our information eco-system. While individual designers may try to tweak product designs, we will not see substantial changes until the underlying profit incentives change, or ethical behavior becomes a grassroot value.

> In some sense it is our ethical duty and professional responsibility to proactively identify and remove the potential for harm from advancing the technology frontier.

Guidance and Possibilities

The field of AI ethics is urgently calling for tangible action to move from high-level abstractions and conceptual arguments towards applying ethics in practice and creating accountability mechanisms. However, lessons must be learned from the shortcomings of AI ethics principles to ensure the future investments, collaborations, standards, codes, or legislation reflect the diversity of voices and incorporate the experiences of those who are already impacted by the biased algorithms[102].

In this section, we will discuss a few sets of guidelines and possibilities that organizations may consider addressing ethical dilemma. These possibilities help only when the leadership or ownership intends to be ethical.

Ethics in Digital Transformation – Santa Clara Guidance

Brian Patrick Green, Director of Technology Ethics at the Markkula Center for Applied Ethics at Santa Clara University has provided one of the most comprehensive guidance to do the right things in the right way. As of Jan 2021, he provides 16 issues to consider[103].

Technical Safety – The first question for any technology is whether it works as intended. Will AI systems work as they are promised, or will they fail? If and when they fail, what will result from those failures? And if we depend on them, will we be able to survive without them?

Transparency and Privacy – Once we have determined that the technology functions adequately, can we understand how it works and properly gather data on its functioning? Ethical analysis always depends on getting the facts first, only then can evaluation begin.

Beneficial Use & Capacity for Good – The primary purpose of AI is, like every other technology, to help people lead longer, more flourishing, more fulfilling lives. This is good, and therefore where AI helps people in these ways, we can be glad and appreciate the benefits it gives to us.

---

[102] Lessons learned from AI ethics principles for future actions; M Hickok; Opinion paper, AI and Ethics Vol 1, pp 41–47, Oct 06, 2020. https://link.springer.com/article/10.1007/s43681-020-00008-1
[103] Artificial Intelligence and Ethics: Sixteen Challenges and Opportunities; Brian Patrick Green; https://www.scu.edu/ethics/all-about-ethics/artificial-intelligence-and-ethics-sixteen-challenges-and-opportunities/

Malicious Use & Capacity for Evil – A perfectly well functioning technology, such as a nuclear, when used as a weapon, can cause immense evil. Artificial intelligence, like human intelligence, can be used maliciously, there is no doubt, e.g., lethal autonomous weapons.

Bias in Data, Training Sets, etc. – neural networks effectively merge a computer program with the data that is given to it. This has many benefits, but it also risks biasing the entire system in unexpected and potentially detrimental ways. (More on this later).

Unemployment / Lack of Purpose & Meaning – Automation of industry has been a major contributing factor in job losses since the beginning of the industrial revolution. AI will simply extend this trend to more fields, including fields that have been traditionally thought of as being safer from automation, for example law, medicine, and education. Attached to the concern for employment is the concern for how humanity spends its time and what makes a life well-spent. How will society prevent unemployed from becoming disillusioned, bitter, and swept up in evil movements?

Growing Socio-Economic Inequality – Those who control AI will also likely rake in much of the money that would have otherwise gone into the wages of the now-unemployed, and therefore economic inequality will increase. This will also affect international economic disparity, and therefore is likely a major threat to less-developed nations.

Environmental Effects – Machine learning models require enormous amounts of energy to train, so much energy that the costs can run into the tens of millions of dollars or more. If this energy is coming from fossil fuels, this is a large negative impact on climate change, not to mention being harmful at other points in the hydrocarbon supply chain. It is possible to make AI a net positive for the environment, but only if it is directed towards that positive end, and not just towards consuming energy for other uses.

Automating Ethical Decision Making – As AI agents are given more powers to decide, they will need to have ethical standards of some sort encoded into them. AI will operate so much faster than humans can, that under some circumstances humans will be left "out of the loop" of control due to human slowness. This already occurs with cyberattacks, and high-frequency trading (both of which are filled with ethical questions which are typically ignored).

Moral Deskilling & Debility – Because one of the uses of AI will be to either assist or replace humans at making certain types of decisions (e.g. spelling, driving, stock-trading, etc.), we should be aware that humans may become worse at these skills. In its most extreme form, if AI starts to make ethical and political decisions for us, we will become worse at ethics and politics. We may reduce or stunt our moral development precisely when our power has become greater and our decisions the most important.

AI Consciousness, Personhood, and "Robot Rights" – Morally, we can expect that technologists will attempt to make the most human-like AIs and robots possible, and perhaps someday they will be such good imitations that we will wonder if they might be conscious and deserve rights – and we might not be able to determine this conclusively. If future humans do conclude AIs and robots might be worthy of moral status, then we ought to err on the side of caution and give it.

Artificial General Intelligence and Superintelligence – If or when AI reaches human levels of intelligence, or exceeds to become superintelligence, it will mark the dethroning of humanity as the most intelligent thing on Earth. We have never faced (in the material world) anything smarter than us before. We ought to keep this in mind because AI is a tool, there may be ways yet to maintain an ethical balance between human and machine.

Dependency on AI – Intelligence dependence is a form of dependence like that of a child to an adult. Much of the time, children and elderly rely on adults to think for them. Now imagine when middle-aged adults who are themselves dependent upon AI to guide them, there would be no human "adults" left—only "AI adults." Humankind would have become a race of children to our AI caregivers. If in an unfortunate instance, our AI parents ever malfunctioned, we could become like lost children not knowing how to take care of ourselves or our technological society. This "lostness" already happens when smartphone navigation apps malfunction (or the battery just runs out), for example.

AI-powered Addiction – Smartphone app makers have turned addiction into a science, and AI-powered video games and apps can be addictive like drugs. AI can exploit many human desires and weaknesses including purpose-seeking, gambling, greed, libido, violence, and so on. So many of us are "addicted" to one app or another, we know we are being exploited and harmed. This is something that app makers need to stop doing: AI should not be designed to intentionally exploit vulnerabilities in human psychology.

Isolation and Loneliness – Technology has been implicated in so many negative social and psychological trends, including loneliness, isolation, depression, stress, and anxiety, that it is easy to forget that things could be different, and in fact were quite different only a few decades ago. Loneliness can be helped by dropping devices and building quality in-person relationships. In other words: caring.

Effects on the Human Spirit – All the above areas of interest will have effects on how humans perceive themselves, relate to each other, and live their lives. But there is a more existential question too. If the purpose and identity of humanity has something to do with our intelligence (as several prominent Greek philosophers believed, for example), then by externalizing our intelligence and improving it beyond human intelligence, are we making ourselves second-class beings to our own creations?

Ethical Principles for AI – USA DoD

The U.S. Department of Defense officially adopted a series of ethical principles[104] for the use of Artificial Intelligence on Feb 24, 2020, following recommendations provided to Secretary of Defense Dr. Mark T. Esper by the Defense Innovation Board in October 2019. Those recommendations came after 15 months of consultation with leading AI experts in commercial industry, government, academia, and the American public that resulted in a rigorous process of feedback and analysis among the nation's leading AI experts with multiple venues for public input and comment.

These principles encompass five major areas: **Responsibility, Equity, Traceability, Reliability, and Governance.** You can adopt those to your sector. This adoption of AI ethical principles should align with the organizations growth, digitalization strategy, and the lawful use of AI systems in the host state/country. The adoption will enhance the organization's commitment to upholding the highest ethical standards, while embracing the strong history of applying rigorous testing and validation of inspection technology innovations and methods.

While the existing ethical frameworks provide a technology-neutral and enduring foundation for ethical behavior, the use of AI raises new ethical ambiguities and risks. These principles address these new challenges and ensure the responsible use of AI by the organization.

The AI ethical principles encompass five major areas adopted from DoD and the sixth one which is data specific has been added here:

Responsible – Company personnel will exercise appropriate levels of judgment and care, while remaining responsible for the development, deployment, and use of AI capabilities.

---

[104] DoD Adopts Ethical Principles for Artificial Intelligence; US DoD; https://www.defense.gov/Newsroom/Releases/Release/Article/2091996; Feb. 24, 2020.

Equitable – The company will take deliberate steps to minimize unintended bias in AI capabilities.

Traceable – The company's AI capabilities will be developed and deployed such that relevant personnel possess an appropriate understanding of the technology, development processes, and operational methods applicable to AI capabilities, including with transparent and auditable methodologies, data sources, and design procedure and documentation.

Reliable – The company's AI capabilities will have explicit, well-defined uses, and the safety, security, and effectiveness of such capabilities will be subject to testing and assurance within those defined uses across their entire life-cycles.

Governable – The company will design and engineer AI capabilities to fulfill their intended functions while possessing the ability to detect and avoid unintended consequences, and the ability to disengage or deactivate deployed systems that demonstrate unintended behavior.

Data Management – The company personnel will honor the data acquisition, transfer, storage, analysis, processing, security, and ownership/**sharing** rights as determined by company policy and contractual obligations.

Ethics Guidance for Trustworthy AI – EU

On 8 April 2019, the High-Level Expert Group on AI presented Ethics Guidelines[105] for Trustworthy Artificial Intelligence, requiring that AI should be:

Lawful – respecting all applicable laws and regulations,
Ethical – respecting ethical principles and values, and
Robust – both from a technical perspective and social environment.

---

[105] Ethics Guidelines For Trustworthy AI; European Commission; https://digital-strategy.ec.europa.eu/en/library/ethics-guidelines-trustworthy-ai Mar 8, 2021.

The Guidelines put forward a set of 7 key requirements that AI systems should meet in order to be deemed trustworthy. A specific assessment list aims to help verify the application of each of the key requirements:

Human agency and oversight: AI systems should empower human beings, allowing them to make informed decisions and fostering their fundamental rights. At the same time, proper oversight mechanisms need to be ensured, which can be achieved through *human-in-the-loop, human-on-the-loop, and human-in-command* approaches.

Technical Robustness and safety: AI systems need to be resilient and secure. They need to be safe, ensuring a fallback plan in case something goes wrong, as well as being accurate, reliable and reproducible. That is the only way to ensure that also unintentional harm can be minimized and prevented.

Privacy and data governance: besides ensuring full respect for privacy and data protection, adequate data governance mechanisms must also be ensured, considering the quality and integrity of the data, and ensuring legitimized access to data.

Transparency: the data, system and AI business models should be transparent. Traceability mechanisms can help to achieve this. Moreover, AI systems and their decisions should be explained in a manner adapted to the stakeholder concerned. Humans need to know that they are interacting with an AI system and must be informed of the system's capabilities and limitations.

Diversity, non-discrimination and fairness: Unfair bias must be avoided, as it could have multiple negative implications, from the marginalization of vulnerable groups to the exacerbation of prejudice and discrimination. Fostering diversity, AI systems should be accessible to all, regardless of any disability, and involve relevant stakeholders throughout their entire life circle.

Societal and environmental well-being: AI systems should benefit all human beings, including future generations. It must hence be ensured that they are sustainable and environmentally friendly. Moreover, they should consider the environment, including other living beings, and their social and societal impact should be carefully considered.

Accountability: Mechanisms should be put in place to ensure responsibility and accountability for AI systems and their outcomes. Auditability, which enables the assessment of algorithms, data and design processes plays a key role therein, especially in critical applications. Moreover, adequate an accessible redress should be ensured.

This guidance has been translated into an assessment tool called ALTAI[106] – Assessment List on Trustworthy Artificial Intelligence.

AI Principles – Microsoft

Microsoft has identified six principles[107] for AI implementation:

Fairness – AI systems should treat all people fairly,

Reliability & Safety – AI systems should perform reliably and safely,

Privacy & Security – AI systems should be secure and respect privacy,

Inclusiveness – AI systems should empower everyone and engage people,

Transparency – AI systems should be understandable, and

Accountability – People should be accountable for AI systems.

The principles for responsible AI are put into practice through three groups:

Office of Responsible AI (ORA): sets the rules and governance processes, working closely with teams across the company to enable the effort.

AI, Ethics, and Effects in Engineering and Research (AETHER): Advises the leadership on the challenges and opportunities presented by AI innovations.

---

[106]ALTAI – The Assessment List on Trustworthy Artificial Intelligence; European Commission; https://futurium.ec.europa.eu/en/european-ai-alliance/pages/altai-assessment-list-trustworthy-artificial-intelligence

[107] Responsible AI; Microsoft; https://www.microsoft.com/en-us/ai/responsible-ai; Accessed Aug 2021.

Responsible AI Strategy in Engineering (RAISE): a team that enables the implementation of Microsoft responsible AI rules across engineering groups.

Immersive AI Education – Harvard University

Harvard University is bringing ethical reasoning into the computer science curriculum, through a program called Embedded EthiCS[108]. This program meets the challenge of making ethical reasoning integral to computer science education with a distributed pedagogy that introduces ethics directly into standard computer science courses across the curriculum. It works by embedding philosophers into courses to teach a module for the course that explores an ethical issue that the course material raises. In a data systems class, the philosopher might explore issues of privacy in large, distributed systems. In a programming languages course, she might ask students to consider ethical specifications and functional ones. In a human-computer interaction course, she might explore whether software engineers should design systems that are accessible to visually impaired users. In a machine learning class, she might explore how solving problems using machine learning can lead to inadvertent discrimination. In a networks class, she might explore the issue of censorship on social media platforms.

Embedded EthiCS distributed pedagogy program offers three advantages over stand-alone courses:

- It shows students the extent to which ethical and social issues permeate virtually all areas of computer science,
- It familiarizes students with the wide range of ethical and social issues arising across the field, and
- It provides students with repeated practice reasoning through those issues, communicating their positions, and designing ethical systems.

---

[108] Harvard University Programs; https://embeddedethics.seas.harvard.edu/about; Accessed Aug 2021.

AI and User Trust – NIST

The National Institute of Standards and Technology (NIST) has released a draft document on Artificial Intelligence and User Trust (NISTIR 8332)[109], intended to examine how humans experience trust as they use or are affected by AI systems. NIST's authors identify nine characteristics that define AI system trustworthiness: **accuracy**, **reliability**, **resiliency**, **objectivity**, **security**, **explainability**, **safety**, **accountability**, and **privacy**. The document asserts – If the AI system has a high level of technical trustworthiness, and the values of the trustworthiness characteristics are perceived to be good enough for the context of use, and especially the risk inherent in that context, then the likelihood of AI user trust increases. It is this trust, based on user perceptions, that will be necessary of any human-AI collaboration.

According to NIST co-author Brian Stanton, the issue is whether human trust in AI systems is measurable — and if so, how to measure it accurately and appropriately. *"Many factors get incorporated into our decisions about trust,"* he said. *"It's how the user thinks and feels about the system and perceives the risks involved in using it."* He explained that NIST's proposed model for AI user trust is based on others research and the 'fundamental principles of cognition.'

> Good news – These guidelines appear very similar, well thought out,
> and portable across industries with minimal modifications.
> Bad news – We should be prepared to learn and adapt.

---

[109] NIST IR 8332, https://nvlpubs.nist.gov/nistpubs/ir/2021/NIST.IR.8332-draft.pdf; June 2021.

Building and Sustaining Ethical Machines

When a cyber-physical loop of the 4th revolution, becomes fully automated with no human in the loop, the programming and learning of the machines must be robust and dependable. The system should operate effectively and efficiently with parameters and be able to safely abort and raise concerns when it steps outside a pre-defined boundary. Organizations that own and operate such systems should be able to spot unacceptable data trends and tendencies and over-ride automation.

Some key questions that we could ask under various categories include, but not limited to, the following:

Starter qualifying questions –

- o Is it the right thing for the customer, and other affected parties?
- o Is it the right thing for the business owners, and the employees?
- o Is it the right way to do things?
- o Can the product/service hurt the consumer, society, or the planet?

Asking questions to build a robust learning machine –

- o Can the machine spot a Conflict of Interest and an ethical situation, if possible?
- o Can the machine monitor its own performance and raise alarm when suspect?
- o If something is too good to be true, can the machine raise an alarm?
- o Can the machine recognize bad or inadequate input to act upon, so that it learns from relevant situations only, even with small data set?
- o Can the machine be aware of failure modes and effects?
- o When machines are connected, should they share the learning? Shared learning could reduce the bias but increase the risk of widespread poor action in case of bad machine judgment.
- o Can the legal and contractual items be built into the logic?
- o Can we isolate bad data over time, unlearn, and relearn from the relevant data set?

Asking questions to isolate programmer's ethics from the program logic –

- o Should we train or certify programmers on ethics?
- o Does the development team understand the value of diverse opinions, and trained to invite and resolve difference?

Asking questions to isolate machine trainer's ethics from the machine learning algorithms –

- o Is there adequate diversity in the team that is training the machine?
- o Are we able to screen data before it is used for learning?
- o Are we able to identify and remove unintentional bias?

Checking if the Validation Testing plan is adequate –

- o What is the minimal set of validation testing required?
- o Is the testing and validation being done by a diverse team?
- o Should the system be tested periodically, just like human recertification, besides initial validation test?
- o Should we run validation on known and understood ethical situations?
- o How much testing should be done with bad input to make the system robust?
- o Should we test the machine on new ethical situations? Who decides those situations and preferred answers?
- o Should the machine test itself and report periodically?
- o Are there any "gray" areas that make separating domains difficult?

This list of questions will never be complete and each development team and adopting organization will need to review, expand, and revise on this starter set. Perhaps each periodic test will help refine it even further.

Digital Transformation Review Board

Ethics is complicated, and context dependent. It needs to include discussion with diverse perspectives from many stakeholders. Because of the ethical questions with research projects, Institutional Review Boards (IRBs) are being put into place mandating an ethics check prior to conducting research with human subjects. Concerns with the power and responsibility of companies such as Facebook and Google regarding security and personal information have led to the creation of data protection laws. According to an article by The International Association of Privacy Professionals (IAPP)[110], data protection laws are often vague, out of date or require companies not only to comply with specific requirements but also to assess and respond to risk and to be "fair" and "transparent."

Therefore, Data Review Boards, or sometimes called "ethic review boards", are gaining ground as a model to consider risk in programming, especially regarding AIs, MLs and ANNs. We would like to think of Digital Transformation Review Board (DTRB) to assure integrity and quality in data processing, on lines like Materials Review Board or Design Review Board for product quality. The Board assessment structure would address areas including but not limited to ethical design concerns, analysis of data sets and technology and programmer training. DTRBs could analyze the ethical design, implementation, manufacture, and operation of automated systems as well as technicians and practitioners of the systems.

Once after an initial review, the DTRB could evaluate how the systems AI, ML, and ANN operate in the future and if variation introduces potential risk from an undetected ethical gap. The time and cost of DTRBs would be offset by the prevention of undetected defects and their failure.

---

[110] Why data review boards are a promising tool for improving institutional decision-making; F Cate; R Dockery; S Crosley; *Privacy Perspectives,* The International Association of Privacy Professionals; https://iapp.org/news/a/why-data-review-boards-are-a-promising-tool-for-improving-institutional-decision-making/; Feb 28, 2020.

DTRB Constitution

For DTRB to be effective, the norms and constitution needs to be well-defined and governed. We have learned the source of bias and need for diversity in development and training of industry 4.0 systems. On similar lines the DTRB should have the required diversity. DTRB can include:

- Subject matter experts,
- AI/ML expert in developing algorithms and data management systems,
- Behavioral scientists, and humanities specialists,
- Data security expert,
- Legal counsel,
- Diversity, Equity, and Inclusion champion,
- User/consumer representative, and
- Maybe, an inexperienced professional to provide a fresh set of eyes, and question status quo.

DTRB Norms

DTRB is the focal point for coordinating implementation of digital ethical principles in digital-physical eco-system. The norms for the Digital Transformation Review Board will evolve as we collectively build experience. Here are a few to start with. DTRB should

- Interface with Technology Reviews and Strategy cycle,
- Have a cadence tied to new systems development and application, as well periodic review of learning systems in the field,
- Be empowered to act in good faith of stakeholders internal and external, reporting directly to the highest levels of organization, or external governing body such as the board,
- Not have any conflict of interest, in evaluating risks and benefits, and
- Consider external participation, if deemed necessary to ensure integrity of the process.

Let's Summarize

Summary of Perspectives

Moral organizations create new technologies for the sake of something good. It can address many of the existing ethical situations, but also create some new unknown scenarios. To be effective, we need to make some conscious decision, in accord with ethics. Since AI can be so powerful, the ethical standards we give it better be good, be it in the form of guidelines or regulations for developers and trainers.

Algorithmic bias has already been discovered, for example, in areas ranging from criminal punishment to photograph captioning. These biases are more than just embarrassing to the corporations which produce these defective products; they have concrete negative and harmful effects on the people who are the victims of these biases, as well as reducing trust in corporations, government, and other institutions which might use these biased products. Algorithmic bias is one of the major concerns in AI right now and will remain so in the future unless we endeavor to make our technological products better than we are. As one person said[111] at the first meeting of the Partnership on AI, *"We will reproduce all of our human faults in artificial form unless we strive right now to make sure that we don't."*

To quote Brian Green again on Aristotle, *"Humans have moral characters and we become what we repeatedly do."* So, we ought not to treat AIs and robots badly, or we might habituate ourselves towards having flawed characters, regardless of the moral status of the artificial beings we are interacting with. In other words, no matter the status of AIs and robots, for the sake of our own moral characters we ought to treat them well, or at least not abuse them.

---

[111] The *Partnership* on AI to Benefit People and Society; Inaugural Meeting, Berlin, Oct 23, 2017.

The ethics of AI and robotics is a noticeably young field within applied ethics, with significant dynamics, but few well-established issues, and no authoritative overviews[112] although governments[113, 114, 115] are providing guidance and assessment of societal impact[116, 117, 118].

Summary of Possibilities

It will be a great day, when ethics built into the system will stop unethical people from harming the society. The story of twitter bots[119] spreading misinformation about the pandemic on social media and pushing America to reopen is quite disturbing.

Organizations in pursuit of digitalization need to understand ethical situations and address them. Well-established ethical principles will empower defenders of ethics, consumers with risk management mindset, and people responsible for technology review and validation. While we as

---

[112] Ethics of Artificial Intelligence and Robotics; https://plato.stanford.edu/entries/ethics-ai/ Apr 30, 2020.

[113] High-Level Expert Group on Artificial Intelligence: Ethics Guidelines for Trustworthy AI; European Commission; accessed Apr 9, 2019.

[114] Statement on Artificial Intelligence, Robotics and 'Autonomous' Systems; European Group on Ethics in Science and New Technologies; European Commission, Directorate-General for Research and Innovation, Unit RTD.01. Mar 9, 2018.

[115] DoD Adopts Ethical Principles for Artificial Intelligence; US DoD; https://www.defense.gov/Newsroom/Releases/Release/Article/2091996; Feb. 24, 2020.

[116] AI4People—An Ethical Framework for a Good AI Society: Opportunities, Risks, Principles, and Recommendations; F Luciano, J Cowls, M Beltrametti, R Chatila, P Chazerand, V Dignum, C Luetge, R Madelin, U Pagallo, F Rossi, B Schafer, P Valcke, and E Vayena; Minds and Machines, 28(4): 689–707, 2018.

[117] Responsible AI – Key Themes, Concerns and Recommendations for European Research, and Innovation; S Taylor, M Boniface, and B Pickering; https://www.researchgate.net/publication/329163201_Responsible_AI_-_Key_themes_concerns_recommendations_for_European_research_and_innovation July 2018.

[118] Ethical and Societal Implications of Algorithms, Data, and Artificial Intelligence: A Roadmap for Research; J Whittlestone, R Nyrup, A Alexandrova, K Dihal, and S Cave; Cambridge: Nuffield Foundation, University of Cambridge; 2019.

[119] Nearly half of Twitter accounts pushing to reopen America may be bots; Karen Hao; https://www-technologyreview-com.cdn.ampproject.org/c/s/www.technologyreview.com/2020/05/21/1002105/covid-bot-twitter-accounts-push-to-reopen-america/amp/; May 21, 2020.

individuals may struggle to decide what are the ethical rules, who writes them, and will everyone abide by them; we are sure that they will be a collective wisdom, and learning, just like other social norms have been in the past. These ethical rules will likely include elements and/or define instances to agilely validate their own relevance because of the impact of accelerated technological development and innovation.

Existing Code of Ethics with most professional bodies, predates the 4th revolution and needs to be updated to address the powerful influence of significant human-machine systems. This chapter touched upon ethics of technology as if human thinking stays unaltered through the next revolution. The change in human behavior triggered by their interaction with AI should also be addressed. This chapter has reviewed current perspectives and discussed a few possibilities such as the creation of Digital Transformation Review Board for governance of key AI principles, that may be derived from EU or DoD's recommendations.

Why it Matters?

Those who fund, develop, and deploy AI also shape its role in society. Understanding their ideas can help ensure that this technology makes things better, not worse. Most of us have good intentions. Often, we aren't the ones who decide how the technology will be used, but we can decide what we will and won't build.

Special Acknowledgement

Part of this chapter is a collaborative work with Tracie Clifford in context of NDE 4.0 and has been published in a handbook.

Reference: *Ethics in NDE 4.0: Perspectives and Possibilities;* Handbook of NDE 4.0, Springer; Editors-in-Chief: Norbert Meyendorf, Nathan Ida, Johannes Vrana, and Ripi Singh, Oct 2021.

Let's Take a Selfie

 # The revolutions/eras have the following effect on ethics –

☐ No effect.
☐ Additional considerations, to everything that is already in practice.
☐ Totally new way of separating right from the wrong.
☐ It does not matter. We just follow the policies, laws, and regulations.
☐ Create new roles and responsibilities in the organization.

 # I understand how digitalization needs to address –

☐ Meta-ethics.
☐ Applied ethics.
☐ Normative Ethics – Virtue theory.
☐ Normative Ethics – Duty theory.
☐ Normative Ethics – Consequential theory.

 # I have the following concerns with AI/ML –

☐ No concerns.
☐ Make us lazy.
☐ Make us dumb.
☐ Eliminate some industries.
☐ Lead to serious inflation.
☐ Large scale unemployment.
☐ Change the balance of power in the world.
☐ Make knowledge and experience inconsequential.
☐ Make a few people enormously powerful.
☐ Misused/abused by bad guys.
☐ Completely take over humanity.
☐ Amplify social issues and divide the world even more.
☐ Take away any sense of 'personal' or pride.
☐ Create serious mental health issues.
☐ …
☐ …

I am concerned about the following issues with data applications –

☐ No concerns.
☐ Bias and fairness.
☐ Feedback loops.
☐ Information integrity.
☐ Privacy and Surveillance.
☐ Language and training.
☐ Information transparency.
☐ Trust.

I have the following views around data regulation –

☐ We need strict regulations, driven by governments.
☐ We should let entities govern themselves, through DTRB approach.
☐ We should let professional bodies rewrite and enforce a code of ethics.
☐ Let individuals decide what they wish to protect/secure and how.
☐ We do not need any regulations.
☐ …

I like the following concepts –

☐ Guidelines from government bodies such as US DoD, EU, …
☐ Principles developed by corporations for self-regulations, e.g. Microsoft
☐ Idea of a Digital Transformation Review Board.
☐ Idea of education where ethics is embedded into curriculum.
☐ Personal freedom
☐ …

Disclaimer

I am an engineer and not a philosopher and submit that this chapter is just another piece of research to feed the ongoing hard conversation on ethics intended to raise human-machine concerns as we collectively go through digital transformation.
It is not to be treated as a code of ethics for innovation.

---

11. What Next: Human-Machine Confluence

In 2016, a client called me to support then with a conference in automobile sector. Global Human Body Modelling Consortium of 7 auto suppliers were having their annual conference. The entire subject was new to me. I was surprised how the engineering and medical professional had come together to simulate the human body in an event of an automobile crash. They could predict, which ribs would fracture and what other internal damage can occur, something not quite practical with dummy crash tests. We spent the next 2 weeks creating a thought map of possibilities with such a technology. As we added things like internet, cloud, 3D printing, robotics, our imagination went wild. We discovered new solutions in so many industries such as aerospace, health care, sports, defense, garments. Today I can look back and say, well it was all innovative thinking and technologies for a human purpose. I had barely heard the term industry 4.0 at that time, but not started using it in my practice. In 5 years, we have come a long way with digitalization of physical and biological systems.

While most of us are still getting our hands around the fourth industrial revolution (or Digital Transformation) and how humans and machines will work together for the betterment of society. We are also coming across terms Industry 5.0. It is being expressed in different forms, such as, human-machine reconciliation, addressing shortcomings of the fourth revolution, serving large sustainability goals, and quantum computers. In this chapter, we will explore a few slightly different perspectives emerging around Industry 5.0 and an opinion on it.

The Case for Fifth Industrial Revolution

There are a few definitions and descriptions emerging, which can be categorized around '**human role**' and '**human values**.' A few perspectives can be found through blog posts, research reports, conference discussions, and infomercials for self-promotion. Let us look at whatever we have been able to discover on these two aspects.

In the Context of Human Role

Østergaard[120,121] founder of Universal Robots, defined it as the human touch revolution. He says "*The mass customization ... enabled by Industry 4.0 is not enough. Because consumers want more. They want mass personalization, which can only be achieved when the human touch returns to manufacturing. This is what I call Industry 5.0.*" It is being touted as the revolution in which man and machine reconcile and find ways to work together as a part of execution process to improve the means and efficiency of production. Come to think of it, the transition to Industry 4.0 is not overnight, and organizations will go through slow acceptance, which means we will go through man-machine co-working during the adoption of Industry 4.0. This could last a decade for any company for lack of funds and maturity to simply change it all overnight. On similar lines, Industry 5.0 predicts advances by involving the interaction of human intelligence and cognitive computing. But again, that is happening today as a part of the transition and acceptance of artificial narrow intelligence.

Lindsay and Hudson captured a few sentiments and shared a similar thinking in their 2019 article[122]. They discussed perspectives from a few

---

[120] Industry 5.0 – return of the human touch; E H. Østergaard; https://www.universal-robots.com/blog/industry-50-return-of-the-human-touch/

[121] Welcome to Industry 5.0, The "human touch" revolution is now underway; E H Ostergaard; Quality Magazine; https://www.qualitymag.com/authors/3148-esben-ostergaard May 08, 2019.

[122] What is the fifth industrial revolution and how will it change the world? J Lindsay and A Hudson; https://metro.co.uk/2019/06/10/fifth-industrial-revolution-will-change-world-9738825/ June 10, 2019.

thought leaders. Futurist George Muir argues *it will be the AI revolution,* although many of us view that as Industry 4.0. An American professional services firm Genpact believes *it is the moment when humans and machines combine in the workplace* (How does that qualify to be a new revolution compared to what it is happening within the 4th revolution?). Member of European Parliament Eva Kaili thinks that *it's all to do with the potential of quantum computing,* which could be the case when it opens new possibilities in combination with AI or integration of quantum computing with quantum physics.

6G promises a much more versatile machine to machine communication by 2030. That is not showing signs of human return to action. In fact, experts believe that disappearance of certain skills may even make it hard for humans to get back in the loop. The business models around data exchange may become another barrier to the return of the human touch.

My questions are – "*Why aim to take the human out fully to achieve the 4th revolution and then bring the human back to go to 5th revolution. Why not blend the technology mindfully while adopting the 4th revolution?*"

In the Context of Human Values

Looking at the first three revolutions, they all started with the emerging technologies of the time, continued with new products, new industries, and new business forms. Eventually leading to products needed by humans, working conditions desired by humans, resolving old social issues, and creating new ones, and a lot of waste generated by humans. Unfortunately, each industrial revolution accelerated a host of adverse conditions, such as climate change, deforestation, urbanization, landfills, great Pacific Garbage Patch. Many supporters of the fifth revolution claim it to be helpful to the environment, as companies develop systems that run on renewable energy and eliminate waste.

Christoph Roser at AllAboutLean.com graphically[123] pleads the need to not drag out Industry 4.0 and go into '*De-Industrial revolution before it is too late*', without explicitly calling it as fifth revolution.

A recently published report from European Commission defines Industry 5.0[124] as going beyond producing goods and services for profit. It shifts the focus from the shareholder value to stakeholder value and reinforces the role and the contribution of industry to society. It complements the existing 'Industry 4.0' approach by specifically putting research and innovation at the service of the transition to a sustainable, human-centric, and resilient European industry. The concept is clearly derived from the Japanese definition of Society 5.0.

The best argument to support values driven revolution to be defined separate from Industry 4.0 was articulated by Gauri and VanEerden[125] in May 2019, as a collaborative work of The European Sting with the World Economic Forum. "*The march of successive industrial revolutions that the modern world has witnessed, has intensified the risks of dehumanizing economic progress, to the point that we now face an existential threat in both environmental and humanitarian terms. ... The main principles of the 5th revolution include profit with purpose, focus on United Nations Sustainable Development Goals (SDGs) for achieving a flourishing future, closing the gender gap, and scaling, spreading, and becoming increasingly democratized.*"

> All these perspectives are great. I do not think that it is a revolution by itself, rather a responsible or purposeful application of Industry 4.0.

---

[123] https://commons.wikimedia.org/wiki/File:Industry_5.0_diagram.png Dec 2018.

[124] Industry 5.0: Towards more sustainable, resilient and human-centric industry; European Commission https://ec.europa.eu/info/news/industry-50-towards-more-sustainable-resilient-and-human-centric-industry-2021-jan-07_en Jan 2021.

[125] What the Fifth Industrial Revolution is and why it matters; P Gauri, & J V Eerden; May 16, 2019; https://europeansting.com/2019/05/16/what-the-fifth-industrial-revolution-is-and-why-it-matters/

Are We Ready for Industry 5.0?

Cabe Atwell adds humor to the numbering scheme[126], "Industry is being 'versioned' way too willy-nilly. We need versioning control! Without a better way of describing innovation in industry, we are doomed to see more 'upgrading' of industry, since it is an attention-grabber. So, let me now coin the term 'Industry 6.0,' where we never interface with any machine, person, or drafting table/setup. Instead, it's all done in an app. We take a picture of a rough sketch and click 'make it.'" It may happen.

The claims that the developments of Industry 5.0 could fully realize what the architects of Industry 4.0 had only dreamt of at the dawn of the 2010s; makes little sense[127]. You do not need another revolution to complete the job of the previous one. That would be an evolution or continuous improvement or debugging and not a revolution. Within the realm of Industry 4.0, the artificial intelligence and factory robots can assume more human-like capabilities, for a meaningful and mutually enlightening purpose.

The folks with technology and business focus are defining Industry 5.0 as **an effort** to integrate humans with robots to meet the *high demand for individual personalization* or customization. I believe that can still be accomplished by '**mindful digital transformation**' within industry 4.0 rather than obsession for automation and rush for gold.

The folks with heart are defining Industry 5.0 as **an outcome** which is *human-centric, sustainable, and resilient*. That could still be defined as '**purposeful digital transformation**', where purpose is greater than economic metrics and includes social values.

---

[126] Yes, Industry 5.0 is Already on the Horizon; Cabe Atwell; https://www.machinedesign.com/automation-iiot/article/21835933/yes-industry-50-is-already-on-the-horizon; Sep 12, 2017.

[127] Guide to Industry 4.0 & 5.0, https://gesrepair.com/industry-4-and-5; Accessed Aug 2021.

Then there are folks who may have been late to appreciate the big shift, now use it to **grab attention** or attempt to differentiate themselves from the crowd.

Either way, the term **Industry 5.0 being described today does not appear to be a technological revolution** in a traditional industrial sense, but a re-acceptance of humanity that we may have been gradually losing with every industrial revolution, in our obsession for efficiency, productivity, and personal comfort.

The Digital-Physical-Biological Confluence

There is another form of confluence that has been emerging slowly but steadily, which has been eluded in the broader context of 'yet to be named' fifth era.

For many decades we have seen significant advancement in **physical-biological** systems such as prostheses and implants – artificial substitutes for body parts, and materials merged into tissue for functional, cosmetic, orthopedic, or therapeutic purposes. Other areas that capture physical and biological activities are nano-materials, nano biotechnology, biosensors, and bionics. Home blood glucose meter is a simple example of bio-sensor based product for everyday use.

There is a serious research effort in **digital-biological** systems such as **Biocomputers** which use biologically derived molecules, such as DNA and proteins, to perform digital or real computations. We have created smart devices/wearables, Genetic editing, and sequencing. And now we are advancing the technologies to 3D printing of skin and biological organs. Wake Forest Institute for Regenerative Medicine has demonstrated 3D printing of skin cells directly onto burn wounds. Mechanical engineers and computer scientists at the University of Minnesota[128] have developed a 3D printing technique that even captures motion, to print electronic sensors directly on organs that are expanding and contracting. The new 3D printing technique could have future applications in diagnosing and monitoring the lungs of patients with COVID-19.

Bringing Biology into the **digital-physical** systems of the fourth industrial revolution could usher in a next revolution – governed by **digital-physical-biological** confluence for a **humanity purpose**. We just do not know what that would look like. But we have some early indications of various use cases.

Prof Sastry[129] of Berkeley Engineering referred this as cyber-biophysical research frontier in 2015. Over two dozen faculty members from UC Berkeley & UC San Francisco, are collaborating on work that harnesses the power of the Human brain in disciplines spanning neurology and neuroscience, electrical and Mechanical engineering and many more at the Center for Neural Engineering and Prostheses[130].

Intelligent Implants[131] is at the forefront of electrotherapeutic devices to treat disease and aid recovery in bone and other tissues. They pioneer the use of data, engineering, and biologics to bring novel, active and connected medical devices to healthcare. Their integrated devices facilitate treatment for the patient, as well as decision making for the healthcare professional.

Using a "brain-computer interface, Freie Universität Berlin, Germany[132] created a semi-autonomous vehicle which allowed impulses from the brain

---

[128] New discovery allows 3D printing of sensors directly on expanding organs; Research Brief; https://twin-cities.umn.edu/news-events/new-discovery-allows-3d-printing-sensors-directly-expanding-organs; Jun 17, 2020.

[129] The cyber-biophysical research frontier; S. Shankar Sastry; April 16, 2015. https://engineering.berkeley.edu/news/2015/04/the-cyber-biophysical-research-frontier/.

[130] http://www.cnep-uc.org/

[131] https://www.cipherbio.com/data-viz/organization/Intelligent%2BImplants.

[132] The Future of Formula 1 Racing: Mind Controlled Cars; https://www.endurancewarranty.com/learning-center/motorsports/formula-1-mind-controlled-cars/.

to control key parts of a vehicle's operation. This operates by translating electromagnetic signals within a test subject's brain into recognizable patterns that operate software. A quadriplegic racer Rodrigo Hübner Mendes[133] was the first person ever to drive an F1 car using a sensor studded cap over his head that could pick up his brain activity to drive the car, in 2017.

Neuralink[134] is pushing the boundaries of innovation in neural engineering. They are designing the first neural implant that will let you control a computer or mobile device anywhere you go. When it becomes reality, the Neuralink app would allow you to control your iOS device, keyboard, and mouse directly with the activity of your brain, just by thinking about it. Elon Musk argues that our hands limit the bandwidth of communication between humans and computers, and one of his solutions is the ultra-high bandwidth brain-machine interface to connect humans and computers. The hypothesis also supports the need to control Artificial Superintelligence[135], when that emerges.

Over the last couple of decades, we have seen our attire being supplemented with a smart device beyond phone. Innovations in wearables take us to having sensors close to body tracking our health vitals and even delivering active ingredients such as vitamins or medicines to a target location. Examples might include driving gloves with caffeine in them, swimming costumes with built-in sunscreen, or even underwear that delivers needed vitamins.

Another area of confluence is 'virtual travel' wherein virtual reality and game like experience can help you be a tourist along with others to places that may be difficult or unaffordable to travel. This technology played out

---

[133] EMOTIV x Rodrigo Hubner Mendes – Driving F1 car just by thinking; https://www.youtube.com/watch?v=NhmXaeaHkDc; Aug 18, 2017.
[134] https://neuralink.com/
[135] Superintelligence: Paths, Dangers, Strategies; Nick Bostrom, Book, July 2014.

well during pandemic as virtual conferences, focused on human experience close to physical reality.

Global Human Body Models Consortium[136] (GHBMC) of seven automakers and one supplier have been consolidating their individual research and development activities in human body modeling into a single global effort to advance crash safety technology since 2006. These computers models have significant derivative applications in sports, aerospace, healthcare, wearables, forensics, and military as posted on social media by the author[137] in 2016. Figure 3 presents a 5-year-old thought map that has become a trigger for technology roadmap for a few stakeholders. It connects fundamental disciplines with application domains and value proposition through a set of technology enablers. Today the center green band of enablers can be the entire suite of Industry 4.0 technologies.

The digital twin which captures your personal physiological conditions, tracking your health, through wearables, could be a life saver in case of an unfortunate accident. A comparative scan of injured limb with baseline digital model could control robotic assisted surgery while the 3D printer creates the internal implant and external brace. The 3D printed skin right to close surgery can accelerate the healing process. We probably have all the technological elements to meet the fancy creation of science-fiction writer Gene Roddenberry.

A private company Elemance[138] continues to develop and serve this applied innovation in form of proven, validated, finite element human body models, ready for simulation environments. Today, we can approximate them as digital twins of the human body. When combined with other medical history, they could become a powerful personal digital thread.

---

[136] http://www.ghbmc.com/
[137] CAE in Bio-Mechanics – Imagine Next? Ripi Singh, May 4, 2016,
https://www.linkedin.com/pulse/cae-bio-mechanics-imagine-next-ripi-singh/
[138] https://www.elemance.com

Emerging Disciplines

Rapid Modelling – Scaling, Morphing, Reduced Order

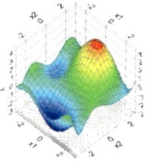

Reusable Response Surfaces

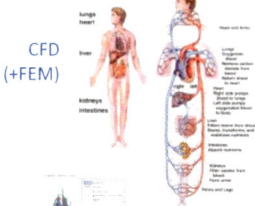

CFD (+FEM)

Probabilistic

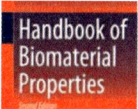

References Data

Aging Models Geometry & Material Morphing

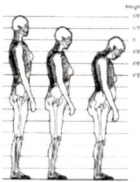

Advanced Rapid Validation And Compliance

Business Models

- Consortium
- Subscriptions
- Models and Data sales

Enabling Technologies

Cloud Computing

Visualization

Wireless

3D Printing

Potential Domains

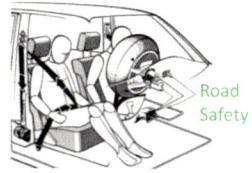

Road Safety

Military Gear Design

Sports Gear Design

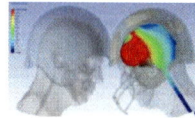

Zero-g Studies

Surgical Implant Design

Smart Wearables Design

Personal Digital Thread here refers to individual physiological model and healthcare history and not behavioral activity captured by Facebook or Amazon etc., although they may even be combined at some point. These personal digital threads can significantly improve long-term healthcare, personalized medicine, precision surgery, besides custom wearables, smart garments, etc. A combination of human body digital twin, understanding of genetics, and opportunity to 3D print organs opens serious opportunities in longevity, quality of life, and questions around ethics, hard to answer at this stage.

Not going too far, imagine a combination of AI based chatbot technology, which learns from a specific individual's history from Facebook, all their direct communications from WhatsApp and text messages, has natural language processing capability to create a digital twin that stays alive after death. Imagine being able to make a video call with your deceased mother, as if she is still around and able to discuss the recent CNN news in the context of your last major career move of physical activity. **Digital Immortality**[139] is certainly possible in near future. How much would you be willing to pay for such a call, and all those who have been accumulating the data will create the wealth in the 5th era?

In some sense many combinations of human-machine integration are on the horizon, not just artificial limbs, and Bio-computers. That would be an era of cyber-physical-biological confluence. And it could be very revolutionary.

---

[139] Digital Immortality and Virtual Humans; M Savin-Baden and D Burden; Postdigit Sci Educ 1, 87–103, 2019.

Xenobots

A remarkable combination of artificial intelligence and biology has produced the world's first living robots[140]. They can perform a range of basic functions, from locomotion and object manipulation to collective behavior. Their creation promises to deliver significant advances in biology and in medicine, in particular. However, it also potentially carries serious risks, where the researchers themselves admit that experimenting with living cells creates the scope for unforeseen consequences.

Despite being described as "programmable living robots", they are actually completely organic and made of living tissue. The term "robot" has been used because xenobots can be configured into different forms and shapes, and "programmed" to target certain objects – which they then unwittingly seek. They can also repair themselves after being damaged.

Possible applications: Xenobots may have great value. Some speculate they could clean our polluted oceans by collecting microplastics. Similarly, they may enter confined or dangerous areas to scavenge toxins or radioactive materials. Xenobots designed with carefully shaped "pouches" might carry drugs into human bodies. Future versions may be built from a patient's own cells to repair tissue or target cancers. Being biodegradable, xenobots would have an edge on technologies made of plastic or metal.

Ethics

Adding biological aspects to an already challenging ethical situation with digital transformation makes ethics an order of magnitude more challenging. Subject of editing genes in human embryos after the disclosure from Chinese biophysicist He Jiankui[141] has been a concern worldwide. The

---

[140] Not bot, not beast: scientists create first ever living, programmable organism; S Coghlan and K Leins; https://theconversation.com/not-bot-not-beast-scientists-create-first-ever-living-programmable-organism-129980 Jan 19, 2020.

[141] 'CRISPR babies' are still too risky, says influential panel; Hiedi Ledford. https://www.nature.com/articles/d41586-020-02538-4; Sept 3, 2020.

technology could one day prevent some serious genetic disorders from being passed down from parents to their children – but, for now, the technique is too risky to be used in embryos destined for implantation. And even when the technology is mature, its use should initially be permitted only to a narrow set of circumstances.

The topic is now too complex for my understanding, and I must leave it out of the scope of this book.

The Case for Sixth Social Revolution

I have not come across this term, and I am not proposing it either, or I guess I am. Where can we go from a super-smart society? Is it where humans do not need to work for a living? Will humanity find a different purpose to stay busy?

The researchers Michael Huberman and Chris Minns published[142] estimates of weekly work hours going back to the late 19th century. This data shows that working hours have steeply declined. Full-time workers in developed countries work 20-30 hours less every week than in the 19th century. If technology can improve productivity by orders of magnitude, we should be able to earn more by working less. When I was growing up, there were no computers and my father worked 6 days a week. He was happy to have Sunday off, because his father worked on the farm all 7 days.

My career so far has been a 5-day workweek. And I have just shifted to a 4-day work week for the next decade. I hope to see this become a norm soon and then perhaps a 3-day week before I die.

Given the technology trends, evolutionary extrapolation, and confluence of multiple technologies such as General AI, Robots, IoT; we may have Robots with Artificial General Intelligence (RAGI). I am now

---

[142] Working Hours; Mark Roser; https://ourworldindata.org/working-hours; Dec 2019.

tempted to predict, we might see a day when RAGIs will create all food and amenities needed for a smart living, smart mobility, smart health, smart manufacturing, and smart energy. RAGIs will maintain each other and build their successor RAGIs. They will also develop renewable energy generators and maintain the transmission through a smart grid, to power themselves and everything else on the planet. And us humans do not need to work at all ...I am getting into imagination overload! I will abort!

The Case for M2H Innovation

If I have difficulty grasping what RAGI can do to humanity, imagine what an Artificial Superintelligence (ASI) with creative power can do for us or do to us when it starts to innovate at rates that we can't even comprehend. We will look at the world around us like a monkey looks at humans with automobiles and mobile devices. It knows something is happening, but cannot comprehend how and why, and so goes his merry way searching for bananas and personal security. Just like humans become a reason for extinction of certain species or having others as household pets, ASI could treat humans the same way.

Tim Urban[143,144] compiled various opinions from thought leaders around evolution of AI in these logical articles. It discusses two thought camps: (a) **confident corner,** where people are buzzing with excitement and can't wait for the future they ever could have hoped for, and (b) **anxious avenue**, where they are nervous and tense, as they think both the extremely good and extremely bad outcomes are plausible.

---

[143] The AI Revolution – The Road to Superintelligence and Our Immortality or Extinction; Tim Urban, https://waitbutwhy.com/2015/01/artificial-intelligence-revolution-1.html ; Jan 22, 2015
[144] https://waitbutwhy.com/2015/01/artificial-intelligence-revolution-2.html ; Jan 27, 2015

Three books worth reading this subject are (1) Superintelligence: Paths, Dangers, Strategies by Nick Bostrom, (2) Our Final Invention by James Barrat, and (3) The Singularity is Near Ray Kurzweil.

My fear is when (not if) ASI gets to a point where it discovers that human greed has been responsible for climate change, loss of many species, imbalance of the ecological system of the planet, social disparities, and other miseries, what will it do?

ASI will surely start with M2H (Machine-to-Human) innovation. But will it continue that way? Will it hurt humans inadvertently or will it be moral and conscious enough to argue what is right and wrong? Will it shut down all transportation and conventional energy plants to reduce carbon emissions and thus putting hospitals in crisis or will it accelerate renewable energy development and create nanobots to help humans deal with it.

ASI will probably take over the control of the planet. In doing so, it might conclude that humans do not deserve to exist in its current form. It could do any of the following (1) Eliminate all humans and save millions of other life form. (2) show mercy by not eliminating us; and just take us back to hunter-gatherer era so we can co-exist with other animals, and the machines that we won't know how to interact with. (3) Solve all sorts of human issues – health, global politics, greed, and anger management, and treat humans like loveable pets.

In some sense when it slips from a Human-to-Human activity into a Machine-to-Human activity, it might slip towards Machine-for-Planet activities. It is a scary thought, but it may be for a greater good.

> If we were to ensure our continued existence and have ASI work for us (An M2H system) we must invest in "**Responsible AI**" otherwise it will be our *final great innovation* or *last challenge*, we will ever face.

Let's Summarize

The current definitions and expressions surrounding Industry 5.0 seem to be purposeful Industry 4.0. It seems more about the responsible application of technology and not something to do with the new technological revolution to change the lifestyle. That trend and focus makes sense to me. While we benefit from advances in science and technology, we also suffer the consequences when the developments are not well thought through. It is extremely hard to go back. Every innovation in any revolution must be governed or regulated with due considerations to ethics, justice, freedom, environment, and human in general.

If you approach Industry 5.0 from the perspective of value creation applications, I believe it to be pre-mature and we need to be cautious of the marketing ploy behind its use. We should let Industry 4.0 mature, get accepted, teach us, and guide us in resolving the current set of safety and quality issues. If you approach it from a research perspective, we must continue to explore and address current limitations and whatever else is unfolding. For now, the next frontier belongs to university, government research labs, and commercial research environment, which may or may not be a mix of digital-physical-biological something!

Special Acknowledgement

This work was encouraged by Norbert Meyendorf, Nathan Ida, and Johannes Vrana, and has been published by springer:

Reference: *Are we ready for NDE 5.0?* Handbook of NDE 4.0, Springer; Editors-in-Chief: Norbert Meyendorf, Nathan Ida, Johannes Vrana, and Ripi Singh, Oct 2021.

Let's take a Selfie

Industry 5.0

- ☐ We need to fully mature Industry 4.0 first.
- ☐ We should let research and government work on it.
- ☐ We do need to define what it should do for us.
- ☐ Please put human at the center of the digital-physical system, and then you can call it whatever.

Digital-Physical-Biological confluence

- ☐ Is a distraction from what is important.
- ☐ Is already here, we just cannot see it.
- ☐ Will change our lives forever.
- ☐ Can lead to immortality.
- ☐ Is a serious ethical issue.
- ☐ …

With all the innovations at break-neck pace,

- ☐ We should just focus on our families, health, and career.
- ☐ We need to keep an eye on purpose, a human focused purpose.
- ☐ We need to align our actions with long-term consequences.
- ☐ Ethics must be introduced as a formal content in every learning.
- ☐ …

12. Let's Define a Human Centric Approach

BEING HUMAN IN THE DIGITAL WORLD IS ABOUT
BUILDING A DIGITAL WORLD FOR HUMANS
— ANDREW KEEN

Before I preach you to define a human-centered purpose, I must practice it myself. So here is my story. When I launched my innovation practice in 2014, my former mentors asked me to write my vision, mission, and values. After a few discussions and some harsh feedback, I wrote these …

Vision: Develop a globally accepted framework for innovation.
Mission: Enable organizations to build a culture of Robust Innovation and Productivity Improvement.
Values: Customer Success, Professional Integrity, and Service Quality.

By the end of the year 2015, I had an Innovation Framework, that continued to develop with every engagement and is the subject of a previous book[145]. I was tracking my success by traditional financial metrics and jobs created by my customers. In Jan 2018, a good friend Brent Robertson asked, *"So… how does it help humanity?"* I could not answer, and I could not sleep well. Over the next few months, I discovered Society 5.0 and UN SDG, and then Global Footprint Network, thanks to a friend Tim Maurer. My mission changed to enabling Purposeful Innovation. In 2019, when I was accepted to be a part of the USA Technical Advisory Group developing ISO 56000 standards for innovation management, I felt I achieved the vision and must look for the **Next One**. At the same time, working for a plastics client, I realized the importance of responsible consumption. During one of the ISO

---

[145] Inspiring Next Innovation Framework; Ripi Singh; Book, OutSkirts Press; Sept 2020.

meetings, I had a conversation with Prof Chen Jin of Tsinghua University, China, who is focused on meaningful innovation. He invited me to Beijing to give a talk on **Purposeful Innovation**. The research to prepare for that talk led to most of the content of another book[146] and my going forward single business statement of **Purpose**:

"Inspiring Purposeful Innovations in Industry 4.0 for Sustainability."

It has been a journey of discovery, learning, and sharing whatever I learn. And the Coronavirus Pandemic has reinforced my purpose.

At the start of 2020, I took this pledge. I will

✓ Focus my business on purposeful innovation to support UN SDG #9 which is *'Build resilient infrastructure, promote inclusive and sustainable industrialization, and foster innovation.'*
✓ Not accept any new client who is not willing to discuss responsible innovation.
✓ Donate all profits from the sale of books towards ocean cleaning (UN SDG #14) or the recovery from the Coronavirus Pandemic.
✓ Minimize consumption of single-use plastic and inspire others to do so.
✓ Be a responsible consumer: remove, refuse, replace, repurpose, reuse, recycle, …
✓ Take every opportunity to educate anyone, anytime, anywhere, about Earth Overshoot Day, through free keynote lectures, classroom courses, social media posts, networking events, or in-person.

> All that brings me to today with
> the H2H innovation coaching practice.

Writing it down helps me to reinforce my belief and holds me accountable. You might choose to do so in the next section.

---

[146] Inspiring Next Innovation Purpose; Ripi Singh; Book, OutSkirts Press; Sept 2020.

Define the Humane Purpose

If you have engaged with all the selfie moments at the end of each chapter; then you will have a good idea of your current state, some idea of the future state, and know enough to draft a human-centric innovation program.

> If You Don't Know Where You are Going,
> Any Road Will Take You There
> — Lewis Carroll

Vision, Mission, and Purpose Statements

I am not a fan of writing vision or mission statements. What makes more sense to me is a purpose you believe in and a leadership charter that you operate on. So, the first step in defining the future state is to confirm your Purpose-Profile Journey; and validate your purpose statement, once again.

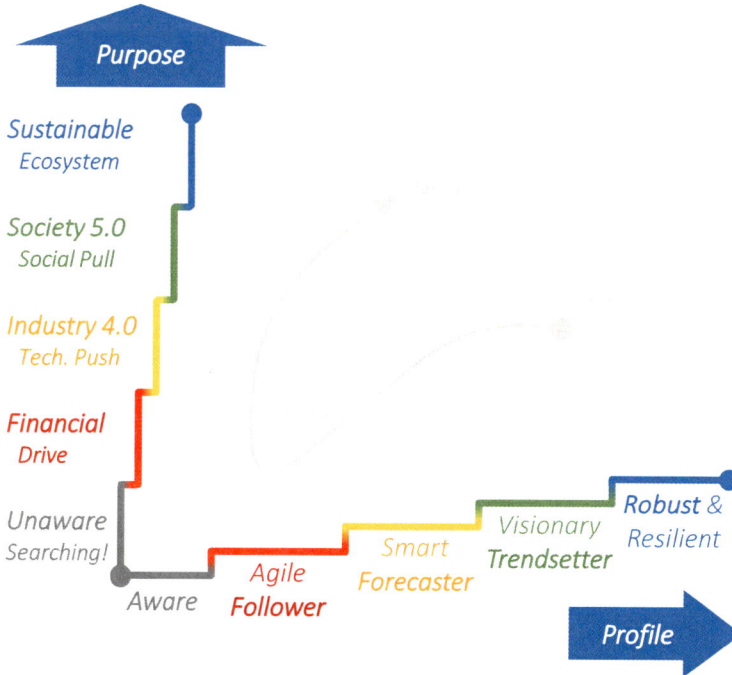

Recap or Rewrite Human-Centric Purpose Statement

Craft your Leadership Charter

One way to define leadership charter is with a Quad Chart, where each of the four boxes define the future state from a different human perspective, along with a list of key activity items. Each quad has a future state perspective as seen from the eyes of that stakeholder and a high-level list of items for the company to focus on. We placed the purpose statement in the center and core values at the base.

Creative Space

Perspective – What should the *customers* say about your value proposition?
List of Items – *Products/services* that you offer to your customers.

Market Place

Perspective – What should the *industry* say about your business?
List of Items – *Markets* and *domains* that you envision to sell to.

Work Place

Perspective – What should the *employees* say about your business?
List of Items – *Employee engagement* focus areas.

Social Space

Perspective – What should the *community/world* say about your business?
List of Items – *Behaviors* to exhibit or *responsible* projects to engage with.

I tested it in the context of my practice, and I found it to be quite useful in bringing clarity of thought, expression of priorities, and alignment.

Creative Space
(Products, Services, and Value Propositions)

Everything Innovation from Purpose to Success

- InnovatePedia – Knowledgebase at the core of all products, services, and solutions
- **Innovation Coaching** – Workshops and Coaching on Purposeful Innovation
- EinFrame & EinStory – Digital Collaborative SaaS Platforms for Innovation & Strategy
- **ISO 56000** – Innovation Management Guidelines: Coaching and Implementation
- NDE 4.0 – Industry 4.0 application for Infrastructure Sustainability & Reliability
- **Inspiring Next Books** – Volume series on Purposeful Innovation
- Innovate Portal – Blogs, Webinars, Videos, Conversations

Market Place
(Industries, Customers, and Beneficiaries)

With this team, you will never go wrong !

- Aerospace and Defense
- Energy and Power
- Healthcare and Medical Devices
- Higher Education and Industry-University Collaboration
- Architecture, Home Remodeling, Manufacturing, IT, Logistics, Education

PURPOSE
Inspiring Purposeful Innovations in Industry 4.0 for Sustainability

Work Place
(Employees, Processes, and Culture)

I want my children to work here

- Engaging respectfully across the board, with all customer, partners, & co-working sites
- Creative and coaching mindset, everywhere, all the time, towards everyone
- Safe and fun for all

Social Space
(Community, Nation, and Earth)

This team knows how to #MoveTheDate & Support UN SDGs

- Include Earth friendly actions in every client project
- Provide valuable content to professional bodies – ISO/TC 279, IAOIP, ASNT, …
- Serve University Advisory Boards, anywhere in the world
- Support select organizations in their efforts on sustainability

Core Values: Fairness * Integrity * Learning * Sustainability

Inspiring NEXT
Purposeful Innovations

Start your H2H Innovation Journey

Ever since I discovered a purpose in my practice, the journey has become a lot more fulfilling. Loss of a client or a project does not bother me as much anymore. The Coronavirus pandemic caused a short-term disruption and a long-term opportunity, to help the community with ideation and innovation. That is what a purpose is – the reason for being that expands beyond fulfilling immediate basic needs.

Create your Implementation Plan

The starter steps include –

Define the Innovation Charter: The leadership charter needs to be interpreted into an activity charter for the innovation team so they can build an implementation plan.

Establish Innovation Dashboard: Measure both the effort and results of the innovation initiative, on a monthly/quarterly basis, respectively.

Identify Innovation Champions: The importance of a Chief Innovation Officer cannot be overemphasized. Until you can find one, the CEO needs to fulfill this role with commitment. Having the wrong individual in this position will drive true innovators out of the company. I have seen a few cases where the role was given to a "favorite executive material" and a few cases where a sales guy did an excellent job of selling himself to gain a good title and salary. One year later, everyone was pointing fingers at each other.

Establish the Team: Build a cross-functional team to kick this off and slowly add other team members to spread the competency. Please pick innovators, early adopters, and a few early majorities. For now, keep the late majority out of the team.

Ensure Diversity: Let the team have the right balance of gender, color, nationality, economic strata, military veterans, age, and other backgrounds that might bring diverse thinking.

Create an Implementation Plan: We discussed earlier how organizations are just like physical matter. The CInO needs to overcome friction and inertia, by putting in energy, and build the momentum. A well-balanced implementation plan comprises the following things, mutually connected.

Create the Innovation Project Portfolio: You need new products and services portfolio for the top line growth of the business. The objective here is to start with the purpose, convert ideas into projects, and mix and match to maintain a growth portfolio.

Establish a Robust Stage-Gate Process: Where the stages are left open to all sorts of innovations, and gates are strictly controlled by a diverse and empowered review team.

Deploy an Innovation Framework: You need innovation management processes to run the innovation projects portfolio effectively and efficiently. The objective here is to build the desired innovation profile.

Establish Ethics Policy: To address innovation in areas where there is no precedence and regulation. It needs to be more than a compliance checklist. It needs a Digital Transformation Review Board.

Put in a Routine to Build the Innovation Mindset: Identify routine and periodic activities, slowly introduce them into your operating system, and periodically review to see the engagement and adapt as needed.

Setup the Innovation Heartbeat: Set up a cadence of activities, to make progress along the various fronts discussed above. If you treat it like an internal program with the CEO as a customer, you will likely manage it with rigor. I typically hear, *"Employees are busy with their day job."* Well then, let us make innovation a part of their day job; Just like we make investing for retirement a part of the budget.

> Lack of plan will cause a false start.

Follow Through on the Plan

Eric Goodman says[147], *"Unlike wine, strategic plans don't have a good shelf life. So, use it and revise it regularly."* Only about half the plans get proper follow through to successful results. Here are some of the important things to greatly improve the chances for successful implementation of your strategy. These are not new to seasoned leaders.

Clearly Communicate the Innovation Charter: Hang it on walls, conference rooms, in your customer presentations. Define department and employee objectives in line with the charter. Anchor your monthly staff meeting around those objectives, performance reviews around those objectives, etc. All the standard management stuff, you already know how to do. Failure to communicate causes confusion and disorientation.

Allocate Resources: A plan without resources is a dream. If you're going to do it, do it right. The best way for leadership to demonstrate priorities is to put resources. Starting with CInO, the Innovation leadership team, with budget, time, and physical space carved out for exploration. Allocate adequate resources to accomplish the plan outlined above. Fewer and focused innovators are better than numerous and nebulous. Lack of resources frustrates those wanting to do something.

Prepare the Organization: Start with the training of all managers to align them with the implementation plan. Then go to an all-hands meeting, share the plan, and immediately ask them to go for open ideation. Announce the date for a Dolphin Tank event. Encourage employees to reach out to the innovation team and ask them to look for upcoming innovation space. Poor preparation leads to anxiety.

---

[147] Strategy Pitfalls; Eric Goodman; http://meridiansuccessgroup.com/strategy-pitfalls/; Feb 18, 2017.

Reward and Recognize: Based on quarterly performance, recognize, and reward the innovation with whatever plan the leadership has established. Lack of recognition causes resistance.

Use an Information Management System: Adopt a system that provides a single page of truth for everyone. The data, information, knowledge, and workflow should be managed and controlled, just like CRM/ERP systems. Refer to EinFrame discussed in Chapter-7.

Buckle Up

Sometimes, the journey starts with a big bang. At launch, there's a burst of energy as people take on assignments. The energy spreads as the details of the transformation emerge and people across the organization begin to see how the change can help the company. Then comes the valley of death, a few months into the program, when energy evaporates. People who were initially excited about participating in the transformation grow tired of the extra work and impatient with the lack of visible results. Enthusiasm gives way to cynicism. This valley of death[148] is a predictable phenomenon, that you can anticipate and manage. As a leader, you need to recognize this and re-energize.

First, look at the journey itself to see if the goals and initiatives are still relevant. Get the team together and ask them to recall what got them excited when they launched the transformation. And do they still have that conviction and ambition?

Second, look at the design of the effort to see if that's where the trouble is. The way the overall program and each of its initiatives are organized and operated can contribute to energy loss. Is senior leadership still involved and

---

[148] Reenergize Change Programs to Escape the "Valley of Death," I Hindshaw and A Gruin; Bain&Co; https://www.bain.com/insights/reenergize-change-programs-to-escape-the-valley-of-death/; Jun 15, 2017.

committed? Do initiative teams have adequate resources? Is the organization identifying key risks and mitigating them? Also, check to see if initiative teams still have a clear idea of top priorities and if they are spending time on activities that produce no tangible results. These are major energy drains.

> Well, you made it through the learning and planning.
> As an innovation leader, I expect you to
> adapt everything to your context and purpose.
> Your commitment is the most important thing.

Now shelve the book for future reference or share it.

Buckle up and enjoy the ride.

IN A REVOLUTION, THE MOST DIFFICULT PART TO INVENT IS THE END
— ALEXIS DE TOCQUEVILLE

Appendix – Innovation Definitions

I can similarly vouch that it is notoriously difficult to define the word 'Innovation.' Over a dozen experts took over 3 years to define it within the ISO platform, now published in ISO 56000. I watched that room debate various terms endlessly in one meeting, in 2019. For me the moment of truth came when one of them casually remarked, *"I can't even define Pizza, that I have been enjoying for 50 years."*

Here are some definitions gathered from various sources on the internet, arranged in alphabetical order by first name. I agree with some of them. After understanding these, you are welcome to add a new one.

Author	Innovation Definition
Avigail Berg	Reorganize the particles with new added components that shift the value to new business opportunities.
Barry Bassnett	Innovation is what happens when creativity has a bottom line.
Bill Flynn	Innovation is the creation of solutions to problems that have opposing requirements.
Braden Kelley	Innovation transforms the useful seeds of invention into solutions valued above every existing alternative.
Christian Terwiesch and Karl T. Ulrich	A new match between a need and a solution.
David Burkus	The application of ideas that are novel and useful.
Dick Lee	Delivering exceptional to the most important customer in the value chain, all the time, every time.
Edson Menezes	Innovation can be a thin line connecting the intuitive, the rational, and the market.

Ellen Weber	An invention or intervention – that shows evidence of a valued solution, garners support of decision makers, and offers mutual benefits for a wider community – by drawing insights from diverse people across several related fields.
Gijs Van Wulfen	Innovation is a feasible relevant offering such as a product, service, process, or an experience, with a viable business model that is perceived as new and is adopted by customers.
Hans Haringa	Innovation: 'something' used by 'some' but opposed by 'many' but over time accepted by all.
Harry Vardis	Ideas that pass through the business model and meet with acceptance by the end users.
Hutch Carpenter	A change in a product offering, service, business model or operations which meaningfully improves the experience of a large number of stakeholders.
Jatin DeSai	Creativity is when you use money to get ideas. Innovation is when you use ideas to make money.
Jeffery Baumgartner	The implementation of creative ideas in order to generate value, usually through increased revenues, reduced costs, or both.
Jorge Barba	Something new or different that delivers value to the world.
Julia Baumgartner	Radical innovation is a new product, process, or system that replaces its accepted predecessor and renders it obsolete.
Kurt Nahikian	Innovation results when a new approach is applied to an old problem that makes lasting and far-reaching changes in behavior.
Lars Christensen	Innovation is to dare to challenge mainstream thinking and behavior pattern.
Madhusudan Rao	Finding Newer & Better bottles to recycle the old wine. End objective remains the same but you want to achieve it in a better way.
Michael Graber	New, organic value creation by applying creativity, in-depth relationships with consumers and customers, and new thinking.
Michele Davies	The creation of new products or services which provide value to the marketplace in one form or another, using existing resources.
Mike Dalton	The organization wide process of finding and profitably serving unmet market needs.
Nick Skillicorn	Turning and idea into a solution that adds value from a customer's perspective.

Irish Firm Orryx	Ideas that are implemented and deliver value.
Paul Hobcraft	The fundamental way the company brings constant value to their customers business or life and consequently their shareholders and stakeholders.
Paul Sloan	Creativity is thinking of something new. Innovation is the implementation of something new.
Peter Balbus	Ideation is applied knowledge; creativity is applied ideation; Invention is applied creativity; and innovation is the successful commercialization or adoption of radical invention.
Ray Meads	A patentable solution (external verified uniqueness) with a differentiated business model that changes the basis of business for that specific industry sector.
Robert Bastarache	Innovation = Value + Creativity + Execution.
Robert Brands	Innovation is: any variation goes, as long as it includes new and it addresses customer needs and wants.
Robert Jacobson	Innovation is seeing things differently.
Sorin Cohn	Innovation is a Renewable Corporate & National Resource to be developed, used & commercialized for economic & social benefits.
Thomas Mathiasen	Innovation: what is new, useful and applied.
Uday Pasricha	Something is innovative when it creates a tangible added value for both user/developer; using existing, wasted or yet unnoticed resources.
Umesh Aherwal	An artistic way of utilizing available resources within the parameters. The word artistic way stands for the well-balanced or proportioned, which requires creative thinking.
Watts Humprey	Innovation is the process of turning ideas into Manufacturable and marketable form.
Reader's personal	

Appendix – Human-AI Collaborative Research

We as humans, are seeing an increasing role of domain specific and focused AI, also known as narrow AI, in engineering design, manufacturing, supply chain, and decision making along the value stream. These intellectual machines are now moving on from assistance to augmentation to becoming more like a partner in research and problem solving. A good indicator is an academic degree program at Carnegie Mellon University. The Master of Science[149] in *Artificial Intelligence and Innovation* program equips students to identify potential artificial intelligence applications and develop and deploy AI solutions to large practical problems. Students work in teams to implement AI systems responsive to market needs.

Collaborative Co-author

I have been using ProWritingAid[150] to work the grammar in this book series for a couple of years. More recently (summer of 2021), Vaibhav Garg had gained access to beta release of the '*Generative Pre-trained Transformer 3*' (GPT-3), an autoregressive language model that uses deep learning to produce human-like text. It is the third-generation language prediction model in the GPT-n series created by OpenAI, a San Francisco-

---

[149] https://msaii.cs.cmu.edu/
[150] TNW News: ProWritingAid sets AI loose to improve your writing like a trusted editor. https://thenextweb.com/news/prowritingaid-sets-ai-loose-to-improve-your-writing-like-a-trusted-editor; July 01, 2021.

based artificial intelligence research laboratory. We also discovered that people have started using it to generate content[151,152,153]. GPT-3 is very powerful, albeit with some striking limitations as well[154]. The power comes from (a) 175 billion parameters, (b) training over a large portion of web pages from the internet, a giant collection of books, and all of Wikipedia and (c) tasks capability that include text classification, e.g., sentiment analysis, question answering, text generation/summarization, named-entity recognition and language translation. The limitations include (a) lack of long-term memory, (b) Lack of interpretability, (c) Limited input size, (d) Slow inference time, and (e) Suffers from some bias, already.

Collaborative Research Method

The GPT-3 provides a robust REST API to access its endpoints. More specifically, Mr. Garg used its completion endpoint using Python bindings to generate and explore the topics pertinent to our collaborative research[155]. To collaborate with GPT-3 on NDE 4.0, we took it up as an innovation project – which means putting it through stages and gates. We kept it simple with detailed actions and gate outcomes presented below.

---

[151] A robot wrote this entire article. Are you scared yet, human? GPT-3; Sept 08, 2020; https://www.theguardian.com/commentisfree/2020/sep/08/robot-wrote-this-article-gpt-3

[152] Can AI and GPT-3 Replace Authors? L Porr; Writer on The Side; https://podcastnotes.org/writer-on-the-side/can-ai-and-gpt-3-replace-authors/ Oct 21, 2020.

[153] I Wrote a Book with GPT-3 AI in 24 Hours — And Got It Published. J Aalho; Jun 12, 2021; https://medium.com/swlh/i-wrote-a-book-with-gpt-3-ai-in-24-hours-and-got-it-published-93cf3c96f120.

[154] What is GPT-3 and why is it so powerful? A Mavuduru; Feb 17, 2021; https://towardsdatascience.com/what-is-gpt-3-and-why-is-it-so-powerful-21ea1ba59811.

[155] Human Factors in NDE 4.0 Development Decisions; Ripi Singh, Vaibhav Garg, and GPT-3; J Nondestruct Eval 40, Article 71; Aug 2021.

Stage-1	AI Agent GPT-3 Capabilities Review and Assessment	**Actions**: Question answering, Text generation, Text summarization, and Ideation. **Result**: Surprisingly good with lots of useful information, and nothing wrong.
Gate-1	**Can GPT-3 Add value?**	~~No,~~ ~~Not Likely,~~ ~~Don't know,~~ Likely, ~~Yes~~
Stage-2	Content with AI-Augmentation	**Actions**: Create an outline of the essay. **Result**: Acceptable Outline, we made some changes. **Actions**: Find best practices in Stage-Gate process. **Result**: Acceptable list but could not match our experience. **Actions**: Identify human factors effecting gate review. **Result**: Extensive list with some valuable new items **Overall:** It validated what we had, added to our draft content, suggested ideas and summarized content.
Gate-2	**Is the content relevant?**	~~No,~~ ~~Not Likely,~~ ~~Don't know,~~ ~~Likely,~~ Yes
Stage-3	Finalize Manuscript and perform AI Check	**Actions**: Assistance with abstract generation **Result**: The abstract made sense, with couple of iterations. It has been used with additional paragraphs to set the context, and novelty of using AI as a co-author
Gate-3	**Does GPT-3 (AI) deserve to be a co-author?**	**Contributions from GPT-3 in this manuscript are at par with an intelligent graduate student or a junior colleague. It has made the manuscript more comprehensive and cohesive.** **Recommend that GPT-3 be treated as a co-author, just like we would have done with an intelligent co-worker.** **This is also being honest to the reader community.**
Stage-4	Publishers' assessment	**Actions**: Review of policy, procedures, and legal implications. **Result:** Acceptable
Gate-4	**Final Decision**	**Accept GPT-3 as a co-author of an AI augmented manuscript**

Outcome of the Gate-3 was merged with the content of the manuscript submitted for publication. Once completed, we used the table of contents to create the abstract. The original abstract created by GPT-3 is shown here. It made sense after a couple of incremental iterations. GPT-3 requires certain parameters and settings, just like any human research assistant would need instructions and boundaries to have a meaningful outcome. Parameters were empirically chosen for suitable results. The abstract generated by GPT-3 was used in the manuscript with additional paragraphs to set the context and define the novelty of using AI as a co-author. The first round at Gate-4 was a conditional go. Human authors received reviewer feedback and incorporated many additions to the manuscript. The final review accepted the application paper that has been published by Journal of NDE Vol 40.

Our Experience

There were human factors during the stage-gates of case study execution as well. We were skeptical about the capability in the beginning and amazed later. During the final review gate and revision stage, despite some experience, there was a noticeable tendency to treat the machine co-author as a tool/special entity, with humanly desire to identify parts of the treatise written by GPT-3 differently. It took special effort for human authors to explicitly check and debias themselves to not treat GPT-3 any differently. Authors conversations with several peers were met with varied levels of curiosity and suspicion. Readers of this case study might feel the same way and may need some time and adjustment to fully absorb the process and impact. The scientific paper and application side were submitted to separate journals. For the application side, considering the importance and relevance of the topic, the journal editors accelerated the review process, but were very conscious of relevance and standard of the content. There was no compromise on quality and acceptability criterion. The science journal presumed AI capability at par with ESL (English as a Second Language) however the detailed copyright editor found very little improvements to AI generated content.

This collaboration was an eye-opening and rewarding experience. It provided a convincing evidence of a powerful human-machine co-working at linguistic and cognitive levels, one which is closer than we think, and more powerful than we conceive. The speed at which the research can be conducted is exponentially faster. This is just like digitalization of the third revolution which had offered an order of magnitude faster access to information as compared to physical libraries of indexed books.

> Ability of AI to connect pieces of information into a coherent story can take human creativity to a whole new level.

Appendix – Ethics Overview

---

*ETHICAL BEHAVIOR IS DOING THE RIGHT THING WHEN NO ONE IS
WATCHING, EVEN WHEN DOING THE WRONG THING IS LEGAL.*
— ALDO LEOPOLD

According to a James Fieser's research published in a peer reviewed online academic resource[156], the field of ethics (or moral philosophy) involves systematizing, defending, and recommending concepts of right and wrong behavior. Philosophers today usually divide ethical theories into three general subject areas: Meta-ethics, normative, and applied ethics.

Meta-ethics investigates where our ethical principles come from, and what they mean. Are they merely social inventions? Do they involve more than expressions of our individual emotions? Meta-ethical answers to these questions focus on the issues of *universal truths*, the will of God, the role of reason in ethical judgments, and the meaning of ethical terms themselves.

Normative ethics takes on a more practical approach, which is to arrive at moral standards that regulate right and wrong conduct. This may involve articulating the *good habits* that we should acquire, the *duties* that we should follow, or the *consequences* of our behavior on others.

Applied ethics involves examining specific *controversial* issues, such as abortion, infanticide, animal rights, environmental concerns, homosexuality, capital punishment, or nuclear war.

Further details can be obtained from the encyclopedia of philosophy.

---

[156] Internet Encyclopedia of Philosophy. https://iep.utm.edu/ethics/; Accessed Aug 2021.

Industry 4.0 is closest to normative ethics and certain parts of applied ethics. There are interesting discussions and research to explore if technology elements such as "robots" or "AI" should be considered in the mix of along with "human subjects."

Normative Ethics

Normative ethics involves arriving at moral standards that regulate right and wrong conduct. It is a search for an ideal litmus test of proper behavior. The key assumption in normative ethics is that there is only one ultimate criterion of moral conduct, whether it is a single rule or a set of principles. Over the years, three theories have developed within normative ethics.

Virtue theory stresses the importance of developing good habits of character. Important virtues today are *wisdom, courage, temperance, justice, fortitude, generosity, self-respect, good temper, and sincerity*. In addition, we should avoid acquiring bad character traits, such as *cowardice, insensibility, injustice, and vanity*. The central role of virtues is grounded in and emerge from within social traditions, and this creates differences around the world, across industries, cultures, and professional communities.

Duty theories are based on foundational principles of obligation. They are also sometimes called non-consequentialist since these principles are obligatory, irrespective of the consequences that might follow from our actions.

Consequential theory calls for us to determine our moral responsibility by weighing the consequences of our actions. This normative principle requires that we first tally both the good and bad consequences of an action. If the good consequences are greater, then the action is morally proper. If the bad consequences are greater, then the action is morally improper.

Ethics and Morals

Ethics are often confused with morals. Some of the conversation above might seem like discussing morals. As society started getting more structured, the distinction got wider. Today, we can say that ethics are applied formally by statutory, regulatory, codes, and standards organizations. Ethics can also be seen informally in social groups and certain professions. While the morals are our personal behavior and beliefs of how to be "good." Morals refer mainly to guiding principles, and ethics refer to specific rules and actions, or behaviors[157]. A moral precept is an idea or opinion that is driven by a desire to be good. An ethical code is a set of rules that defines allowable actions or correct behavior.

A person's idea of **morals** tends to be shaped by their surrounding environment (and sometimes their belief system). Moral values shape a person's ideas about right and wrong. They often provide the guiding ideas behind ethical systems. That is where it gets tricky … morals are generally viewed as the basis for ethics. A moral person wants to do the right thing, and a moral impulse usually means best intentions.

Ethics are distinct from morals in that they are much more practical. An ethical code for an organization or human collective does not have to be moral. It is just a set of rules that people who belong to that collective should follow and has nothing to do with cosmic righteousness or a set of beliefs.

It is important to know that what is ethical is not always what is moral, and vice versa. For example, Omerta is a code of silence that developed among members of the Mafia. It was used to protect criminals from the police. This follows the rules of ethically correct behavior for Mafia, but it can also be viewed as wrong from a moral standpoint. A moral action can also be unethical. A lawyer who tells the court that his client is guilty may act out of a moral desire to see justice done, but this is deeply unethical because it violates the attorney-client privilege.

---

[157] https://www.dictionary.com/e/moral-vs-ethical/

Appendix – Perceptions Unfolded

The predictions from proven leaders of their time, in their domain of excellence, have turned out to be incorrect. There are many reasons for that.

- We have biases anchored around our experience.
- It is easier to spot quick changes as compared to gradual ones.
- We are poor at understanding the confluence of multiple factors changing at the same time.
- We are poor at predicting changing human needs and response to breakthroughs.

> If companies like Google and Apple can have their share of failed projects, leaders can have their share of failed predictions.

Here are some interesting historic quotes from leaders of the industry that I have compiled from various sources on the internet and would like to share with a humbling perspective that how difficult it can be to predict, rather than being judgmental.

Through the 1st Industrial Revolution

(1800s) How, sir, would you make a ship sail against the wind and currents by lighting a bonfire under her deck? I pray you, excuse me, I have not the time to listen to such nonsense. — Napoleon Bonaparte.

(1830) Rail travel at high speed is not possible because passengers, unable to breathe, would die of asphyxia. — Dr. Dionysius Lardner.

(1864) No one will pay good money to get from Berlin to Potsdam in one hour when he can ride his horse there in one day for free. — King William I of Prussia.

Through the 2nd Industrial Revolution

(1876) The Americans may need the telephone, but we do not. We have plenty of messenger boys. — William Preece, British Post Office.

(1876) This 'telephone' has too many shortcomings to be seriously considered as a means of communication. The device is inherently of no value to us. — Western Union.

(1880) Everyone acquainted with the subject will recognize [the light bulb] as a conspicuous failure. — Henry Morton, Stevens Institute of Technology, on Edison's light bulb.

(1889) Fooling around with alternating current (AC) is just a waste of time. Nobody will use it, ever. — Thomas Edison.

(1895) Heavier than air flying machines are impossible. — Lord Kelvin, President of the British Royal Society.

(1901) I must confess that my imagination refuses to see any sort of submarine doing anything but suffocating its crew and floundering at sea. — H.G. Wells, British novelist.

(1903) The horse is here to stay, but the automobile is only a novelty, a fad. — President of Michigan Savings Bank to Henry Ford's lawyers.

(1916) The cinema is a little more than a fad. It's canned drama. What audiences really want to see is flesh and blood on the stage. — Charlie Chaplin.

(1921) The wireless music box has no imaginable commercial value. Who would pay for a message sent to no one in particular? — Associates of David Sarnoff, early radio pioneer.

(1926) Such a man-made voyage [rocket travel] will never occur, regardless of all future endeavors. — Lee DeForest, American inventor.

(1927) Who the hell wants to see actors talk. – H M Warner of Warner Brothers.

(1932) There is not the slightest indication that nuclear energy will ever be obtainable. That would mean that the atom would have to be shattered at will. — Albert Einstein.

(1933) There will never be a bigger plane built. — Boeing engineer, after the first flight of the twin-engine 247 that held 10 people.

(1936) A rocket will never be able to leave the Earth's atmosphere. — The New York Times. The Times published a correction in 1969.

(1946) Television won't last, because people will soon get tired of staring at a plywood box every night. — Darryl Zanuck, 20th Century Fox.

(1955) It'll be gone by June. — Variety Magazine, on rock-and-roll.

(1955) Nuclear powered vacuum cleaners will probably be a reality within 10 Years. — Alex Lewyt, President of the Lewyt Vacuum Cleaner.

(1959) The world potential market for copying machines is 5,000 at most — Executive at IBM to the founders of Xerox.

(1961) There is practically no chance communications space satellites will be used to provide better telephone, telegraph, television or radio service inside the United States. — T.A.M. Craven, FCC commissioner.

(1962) We don't like their sound, and guitar music is on the way out. — Decca Recording Company on declining to sign the Beatles.

(1968) The Japanese auto industry isn't likely to carve out a big slice of the USA market. — Businessweek magazine.

Through the 3rd Industrial Revolution

(1943) I think there is a world market for maybe five computers. — Thomas Watson, Chairman of IBM.

(1977) There is no reason for any individual to have a computer in his home. — Ken Olson, President of Digital Equipment Corp.

(1968) Remote shopping, while entirely feasible, will flop — Time magazine.

(1995) I predict the internet will soon go spectacularly supernova and in 1996 collapse. — Robert Metcalfe, Founder of 3Com.

(1995) The truth is no online database will replace your daily newspaper. — Cliff Stoll. Newsweek article titled 'The Internet? Bah!'

(2003) These Google guys want to be billionaires and rock stars and go to conferences and all that. Let's see if they still want to run the business. in two to three years. — Bill Gates, Chairman of Microsoft.

(2005) There's just not that many videos I want to watch. — Steve Chen, co-founder of YouTube, upon selling his own company to Google.

(2007) There's no chance that the iPhone is going to get any significant market share. No chance. — Steve Ballmer, Microsoft CEO.

Through the 4th Industrial Revolution

(2014) Once unfriendly superintelligence exists, it would prevent us from replacing it or changing its preferences. Our fate would be sealed. … A badly designed AI system will be impossible to correct once deployed – Nick Bostrom in his book Superintelligence.

(2018) I do think we need to be very careful about the advancement of AI. As AI gets probably much smarter than humans, the relative intelligence ratio is probably similar to that between a person and a cat, maybe bigger. — Elon Musk.

(2019) It's impossible that humans could be controlled by machines. They're machines that are invented by humans.—Jack Ma, Alibaba. One of these two (Jack Ma and Elon Musk) will be wrong by 2050.

(2010s) The aerospace industry will never accept 3D printed parts — various executives and thought leaders.

(2014) 3D printer drones will take to skies by 2040. — BAE scientists.

(2015) Human colony on Mars by 2039. — Buzz Aldrin.

(2018) We will have 1 Trillion humans in the solar system. – Jeff Bezos.

(2019) We will go to a 4-day workweek by 2030, and 3-day by 2040. — Ripi Singh.

(2020) Reader's prediction

> A lot of what we say before a revolution is wrong after the fact.

About the Author

Dr. Ripi Singh, is an innovation coach with 5 years of experience and 30 years of learning in product, process, and people leadership; spanning aerospace & defense, renewable energy & power, advanced manufacturing, healthcare and medical devices, IT, and the art of learning itself. His coaching practice has a purpose – Industry 4.0 for Sustainability.

Ripi helps his clients bring affordable innovation into their culture using a holistic approach described in the Inspiring Next Innovation book series. His service spans across mentoring young minds to coaching business owners; startups to growth companies; commodities like garments to futuristic technologies like drones. He engages in global projects in Germany, India, Singapore, China, and the United States. He supports local eco-system development through collaborative innovation spaces in State of Connecticut. Some of his friends jokingly call him Ripi 4.0.

Ripi 3.0 served the corporate world as Director R&D Alstom Power (now General Electric), as Advanced Technology Manager for United Technologies, and as Chief Engineer at Karta Technologies. During those 16 years, he successfully delivered advanced technologies on high impact and leading-edge aviation and energy programs. He also performed foundational research on aviation system sustainment and life extensions in collaboration with industry and universities.

Ripi 2.0 was an academician, serving in the Faculty of Aerospace Engineering, and supporting aerospace industrial sector in Bangalore India. Over a decade, he did fundamental research in materials fatigue and fracture mechanics necessary for flight safety; and contributed to USA Navy and EU projects in the 1990s.

Ripi 1.0 was making working models of earthmoving machinery in middle and high schools for science fairs and exhibitions in India, even before he was exposed to a calculator during sophomore engineering.

Ripi has been felicitated with many national and corporate honors, authorship of 100+ publications, 300+ lectures, two patents, and other accolades. He has won the *'President of India Cash Prize'* for outstanding research, *'Calcutta Convention Award'* for excellence in Technical Education, *'Tata Fellowship'* for Research; All these national recognitions qualified him for naturalized citizenship of the USA under the category of *'Outstanding Researcher with Extraordinary Ability.'*

Ripi serves on Technical Committee 279 as USA Expert delegate to ISO 56000 on Innovation Management Guidance, Chair of NDE 4.0 for American Society for Non-Destructive Testing, Guest editor for Springer on NDE 4.0, Industrial advisory board for Entrepreneurship and Innovation at University of New Haven, University of Hartford, Southern CT state University, Tsinghua University, and International Association of Innovation Professionals. He holds a BS, MS, and a Ph.D. in Aerospace Engineering, a post-doc from Georgia Tech, and an Executive MS in Business Strategy from RPI, always with the highest GPA.

Ripi's wife Anu Kaur is a cancer research scientist, and they have one son Amanjot Singh, a practicing mechanical engineer. Ripi loves travel, music, dance, and photography. His study of different faiths has taken him to Vatican City, Jerusalem City, Salt Lake City, Amritsar, Badrinath, Tirupati, and many other popular religious shrines around the world.

Look out for more titles in Inspiring Next Series from Ripi Singh

- ✓ Inspiring Next Purposeful Innovation, Dec 2020
- ✓ Inspiring Next Innovation Purpose, Aug 2020
- ✓ Inspiring Next Innovation Value Chain, Aug 2020
- ✓ Inspiring Next Innovation Framework, Aug 2020
- ✓ Inspiring Next Innovation Mindset, Aug 2020
- ✓ The World of NDE 4.0: Let the Journey Begin, Sept 2021
- ➢ **Inspiring Next Human to Human Innovation, Sept 2021**
- • Inspiring Next Multi-Vitamins for Healthy Innovation, Dec 2021
- • Inspiring Next Innovations in Energy Systems, Sometime in 2022
- • Inspiring Next Enriched Living, Sometime in 2022

Just sharing some personal perspectives as I close this volume.

Consultant	✓ Coach
Solves Client's problem	Builds client's competency to solve the problem
Transaction relationship, finite duration, with defined deliverable and closure	Empathic relationship, longer lasting, with no defined end point
Tangible, visible, explicit solution outcome	Intangible, invisible, implicit competency building
Expected to be more competent than the client on the subject of transactions	Expected to make the client more competent than client believes possible on their subject
Protective of his skills, tools, and tricks	Shares his skills to develop the client
Vested in the task outcome	Vested in client success
Solution speed controlled by the consultant	Developmental pace controlled by the client
Good for solving a problem	Required to search the right problem

Motivation	✓ Inspiration
External pull to perform & accomplish	Internal drive or urge to pursue
Pulled towards a goal or an objective	Driven towards a purpose
Rewards are generally visible & tangible	Rewards are invisible & intangible
Aligned with management styles	Aligned with leadership attitude
Good for improving productivity	Required to foster innovation

Business	✓ Practice
Sells a product or service	Professionals provide services
Focus on financial gains as KPI	Serves a social or professional purpose
Focus more directed at commodity	Focus more on customer solution
Management structure aimed at sales	Structure build around competencies
Generally, charges & collects in advance	Generally, charges by hour afterwards

Teacher	✓ Guru
Gives structured information.	Awakens the intelligence & awareness
Takes responsibility for your growth	Makes you responsible for your growth
Gives you things you do not have and require	Takes away things you have and do not require
Answers your questions	Questions your answers
Requires obedience and discipline from the pupil	Requires trust and humility from the pupil
Clothes you and prepares you for the outer journey	Strips you naked and prepares you for the inner journey.
Guide on the path	Pointer to the way
Sends you on the road to success	Sends you on the road to freedom
Explains the world and its nature to you	Explains yourself and your nature to you
Gives you knowledge and boosts your ego	Takes away your knowledge and punctures your ego
Instructs you;	Constructs you
Sharpens your mind	Opens your mind
Reaches your mind	Touches your spirit
Instructs you on how to solve problems	Shows you how to resolve issues
A systematic thinker	A lateral thinker
Leads you by the hand	Leads you by example
One can always find a teacher	But a Guru has to find and accept you
When a teacher finishes with you, you celebrate	If a Guru finishes with you, life celebrates.

Front Cover: A human brain running to offer an innovative solution to serve the needs of a human heart. The inspiration for this graphic came from https://healthybrains.org/healthy-brains-rely-healthy-hearts/. The flaw in the picture is discussed in Chapter-6, page-90 as an example of human factors during content review and decision making.

Trademarks around the term H2H

I did a search for trademarks around the term H2H just before publishing on Sept 03, 2021. System reported back 76 records containing the term H2H. 20 out of those are exclusively H2H and none of them relate to Innovation.

From USPTO TESS Search Sept 03, 2021

Serial Number	Reg. Number	Word Mark	Live Dead
90377731		H2H	LIVE
90245832		H2H	LIVE
90115381		H2H	LIVE
88893352	6199747	H2H	LIVE
88863963		H2H	DEAD
88786499	6140633	H2H	LIVE
88725810		H2H	LIVE
88330549	5889321	H2H	LIVE
88294919		H2H	LIVE
88221459		H2H	DEAD
87920063	6463921	H2H	LIVE
87731782	5789941	H2H	LIVE
86838664		H2H	DEAD
86828623	5438692	H2H	LIVE
86700179	4904975	H2H	LIVE
85766949	4354011	H2H	DEAD
85651190		H2H	DEAD
85361098	4155663	H2H	DEAD
85154277		H2H	DEAD
78676095		H2H	DEAD

I urge readers to think and promote #H2H as a useful term, that helps build the right mindset of sharing/giving, away from exclusivity/ownership.

Made in the USA
Middletown, DE
18 March 2022

62820344R10139